I'LL TRY ANYTHING ONCE

Also by Giles Tippette

The Bank Robber
The Trojan Cow
Saturday's Children
The Survivalist
The Brave Men
The Mercenaries
The Sunshine Killers
The Spikes Gang
Austin Davis
Wilson's Woman
The Texas Bank Robbing Company
Wilson Young on the Run
Wilson's Gold
Wilson's Revenge
Wilson's Choice
Wilson's Luck
Hard Luck Money
China Blue
Bad News
Donkey Baseball and Other Sporting Delights
Cross Fire

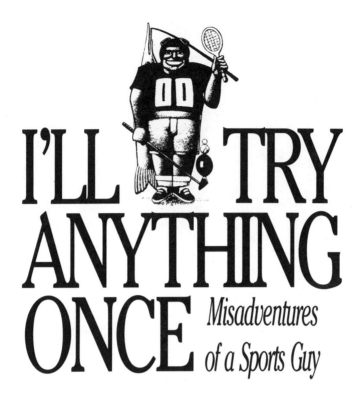

I'LL TRY ANYTHING ONCE
Misadventures of a Sports Guy

GILES TIPPETTE

Foreword by
Carlton Stowers

Taylor Publishing Company
Dallas, Texas

Published by Taylor Publishing Company
            1550 West Mockingbird Lane
            Dallas, Texas 75235

Designed by Hespenheide Design

Library of Congress Cataloging-in-Publication Data

Tippette, Giles.
    I'll try anything once: misadventures of a sports guy / Giles
Tippette.
        p. cm.
    Collection of previously published articles.
    ISBN 0-87833-728-8: $17.95
    1. Sports. 2. Sports—Humor. 3. Tippette, Giles. I. Title.
GV707.T55 1991
796—dc20
                                                    90-21930
                                                    CIP

Printed in the United States of America
10 9 8 7 6 5 4 3 2 1

To Terri Williams and Dr. James M. Thompson
(in order of importance)

Contents

Foreword

It is traditional, I'm told, to spend these opening pages kindly patting the author on the backside and addressing the great pearls of wisdom he has fashioned for those generous enough to have purchased this book. So, best we get that done with:

Giles Tippette is, quite simply, one of those gifted craftsmen whose skills cause others in the business to fall into a blue funk with the appearance of every new title bearing his name. Whether his subject is football or auto racing, deep-sea fishing or making a fool of himself at an old timer's track meet, he writes with the soul of a poet. You could set the guy's words to music, such is the lyrical quality he possesses.

And, with the earlier publication of *Donkey Baseball and Other Sporting Delights* and now *I'll Try Anything Once*, Giles has done me a major house-cleaning favor. Those of us who pay the mortgage and buy our sixpacks with the written word are constantly on the lookout for the good works of others. When a particularly well-written piece appears it is our pack-rat tendency to clip it and file it away—either as an example of what this business is all about or, honestly, as something from which to crib at a future date. Over the years, I have amassed a sizeable file of Giles Tippette stories from hither (like *Texas Monthly*) and yon (*Sports Illustrated*). The man has been selling his autobiography in 5,000-word increments for years.

Thanks to the wisdom and packaging of Jim Donovan and Taylor Publishing, I can clear space in the filing cabinet, tossing away the ripped-out magazine pages. No longer will I have to dig out tattered articles and insist that friends and neighbors get acquainted with Tippette's marvelous style. Now I can send them directly to the nearest bookstore with the promise they'll get their money's worth. Which is to say I'm delighted that Giles took a respite from his fictional pursuits to compile his best non-fiction into book form. So, too, will anyone be who takes a peek inside these pages.

What Giles Tippette is is one helluva writer. Who he is is a bit more difficult to explain.

Without revealing his age, suffice it to say he's younger in mind than in body. If Peter Pan had been an athlete, he would have grown up to be Tippette. Giles, for all his wisdom and worldliness, has not come to grips with the fact that muscles grow less supple and more likely to ache and tear when one gets a bit longer in the tooth. He has not learned to understand that those of us who can remember when Harry Truman was president can no longer jump as high, run as swiftly, or hit the inside curve ball as often as we once did.

Giles Tippette is still a fiercely dedicated jock; his competitive juices continue to burn brightly. Given the option of winning an Olympic gold medal or the Pulitzer Prize, Tippette would have no difficulty making a choice. For all of us who call him friend it is a state of affairs which has caused suffering and no small measure of pain.

Take, for example, the Great Tennis Showdown, staged some years back in Kerrville, Texas.

During one of our occasional fishing expeditions (which never ended until Giles had caught the largest bass, regardless of the hour or other pressing matters), I unwisely mentioned that I'd begun playing tennis. An innocent remark about an activity whose primary purpose was to eliminate a couple of inches from the waistline turned into a full-blown challenge.

"When do you want to play?" Giles asked.

This from a guy who didn't even own a tennis racquet.

I'll spare you the O. Henry ending to this anecdote by jumping directly to an admission of defeat. The very next day Giles visited his local sporting goods dealer to purchase a racquet, wristbands, and a couple of cans of balls. Then he proceeded to run me ragged on the court.

To hear him tell it, I was reduced to gasping surrender. I don't recall it being quite so bad.

But that's Giles—ageless athlete and great storyteller. The combination, you'll learn as you read on, is unbeatable.

—CARLTON STOWERS

Introduction: Blood, Sweat, and Cheers

P laying sports is a good deal like sex; sometimes it can be great, and even when it ain't it's still better than yardwork.

In my lifetime, beginning at an awfully early age, I've played most sports. Some I was terrible at, some I nearly worked my way up to average at and in a very few instances, I got lucky enough to make all the failures of no account. I don't mean I did anything that was likely to put me in anyone's hall of fame, but there were those few bright, glittering moments—setting a record in track, catching the pass for the first down when your quarterback had to make a desperation throw, bringing the runners around with a hit in the last of the ninth when you were already 0-for-4 and you knew the coach was thinking of pinch hitting for you. Believe me, on the latter, I've hustled into the batter's box on many an occasion before he could quite make up his mind.

But the time on the field was only part of it. Sometimes locker rooms and athletic dorms could be a lot more dangerous than any arena a young boy might wander into. And that was part of my problem. Through a few mix-ups and certainly, as my mother still likes to say, through no intellectual capacity on my part, I got skipped a couple of grades. And because I'd started school when I was four years old (I think that was Mother's way of getting me out of the house), I graduated from high school when I was fourteen and turned fifteen doing two-a-days at John Tarleton Junior College—not a good place, what with all the returning Korean veterans, to be a skinny, underage kid whose only known attribute was foot speed. But it wasn't just John Tarleton, it was every place I played or rodeoed. It seemed like I could never catch up with my age. It seemed like it took nearly thirty years of dedicated dissipation before I even began to look as old as I should have been before a lot of grammar school administrators got all fouled up and jerked me ahead. No telling what I would've accomplished if I had come out of school at the proper time. I probably would've made All-American or at least started for the St. Louis Cardinals.

But going back to those locker rooms and athletic dorms, they were sure not places to look like an easy mark. Not that the pranks that got pulled were deadly, they were merely vicious. Still, you've never known a thrill until you've unwittingly pulled on what you thought was a clean jockstrap that someone had thoughtfully loaded up with Red-Hot, or used toilet paper that had been liberally sprinkled with rosin powder.

Just little things like that.

Athletes play hard on the field, and when they play jokes they play even harder. I once had a roommate who was appropriately nicknamed "Pig." Every time he'd come home from a date he'd tack another pair of panties on the wall by his bunk. As his collection grew we all got more and more impressed, that is until I found a sales slip from J.C. Penney's that he'd carelessly neglected to dispose of.

He had another endearing little habit, too. We had steam radiators in the hall, and when Pig felt like it was too far to the communal bathroom at the end of the hall he'd urinate on one of those hot steam radiators. When a howl went up he'd claim I'd done it. I got several severe broomings from some very large senior linemen. Finally I went to the supply room at the field house and got a baseball bat and came back and sat down on my bunk. I showed it to Pig and said, "Now, Pig, I know I can't whip you. You're older and stronger and you outweigh me by sixty pounds. But you pull that stunt in the hall again and get me blamed and I swear I will beat you to death in your sleep." He must have believed me because he never did it again.

But those were just some of the pranks. There was a lot of good stuff. I remember when I lost my scholarship at Del Mar College because of a disagreement with the coach. (He wanted me to do it his way and I had other ideas.) I got barred from the athletic dining hall. Well, if three of my ex-teammates hadn't smuggled me food I would've starved to death because I was flat broke. I don't know how clean a steak is coming out of somebody's pocket but I wasn't so fastidious in those days.

And, no matter what sport, when we took to that field we all knew we were wearing the same color uniforms. That's a feeling I still wish I had in my life and probably the single biggest aspect I remember.

But then there's been another side to my life in sports, and it's been almost as big a part as playing. That part is writing about athletics and the people I played with and against—the people I got to know and some I got to wish I didn't know. I also got to go into a lot of locker rooms that it's doubtful I'd have seen as a player—like most NFL and major league baseball dressing areas. I think a stronger word than "doubtful" applies. I just don't want to use it.

Being a sportswriter has other advantages. For instance, you can go into the pressbox, and a pressbox is a wondrous thing. It's easily the best seat in the house, it's free, you get free parking and they will help you dissipate by giving you all the "iced tea" and other potables that you want. They even feed you dinner (or lunch depending on the time of the game). Of course, that's in the pros. In college pressboxes they are not allowed to give you iced tea, but they'll give you all the Coke you can drink.

Then they have runners who bring you the game statistics as fast as the Sports Information Director (SID) can crank them out. I guess the theory there is that you are either not sure which game you're at or you're too busy visiting with the other writers to pay much attention.

The only other alternative to the above two theories is that SIDs, as a general rule, don't think writers are too bright. They think we need to be fed information to make sure we get it right even though the game is going on before our very eyes. But it's ingratitude to whip a borrowed mule, so I'll let that go.

All of the stories in this book are true. Some of them are good, honest stories about real sportsmen. Some of them are about me. I'm afraid those that feature some part of my background don't leave me coming off very well.

But, then, as my wife likes to constantly say, "Serves me right." Me, not her.

1

I Get a Charge from Kenny Rogers

---

*T*o tell you the truth, I wish I could have played basketball. I never understood why I couldn't. I'm reasonably coordinated in most sports and can even get around a china shop without running up a horrendous bill in breakage. But basketball has always defeated me. Maybe it goes back to the days when I was way too tall for my age and my agility, and those little guys could get around me and make me look silly. Whatever the reasons, I developed early on an intense dislike for the game and it hasn't slackened any since. I dread that time between football season and baseball's beginning, because there is nothing but game after game of roundball. Does the season ever end? I mean, is there actually a day in these United States where some place at some time someone is not playing that silly game? I don't think so.

In the story that follows I've given you one main reason, and just touched on a few of the minor reasons, why I don't like the game. Come around some day; we'll go out for a beer and I'll tell you about half a dozen others.

As a man who prides himself on having played most sports with some degree of success, I hate that basketball has to be the exception.

But then there's snow skiing, too. You don't want to get me started on snow skiing.

A lot of people have asked me why I don't like basketball. Or maybe I've told a lot of people I don't like basketball. I can't see where it makes much difference except to the very picky.

But being as I'm a sportswriter, it is probably not fitting that I should have a prejudice against what some people call a major sport, unenlightened as they may be.

I, however, have my reasons. The first that comes to mind is the same reason I don't like Kenny Rogers, and not just for his singing, either. Though I don't really much care for that, now that you mention it.

This particular incident occurred back in about 1971 in Houston. Kenny Rogers and his band had come to town to do a concert that was sponsored by a Houston radio station. It seemed that one of his band's habits, whatever town they were in, was to get up a game between themselves and certain members of the local media. I don't know if they did this because they liked basketball so well or because they wanted to prove that it was possible to smoke those funny cigarettes and still play the game.

Anyway, they seemed pretty serious about it. They even had their own uniforms and claimed to know some set plays. They said it was their way of staying in shape against the grueling excesses of the road.

Now ordinarily I would not have become involved in such an enterprise. I already had several vile experiences with basketball under my belt and wasn't looking to increase the carnage. But it so happened that the main luminaries of the sponsoring radio station were a disc jockey team named Hudson and Harrigan. I didn't know Harrigan very well, but I had good reasons for carrying a well-concealed grudge against Mack Hudson. We played golf nearly every day and he always insisted on driving the golf cart, although he had about the same mechanical aptitude as Truman Capote. For instance, he waited until I'd bought a new set of clubs and a new golf bag before he managed to drive us into a four-foot-deep creek.

We just stood there, water streaming off us, up to our waists in the creek. I stared at Hudson. With malice. All he could say was, "You better not leave your new clubs in that water too long. I don't think it's good for the grips."

So when he invited me to be on the media team I accepted. I accepted because I knew something Hudson didn't know. I may be 6'3" and I may have had a fair athletic career, but there was a point he hadn't considered.

I can't play basketball.

I don't mean average; I don't mean just a little; I mean not at all.

And I knew he was counting on me to help carry the team, because I knew just what kind of help he could expect from the rest of the media. A couple of years before I'd had occasion to manage and play third base for a fast-pitch softball team called the Press Club Spikes. I was able to take this team to the finals of the city championship, but it wasn't with the help of any members of the media other than my modest self. The idea was that the team would be composed of members of the Press Club, but it became obvious, after a couple of practices, that the news-gathering ability of the Houston press, radio and television resources would be greatly hampered if I let too many of these people stay on the field. I don't mean that they were just slow and small and nonathletic, I mean that they were in danger from any object that was thrown at them, pitched at them or hit at them. And then there was the question of running in a straight line without falling down, not to mention the business of swinging a bat without needing to see a chiropractor the next day. Forget about sliding; none of them ever got on base anyway.

So I filled the team up with ringers and we did all right. Naturally I didn't tell Hudson any of this. I figured he'd find out in due time.

Besides, how tough could a bunch of musicians be?

Elvin Hayes, the great college and professional basketball player, was to be our coach. Naturally we didn't hold any practices because there wasn't time, but mainly because none of us could have stood it. We'd have been worn out to the point where we couldn't play the game.

So Elvin just had to pick blindly and, judging from what he must have seen, he probably should have done it blindfolded.

Since I was by far the biggest, he automatically designated me as center. Later, when I could get him aside, I quietly confided my problem to him. He said, "What do you mean you can't play basketball?"

I said, as helpfully as I could, "Well, I mean I can't dribble the ball, I can't pass and I can't shoot. Did I leave anything out?"

He gave me a look. "No," he said. "I guess that just about covers it. Can you play defense?"

"I guess," I said. "I've got good reflexes."

He said, "Then you just lay back and stuff up the paint on your end."

I knew he was talking about something, but I wasn't entirely sure what he meant. I said, "Uh, what's the paint?"

The looks were turning strange now. He said, "Have you ever seen a basketball game?"

"Not many."

"The paint is the lane." he said. "The center. That stuff in front of the free throw line and between those other two lines. The place where the floor ain't the same color as the rest of the floor."

"Ah," I said, nodding as if I understood.

"Just don't let them drive up the middle on you."

But another problem had arisen besides my ignorance and ineptitude. It was a problem we would have never imagined in a million years, but, given the character and social consciousness of musicians, we should not have been too surprised by. Now a caravan the size of Kenny Roger's band roughly comprises about a hundred people, all the way from road managers and advance men to electricians and guitar tuners—maybe, for all I know, even food tasters. That's not counting the band itself.

But they claimed they didn't have enough people to play the game. Not enough people? We had churches in Houston with a lot smaller membership than that band had.

Yet they claimed they needed one more player. It turned out to be Dan Pastorini, now a drag racer, but then the quarterback for the Houston Oilers and a large, good athlete. Rogers claimed he could play the guitar.

Well, hell, if we'd known that was within the rules we would've given press credentials to half the University of Houston basketball team and claimed they were all journalism students or, at the very least, writing a book.

But they ran Pastorini in on us right before the game and it was too late for any countermeasures—except for psychological ones.

For some reason both teams dressed in the same dressing room. It was the girls' dressing room of the gym, as I remember. And that was either because the boys' dressing room was under refurbishment, or there were more electric outlets in the girls'.

I think it was the latter. Hudson and I sat over in a corner watching Pastorini and the boys in the band blowdrying their hair. We sat there snickering and making *sotto voce* remarks like, "This is the first time I've ever seen a team showering and shampooing *before* a game," and, "Have you ever seen more blowdryers outside of a beauty parlor?" or, "Have you ever seen more *hair* outside of a beauty parlor?"

By and large everybody ignored us except Pastorini, who cast a couple of cool, appraising looks in my direction. Right then and there I should have realized that if there was to be any retribution for this irreverent lack of awe it was going to come my direction rather than toward the midgets on my team. Pastorini was just as tall as I was and maybe ten pounds heavier. He was also in shape, something I couldn't quite claim.

What the hell. It was just a bunch of musicians, and they'd be so worried about getting their hair messed up or one of their picking fingers hurt that they'd be afraid to "drive the middle." Whatever the hell that meant.

However, I am being unfair about one matter. I have indicated that Kenny and his band had shampooed and showered before the game. Strictly speaking this was true, but it could be looked at another way. Anyone that knows basketball knows you go out and take your warm-ups and then come back in the locker room and get ready for the game. Normally this time is reserved for the team to go over their strategy again and for each player, in his own way, to get ready to give his best. Well, since neither of us had any strategy, and our best wasn't going to matter, I could see where Kenny and his team would spend the time grooming themselves and changing into fresh uniforms. Why not look your best?

Rogers really was a big draw. The tickets weren't free, but they were going for a very nominal amount and the proceeds were going to charity, so we were expecting a fairly large crowd. There had even been a couple of thousand in the stands while we were taking our warm-ups, so it was only natural to expect a great deal more by game time. Therefore, who were Mack Hudson and I to snigger about a guy blowdrying his hair before a game? I guess we had just never seen anyone do something like that before.

Good thing he did, though, because there were about eight thousand fans in the stands when we came out to start the game. Either they were fanatical basketball fans or they were there hoping someone would sing.

My big moment came in the first play of the game. I out-jumped Pastorini on the tipoff. Didn't much matter though, as one of our players took a wild shot from somewhere near mid-court that never came anywhere near the basket. Then the other team started playing and it became sadly apparent that they knew what they were doing.

Now, one thing I've observed about basketball is that there's a lot of running—up and down and back and forth and side to side and even in circles. At first I tried to follow the ball downcourt and even managed to grab a few rebounds, not that it did much good since somebody usually took it away from me before I could pass it off. We only had one player who seemed to have the slightest idea what he was doing. That was Dan Lovett, who is, I believe, now with ABC. But Lovett is only about 5'2" and not a hell of a lot of help other than to run around yelling, "Ball! Ball! Ball!"

Hell, I'd have loved to have thrown him the ball if I could have just kept hold of the damn thing for more than two seconds.

But we, or I, had a bigger problem. None of us were, to say the least, in what you'd call tip-top condition. I'd been training by reading without my glasses and doing twelve-ounce curls with a can of Budweiser, but we all smoked and dissipated when we got the opportunity, and this constant activity was taking its toll. We had a squad of about twenty players on our media side, but my problem was that the next guy anywhere near my height was Paul Harrigan, and he was only 5'8" and nearly spastic.

So I stayed in a great deal more than I wanted to. Finally, when I did get a chance to get a short breather, Elvin said to me quietly, "It sure is a good thing you ain't black."

I asked what he meant by that. He said, "We'd have to get you bleached, the way you play basketball."

I think by halftime we'd scored ten points. I, somehow, unaccountably, had scored four. The musicians had like thirty-something. It wasn't a real close game.

But it didn't seem to matter to the fans. They screamed every time Pastorini got the ball, and they screamed even louder when Rogers was even in the vicinity of the play. I think we were sort of intimidated.

And then it happened. The play that was to turn the game around.

Oh, I don't mean the score. That was a foregone conclusion. I mean the texture and character of the game.

Early in the second half I was doing what I was supposed to be doing, standing in the middle of the "paint," jamming up the middle. The musicians were coming at our basket, Kenny Rogers took a pass at the top of the key and started a drive up the middle, coming straight at me. Well, normally, him being the star and all, I would have gotten out of the way so the crowd could cheer and have a good time. But in this instance I was so tired I was just a half second late, and Kenny Roger's big foot came down on top of the instep of my right foot, damn near breaking the arch.

I screamed, I screamed like hell. The reason I screamed was it hurt like hell. Kenny Rogers may be a musician, but he's a musician who weighs a half ton.

It was also a foul. I had position on Rogers and he charged straight into me. But no foul was called. Even mild-mannered Elvin Hayes could see it was wrong and came out on the court to argue with the referee. The crowd could see it was a foul, too, and I was gratified to hear, even though Rogers scored on a layup, a great silence.

Elvin helped me limp over to the sideline and put Paul Harrigan in. Well, I watched for a while, but then I saw that Harrigan was in even more danger than I was. I asked Elvin if I could go back in and just stay under my basket and play defense. I knew I couldn't run. But although the pain had subsided to where a few shots of morphine might have controlled it, my anger was about to go over the top.

Elvin thought it was a fine idea. So I limped back out onto the court, getting a rather nice round of applause. The last thing Elvin said before I left the sidelines was to "play a little football with 'em." That I understood.

I also threw in a little baseball. I used to be a third baseman, and one of the most effective ways to stop a runner rounding third from scoring is to give him a gentle little nudge with your hip. His momentum will do the rest. Of course it's illegal as hell, and if the umpire catches you he's going to allow the run. But if he doesn't catch you, you might can tag the runner out before he recovers. Of course this can lead to some ruffled feelings, but what you want to do, if you're the third baseman, is to walk around looking innocent and talk about the poor fellow's bad luck in stumbling over the bag.

I got Pastorini with a hip when he tried to drive the lane on me. It nearly sent him into the nickel seats and, if Houston Oilers owner Bud Adams had been watching, I think it would have given him a bad moment. I got a foul out of it, but Pastorini got a couple of skinned knees. Fortunately it didn't affect his hair. Every strand stayed in place. A man with a canful of hair spray at his disposal doesn't take any chances.

Rogers I didn't get until almost the start of the fourth quarter. He came driving in from the right forecourt and I moved to that side of the basket, stepping out just a little and going down instead of going up with him. He tried to jump high above me and, as he did, I stood up.

Now, I don't know if little men fall lightly, but I can guarantee you that fat men fall heavily. He went down like two hundred pounds of Silly Putty hitting that hardwood floor. I remember that there was a collective gasp from the audience. After all, the concert was the next night and I might have knocked the voice out of ol' Kenny. But they needn't have worried. As he got up the things he was yelling at me were assurance enough that the man would be heard without benefit of a microphone.

Funny, he hadn't said a word to me when he'd sprained my arch. Why this sudden interest in my ancestry? I hadn't been curious about his.

After that I was all elbows and shoulders and knees under our basket. They kept on scoring, but they weren't getting any cheapies. In fact, they seemed downright reluctant to come in close.

Of course I was drawing fouls, but a curious thing happened. I drew four and then they stopped, one short of fouling me out of the game. I don't know what caused it. I saw Elvin talking to one of the referees (no doubt telling him I was confused about what game I was playing), but I can't say for sure that's what it was. Maybe it was the change in the crowd. All of a sudden they seemed to take notice that there were some other players on the court besides Rogers and Pastorini et al. On the rare occasion they would even give a kind of mild cheer when our side scored.

But that's not what stopped the referees from calling fouls on me. My style of play gradually spread to my own team, inept though they were, and then, like a head cold, went over to the musicians. The last five minutes of play bore little or no resemblance to the game they cutely call "hoops."

I think the reason the referees weren't calling the fifth foul on me was that there were so many others going on it would have seemed redundant. I think they just threw up their hands and said to hell with it.

Besides, the crowd was having an enormously good time.

They beat us, of course. I don't know what the final score was, but I think their end was about twice the size of ours. It didn't matter, though, because I think we heavily outscored them in the main category—bumps and bruises delivered.

In the end they weren't very good sports about it. We had a couple of cases of beer iced down in the locker room. We'd envisioned us all getting together for a nice communal shower and then sitting around drinking beer and discussing the ball game, the media game and the music game.

But the other side didn't want to play. Kenny Rogers' several factotums came into the locker room, gathered up all their stuff, and departed without a word. We heard that the rest of them just got into their limousines, still hot and sweaty, and drove off.

Hudson said, "Hell, I was looking forward to watching them blowdry their hair again."

That's just one of the reasons I've got for not liking basketball. The others are worse. In fact, I can't think of a single good encounter I've ever had with anything pertaining to basketball. That includes the fact that the first woman who ever cheated on me (that I know of) did so with a basketball player.

You may begin to see why I don't have a real round spot in my heart for the particular sport, especially in view of the fact that I was once drafted into the ultimate embarrassment, a donkey basketball game.

But enough self-flagellation.

My arch still aches sometimes. But that's not a sign of rain. It means in the next ten minutes they're going to play a Kenny Rogers record on the radio.

2
420 Miles
of Madness

---

*O*f all the sporting events I have ever covered, watched or participated in, I consider this by far the most grueling, the most dangerous, the most foolhardy and, easily, the one most deserving of admiration.

A strong statement. I have seen the grace and cruelty of the boxing ring, the brutal strength of the football field, the finesse and timing of the baseball diamond, the unreal stamina of the marathon runner, the speed and agility of the hurdler, the senseless pursuit of the bull rider in rodeo, the grace under penalty of death of the matador. In short, almost every type of athletic endeavor there is.

But nothing to match the Texas Water Safari.

Hell, it nearly finished me off just covering it for a magazine story.

I had been reading about it in newspapers for several years, with emotions varying between horror and admiration, when Bill Broyles (then the editor for Texas Monthly, now the co-creator of TV's "China Beach") called and asked me to go down and do a piece on the race—if it can be called that. I figured, what the hell. How bad could it be? I was a little troubled, however, by exactly how you covered an event that transversed 420 miles of backwoods swamps and rivers and creeks. I mean, they don't exactly have press boxes available for the comfort of the attending media for such events.

But Broyles assured me it would be a piece of cake, nothing to it. I have since discovered that Broyles is one of the biggest liars and con artists who ever masqueraded as a nice guy.

But I went, confident that all would be arranged as Bill had promised. My first pleasant surprise was to find that I was going the whole way, in some sort of a skiff equipped with an outboard motor. I hadn't counted on that. I also hadn't counted on my guide, an estimable fellow named Butch who had the skiff provisioned when I arrived. All of the provisions were beer. I like a little beer as well as the next fellow, but I sort of thought we ought to take along a little food for a pull of 420 miles. Butch said vaguely that we'd find some along the way.

I don't know what he had in mind, but I knew I wasn't going to eat it.

The race got started and, after that, it sort of turned into a blur. Of course, with our outboard motor, we normally should have had no trouble keeping up with the contestants. But Butch had neglected to tell me about the rapids we couldn't run in the skiff, or the waterfalls we couldn't go over, or the little tangled bayous we'd encounter, or the shallow water we couldn't get through. We spent as much time getting that skiff out of the water, loading it on the trailer that was following us, and then putting it back in the water, as we did doing anything else. Some seventy hours later it was over. I do not recall us ever finding anything to eat along the way. As it turned out, I was so tired I didn't care.

Some time later, after the story came out, I was back in Houston when a lawyer, a man who himself had competed in the race a year or so before, called me. He was looking for a partner—would I be interested in joining him in next year's race? I went to lunch with the man and we sat there, sounding just as sane as you please, talking about actually entering that man killer. Somewhere between the last course and when the bill arrived it suddenly came to me that it had almost killed me just trying to cover the thing. Now he was talking about entering it as a contestant.

Enter it? With sanity returning I realized I'd just as soon enter a *spirited game of "Let's both start running and keep going until one of us dies."*

I got away from that man quick.

They came gliding across the dark bay in their racing canoe, as exhausted as two human beings could be. The crowd of five hundred that had been waiting at the bay front through the long night slowly began to cheer. The Chatham brothers, who had wanted so badly to win themselves, waded out into the waist-deep water to help the winners out of the canoe. Then the brothers half-led, half-carried them up the steps to the bank and eased them down onto a pair of chairs, where they sat for an hour before they could say a word.

The two men had just won an annual canoe race called the Texas Water Safari, which begins in San Marcos and comes down the San Marcos River to the Guadalupe River and then crosses San Antonio Bay to finish, after 420 miles, at Seadrift. It is called a race for lack of a better name, but it's much more than that. It is a test of will and endurance so intense and grueling that even a long-distance swim or a marathon run pales in comparison. I had assumed, because of the length of the race, that the boats would tie up at night and the contestants would camp out and get a little sleep and rest up. But that is not the way it is done. They don't stop for anything. They don't stop to eat, to sleep, to rest, to drink, to visit, or for any other reason. They race. They race without a pause for about two full days.

I have been around sports both as a participant and as a writer for some twenty-five years, and I know through that exposure something about what competitive exertion can do to your mind and body. When I thought about this race I was stunned. A football game, for instance, takes some three to four hours, but the actual time that the ball is in play and the players are going all out is probably less than fifteen minutes. And yet I've seen dressing rooms full of exhausted football players. A marathon runner goes for only two or three hours. And yet some of them can barely move for a week afterward. But the winners of this race would be on the river twenty to thirty times as long as a marathoner.

All the while they would be going at an incredible pace, with no break. They would be sustaining a heart rate of more than 120 beats a minute for almost two days. They would be dehydrated because they could not take in liquids as fast as they would lose them. They would hallucinate. Some of them would collapse from total exhaustion. Along the way they would fight the blackness of the river at night, drag their canoes around quarter-mile logjams, face white water, portage around seemingly innumerable dams, and, worst of all, suffer their bodies to produce that incessant forty strokes a minute.

I had gone to San Marcos three days previously just as the racers were beginning to gather. They ranged in age from eighteen to fifty-one, a mixed group with no apparent common denominator except that they all seemed in remarkable physical shape. Professionally, they were engineers, lawyers, truck drivers, salesmen, even a medical student. Tom Goynes, who owned a canoe livery in San Marcos and was a professional guide, was the only one who could have been considered a professional canoeist.

I had done a little canoeing myself on some white water rivers, but these racing canoes didn't look anything like what I was used to. They were narrower, sleeker, lower. Some of them looked so low that you wondered if there'd be enough freeboard, once they were manned and loaded, to run white water without flooding. I had expected the traditional two-man canoe that is paddled, but there were other craft as well. For instance, two sculling canoes were entered. Sculling canoes are long, racy-looking boats rowed by two men, each using two sculling oars. Looking at the powerful, wide-bladed oars I thought that a paddling canoe wouldn't have a chance to stay up with them. But I was told that wasn't necessarily the case, since the race is actually two races. The upper part is down the San Marcos River, which normally is full of rapids and white water; in rapids the two-man paddling teams have an advantage. It's only after the race enters the Guadalupe, which is wider and much smoother, that the sculling teams have the advantage. A compromise between the traditional canoe and the scullers was the three-man paddling canoe. These are considered almost as fast as the scullers, but, because they are longer, are not quite as maneuverable as the two-man paddlers. Since the river was really high this year, there wouldn't be much white water on the San Marcos. That meant the sculling teams should take the lead almost from the beginning.

There were also several kayaks and a one-man open canoe. None of these boats had a chance to win, so I wondered why they were entered. Owen West, one of the kayakers, told me, "Look, I'm going down this river as a test of myself. And if I have someone else paddling I can never say that I did it by myself."

That was *his* reason for entering the race, but there were perhaps as many other reasons as there were contestants in the race. Yet none of them wanted to talk much about it. I didn't feel many of the racers were consciously trying to prove anything to themselves. Most of them had made the race before, and many of them had been in races all over the United States. They all made an effort to avoid the obvious clichés, and though a number of them tried to explain why they were willing to put themselves through such an ordeal, none really could. Perhaps Mike Wooley came the closest when he said, "It's the way I want to live my life. I like it. I don't like the pain and the agony, but I like myself better for having endured it."

There would be four favorites. Mike Wooley and his partner Howard Gore from Houston were scullers, as were the two Chatham brothers from Seadrift. Then there were the two three-man paddling canoes, one headed by Richard Miller of Houston, the other by Jim Trimble of Victoria. Roy Tyrone of Friendswood and his partner, Scott McDonald of Deer Park, in a conventional racing canoe, were given an outside chance, but most discounted them, as they did a dark-horse two-man team from Oregon, because the river was so high.

It was not immediately obvious, but after a time you began to sense the quiet camaraderie among these men. Since they are competing against each other and are all such fierce competitors, you might think that there would be no such sincere feeling. But it is genuine. I suppose it's because they are not only racing each other. They are racing themselves. But more than that, they are racing the river—a most powerful opponent.

I took a look at the upper part of the river, and even though it was high, there was still plenty of rough water. The rapids are the first and most obvious challenge in the race, a challenge that begins with an ominous sound. From up the river you hear a dull roar ahead, and as you near, the roar becomes louder and louder until you finally come sweeping around a curve, your speed picking up as you're funneled into the narrowing channel. Then ahead you see that jumping, foaming water, and you know there are rocks in it that can knock a hole in your canoe or knock a hole in your head if you capsize and are swept through that angry water.

The race was to begin at nine on a Saturday morning from Aquarena Springs in San Marcos, at the headwaters of the San Marcos River. The night before, all the racers, their families, team captains, and the bank runners had gathered at City Park for the official check-in and canoe inspection. One of the rules of the race is that you cannot take on any supplies along the way except fresh water. All of the teams furnished the race judges—led by John Nabors, a Houston lawyer—with a complete list of everything they would be carrying so that the judges could compare the lists with what was actually in the canoe. At the finish the canoes would be impounded until the judges could determine that there wasn't one item, not even a safety pin, that they didn't have when they started.

The contents of the canoes were interesting, especially the food. Almost every canoe had bananas taped to the thwarts, along with lots of cans of Del Monte pudding and snack packs, in all flavors. They also carried commercial preparations of Nutriment and Gatorade and other fast-energy foods. I was impressed by the extent of the provisions and the thought that had gone into them. Butch Hodges, however, was not. Hodges, who would take me down the river in a motorboat, had won the race in 1976 with his then partner, Robert Chatham, and held the existing course record. He looked at the bananas and the fast-energy food and said, "It don't make any difference what they take. They ain't going to eat a third of it. Oh, they'll eat that first day out, but by night they'll be so tired their systems won't take anything but water. 'Course, they ain't hungry by then, anyway."

If the food would turn out to be superfluous, the water would not. Each racer takes two plastic jugs rigged with long plastic tubes coming out the top. As they paddle, the racers constantly suck up water, especially through the heat of the day. Most of them will drink fourteen gallons of water during the race. One of the main functions of the team captain is to be ready with water along the route. As the canoe nears, the captain wades into the river with the full water containers. One of the racers slings out the empty jugs and the captain swims or wades alongside the canoe, boarding the full jugs. A team captain is the only person who can touch a canoe or the racers. If anyone else does, the canoe is instantly disqualified. But in spite of all they would drink, and in spite of the excellent shape they were in, many of the racers would lose ten pounds before they reached Seadrift.

After the canoes were inspected, John Nabors reiterated some of the rules and spoke of what they should expect along the route. "Stay in the main river," he said, "because we don't want to have to go looking for you. And if you take any shortcuts, especially at night, you're going to get lost." He also stressed the danger at Ottine Dam. "The river gets very crooked and very fast there, and you can be onto Ottine Dam before you know it. And it's a twelve-foot drop, straight down. So be alert."

There was not much talk about the rules. The racers knew the rules by heart and most were obvious. Their purpose was to eliminate any form of assistance, to enhance the challenge. No one questions them. The most basic rule is "Only muscle-powered propulsion of boats or canoes will be permitted." There is no limit on the number of team members, although the logic of the river is such that only two- or three-man teams are competitive. One year a four-man team entered, but they broke their canoe early in the race on the rocks at the Cottonseed Rapids.

The man who probably holds the record for breaking the most boats is Owen West of Houston, who races solo in a kayak. He also holds the record for the most finishes—ten out of ten. Someday he will probably come paddling across the bay to the finish line on a log, having broken his kayak somewhere upstream. Butch Hodges, my guide, has a grudging respect for West. "I don't know how he does it year after year. He'll tear the living hell out of that kayak, trying to go over a dam in it, and then he'll get out on the bank and piddle around and find him some old tin or some sticks or God knows what and get it somehow put back together and there he'll go again." At the racers' meeting West was telling everyone that this was his last race, that at forty-one he was getting too old. Tom Goynes said, "I'll believe that when I see it. I believe I've been hearing that story for the last ten years." Goynes himself has entered eleven times, finishing eight. His would be one of the more unusual teams in the race, for his partner was his wife, Paula, who would be paddling in the stern, the command position in a two-man canoe.

By the time the meeting was over, it was late, especially for people who were about to face 420 miles of river nonstop, and most of them went to their motels and campers to get as much rest as they could—though, as Doug Harrington, the bowman in Rich Miller's boat, said, "It's pretty hard to sleep while you run every mile of that river in your head."

But even though most had gone off to rest, a few racers were still out at Tom Goynes' canoe livery—the unofficial race headquarters and outfitting central—either visiting or working on their canoes. Out in the work shed the team from Oregon was making some last-minute changes. Doug Soules looked disgusted. "We've come twenty-two hundred miles and the canoe still isn't finished."

He had built a wood-strip canoe, a thing of varnished beauty that appeared to be in motion even as it sat on its sawhorses. His partner, Bill Crossland, never seemed to talk, but he had won the National Canoe Championship three times. The Chatham brothers would also be using a homemade boat, one built by Butch Hodges. Along the bow was the name *Delta Dawn*, which had been Butch's favorite song at the time.

And then it was Saturday morning and the canoes were in the water, jockeying to line up in the five rows to which they'd been assigned. In a race of this length the start should not have been that important, but the racers seemed as tense and alert as sprinters on their blocks. On the banks some five hundred people were screaming encouragement. The starter raised his pistol and the field of twenty-eight canoes was away in a froth of water.

The two sculling boats and the Trimble three-man paddling canoe sprinted into the lead. They ran abreast for half a mile, but just as they approached the first bend, the Chatham brothers began to pull into the lead. For the Chathams the race was even more important than usual, if that was possible; their father, who had raced himself and was now in the hospital in serious condition, had asked them to win it. Their determination was clear in their faces as they pulled steadily on the oars. They rounded the first turn with a good fifteen-yard lead on Wooley and Gore, who were second.

But as the river straightened, the Trimble team, paddling furiously, began to edge up on the Wooley canoe. In another half-mile they were cutting the sculling boat's bow wave; showing excellent teamwork, the three men, paddling as one, began to pull on past. Sculling smoothly, Wooley and Gore seemed to settle back to a determined pace.

Behind them the field began to string out. Roy Tyrone and his partner, Scott McDonald, were running fourth, ahead of Miller's three-man team. Behind them came the Oregon team, also showing surprising speed on the initial flat stretch of river.

Most of the racers had been preparing for six months or more for this race. They had different methods of training: lifting weights, jogging, riding bicycles. But the main method was the same: running the river. Some of the racers would put the canoe in the river on a Friday night after work and not get out again until Sunday night, often running two hundred miles, though not at full racing or portaging speed. And it was the portages that were killing when taken at racing speed. During the 420 miles, the contestants would encounter nine dams plus numerous low-water bridges and logjams. The number of portages depends on the level of the river. The logjams, which are the hardest single obstacle, are impossible to foresee. One year Butch Hodges and Robert Chatham, after thirty hours of racing, had to portage a mile and a half around logs and debris before they could put back into the river.

"We were dragging that canoe," Butch said, "and just barely able to do that. It really gets you when you're already so damn tired."

But now the racers were coming into their first serious challenge, Cottonseed Rapids, a long stretch of rocks and white water with a narrow chute exit that must be run very carefully. The Chathams were the first around the turn that leads into Cottonseed. The two hundred spectators on the bank began to yell as they recognized the canoe.

"Come on, Bucky! Come on, Robert! Row that thing!"

They came on with long sweeping strokes, until just before the entrance they began to backwater as Bucky, the bowman, turned in his seat to study the best way to run the water. Without much hesitation he put the canoe through the first of the rapids, guiding it skillfully while Robert, in the stern, responded to his stroke commands.

"Give me some right! A little more right! Now a little left! Now dig!"

Pulling hard now to get steerageway in the swift water, they ran right by a big rock in the middle of the river, cut sideways down a ledge they couldn't top, then made a hard right and came gracefully through the last chute, going on down the river, passing the cheering spectators without a glance, looking very resolute.

Then the Trimble boat rounded the curve. They came on, paddling carefully, the bowman studying the current for the best opening. He took a lead a shade to the right of where the Chathams had entered. Then, as will happen with the longer boats, the stern began to drift with the current. They tried frantically to correct, but it was too late; they were swept broadside into the big rock that the Chathams had negotiated so successfully.

The spectators, who had been cheering, became very quiet as the canoe capsized and the three men went tumbling through the white water. They came up clinging to the side of their flooded canoe, struggling to find footing in the swift water so they could guide their boat to the bank. They slowly disappeared from view around a sharp bend, still swimming alongside their boat.

And then came the Wooley boat with Howard Gore in the bow, turning to guide them skillfully through the same route the Chathams had taken. If anything, they ran the rapids faster than the lead boat. The two-man team of Tyrone and McDonald came next into view. Five seconds later the Oregon crew rounded the bend. Both teams paddled madly for the rapids, each determined to be the first canoe through. While it had seemed that the Wooley scullers had run Cottonseed quickly, these two canoes, now running almost bow to stern, simply flashed through the rocks and white water and were gone.

"That's going to be a race," Butch Hodges predicted.

Next came the Richard Miller three-man team with Doug Harrington in the bow. They came through very cautiously, guarding their boat, hoping to make up speed when they hit the Guadalupe.

Tom and Paula Goynes followed. To their embarrassment, the stern of their boat hit a rock just as they entered the chute, and they overturned. They floated past, clinging to their canoe and looking chagrined. One of the spectators yelled, "Way to go, professional canoe guide!"

And then, amazingly, here came Mike Watson of Freeport, pulling alone in an open two-man canoe. His partner had quit on him at the last minute and he'd decided to try it on his own, a feat that the knowledgeable said could not be done. In a kayak, yes, but not in an open canoe. A spectator said, "I'm absolutely amazed he's made it this far. I'll give ten to one he never gets through Cottonseed."

But he did, running it easily and smoothly, and disappeared down the river. In September he would be entering medical school, and as he had said, this would be his only chance to race the river. The veterans of the river admired his courage, but said he didn't realize what he was facing. The rest of the field came slowly by, Owen West bringing up the rear.

They all continued downstream, heading for Martindale Dam and Staples Dam—both killing portages—then on through rapids and logjams to Fentress and Prairie Lea and on some eighty miles to Luling Dam. At most places the San Marcos would be no more than twenty yards wide and very swift.

Downstream about two miles from Cottonseed Rapids, the three members of the Trimble team were standing next to their crippled boat looking at each other. They had finally beached her and had spent a frantic hour repairing a four- to five-foot gash in the side. Their boat was resinous plastic, very fast but also fragile. Then they had put back in and had made another half-mile before their boat had filled with water. They had worked on her for another hour, but they knew it was no use. Finally they just stood looking at each other, no one wanting to say the obvious. Then, without speaking, they went off one by one to sit privately, thinking their own thoughts. After all their work and preparation, they had missed the very first rapids, hit one rock, and it was all over.

By the time the lead boats reached the bridge at Luling, the racers had been on the river for over five hours and were all thoroughly soaked, but they seemed as fresh as when they had started. The first and second positions had not changed, but the Rich Miller team had passed the Oregon boat and the Tyrone boat, and was now running third, seeming actually to be gaining on the scullers. Several boats back, unbelievably, was Mike Watson, still paddling for all he was worth.

"It's not possible," Butch said. Buster Finke, who had joined us as my assistant guide, said, "He's going to kill himself."

After him were the Goyneses, who had lost time by overturning at Cottonseed Rapids. But now they seemed to be working well together. As the afternoon wore on, the Chatham brothers began slowly to build up a lead over the Wooley team. They were unlikely-looking racers, for Bucky, who is thirty-four, weighs only 130 pounds. His brother, Robert, thirty-six, is only ten pounds heavier. But then, this is a race of endurance and determination, and most of the racers were not very large. Some few might have weighed 180 or 190 pounds, but they were the exceptions.

From Luling it is about twenty miles to Ottine Dam. From there it is another thirty to Gonzales, where the San Marcos enters the Guadalupe. It was already late in the afternoon, and it was important to try to make the portage below Highway 90 before dark, for it was a half-mile nightmare, through brush and vines and bogging mud. It was difficult in the daytime; it was a killer at night. Consequently the lead teams were now digging hard to make it before dark.

Spectators continued to line the banks at each bridge, sometimes four or five hundred of them. They cheered wildly as each canoe sailed past. The Chathams were pulling away from the Wooley team. At this point they were holding a seven-minute lead. "They ain't sprinting," Butch said, "but they're going awful swift."

But Ottine Dam lay ahead and anything could happen there. The portage at Ottine is difficult for several reasons. First, you must go to the bank a good distance back from the dam or risk being swept over it. Then you must somehow muscle the canoe, which weighs anywhere from 60 to 140 pounds, up a steep bank, down a slick clay slope, and through a grove of trees. The portage is difficult enough for a fresh team, much less a team that has been racing for eight hours.

But the Chathams came sweeping up to the bank, backwatering at the last minute. Jumping into the chest-deep water, Robert held the canoe in place while Bucky climbed onto the steep bank. Then, lying on his belly and bending far down, Bucky lifted the prow of the canoe while Robert got the stern up on his shoulder. Together, they worked the boat forward until it was balanced well enough on the bank that Robert could climb up. Then they each grabbed a thwart and began to run the hundred yards down the slippery slope. Butch ran beside them, asking them how they were doing. Robert didn't answer until they'd crashed through the grove of trees and had the boat back in the river. Panting, he said, "We hit a snag and knocked a strip a little loose. We're taking on some water. But we don't want anybody to know."

Bucky slapped his arm and said, "Damn!"

Robert said, "What's the matter?"

"Something bit me."

But by then they were already out in the river, sculling away.

The Wooley team arrived, now eight minutes behind, made a good portage, and were gone. Then came the Rich Miller three-man team, looking more tired than the others. Doug Harrington seemed especially fatigued.

And then, just twelve minutes behind the Miller team, came the Tyrone canoe, racing almost neck and neck with the Oregon team. They hit the bank simultaneously, flashed up and over it, and, carrying their canoes, had a foot race down to the river. Tyrone and McDonald got away perhaps a second ahead, but within a hundred yards the Oregon team had drawn abreast. They disappeared around a bend, both paddling ferociously. The spectators cheered the two-man canoes through the whole portage. Someone wondered if it would be possible for them to catch the Miller team. It was beginning to seem that it might happen.

Two other teams passed and then came Mike Watson. Tall and skinny, but obviously extremely strong, he had a difficult time manhandling his canoe over the tough portage. But he made it and was gone again. Someone said he'd never last the night. But now no one was so sure anymore.

Four boats, including the broken Trimble canoe, had dropped out. At the next vantage point, near Slayden Cemetery, an old abandoned iron bridge spans the river, and the crowd clustered there to watch the racers go by. A great number of supporters from Seadrift were on hand to cheer the Chathams on. The crowd waited in anticipation for the first boat. Butch was organizing a good welcome for them. He had the Seadrift folks gathered together and was going to lead them in "Delta Dawn" when the Chathams came around the bend and then sing them on down the river.

"Here they come!" somebody yelled, and we could see a sculling boat make the bend and head for the bridge. The crowd began to sing:

Delta Dawn,
What's that flower you have on?
Could it be a faded rose from . . .

And then the words died on their lips. It was not the Chathams but the Wooley team. As they passed under the bridge, Wooley looked up and yelled, "Bucky's sick. They think a spider bit him. They're about five miles back pulled over on the bank behind a logjam." He yelled something else, but they were pulling hard and his words were lost in the distance.

And now everyone, especially the Seadrift people, settled down to an anxious vigil. Thirty minutes later, the Chatham canoe rounded the bend with Robert sculling furiously and Bucky collapsed in the bow. My two guides and several other Seadrift men fought their way over a fence and through heavy brush and trees down to the riverbank. Bucky looked bad. He was trembling and his face was ashen. His right arm was badly swollen all the way down from the elbow and his breathing was shallow and irregular. Robert was leaning over his oars panting. He was crying from exhaustion or disappointment or worry over his brother or all three.

Butch knelt by him. "Bucky, we better get you to a hospital."

Bucky didn't say anything, just lay there with his eyes closed.

Robert said, "Maybe he'll be all right. Maybe we can go on in a minute."

But Butch said to Bucky, "I'm not going to touch you unless you say so. Put out your hand and I'll carry you to the hospital. Put out your hand, Bucky."

It took perhaps five minutes, either for the words to sink in or for Bucky to make up his mind. No one on the bank said a word; the only sound was the rippling of the river. But finally, almost imperceptibly, his hand started out. Instantly, Butch grabbed his hand and lifted him out of the canoe. Butch and another man picked him up and started running up the bank with him, taking him to the hospital in Gonzales. The rest of them got Robert, now totally exhausted, up onto the bank and then hauled up the canoe.

Bucky had been bitten by a black widow spider at the Ottine Dam portage. He'd gotten very ill thirty minutes later. After ten hours of racing, Robert had carried his brother around a two-hundred-yard logjam, gone back and dragged their canoe around it, and then single-sculled them five miles down to where he'd banked. As they led him up the bank, his whole body was trembling and he had to have help walking. But he was still talking of going on by himself.

The Richard Miller team passed almost unnoticed. But they were losing ground to the Wooley canoe and looking very tired. Just ten minutes later, Roy Tyrone and Scott McDonald swept under the bridge, running neck and neck with the Oregon team, both crews still paddling like mad. That appeared to be the race to watch, because the three-man team, which seemed to be the only one with any chance of catching Wooley and Gore, was flagging badly. It was not considered likely that a two-man paddle team could catch a sculling canoe, not on the open Guadalupe River, where the scullers had traditionally made their best time. But night was approaching, and anything could happen on the river in the dark, particularly to those long sculling oars sweeping out into the blackness.

The lead boats passed Gonzales just as night came on. The next checkpoint was Hochheim—a lonely, grueling eight hours away. Now in the lead, Wooley and Gore held their steady pace. Their early strategy of pacing themselves was beginning to pay off. The Miller team continued to lose ground, but behind them the fierce race between the two-man canoes continued.

Roy Tyrone later said, "We ran with them all night. They laid in right on our stern, using our lights as well as their own. Try as best we could we couldn't shake them. Every so often we'd start a sprint, but as soon as we did, they'd start one, too. I'll bet there was never a yard separating us for six hours. Of course, they were doing the smart thing. They'd never run the river, not even in practice, and they were using us for guides. Those guys were really good."

But at Hochheim in the early hours of Sunday morning, Tyrone took a gamble. "Our team captain was waiting for us at Hochheim with water, and even though we needed water badly, I decided to pass it by. I had just heard one of the Oregon guys say to the other that they'd slow up for water. Well, as soon as I saw them lose a little momentum, I yelled to Scott to hit it, and we just jumped away from them. Before they could recover we had a twenty-yard lead. We made a fast portage and just went on from there. After that they kept losing ground."

But more important, Tyrone and McDonald had gained an un-believable amount of time on the Wooley team. The sculling team came through Hochheim at 2:55 A.M., and Tyrone and McDonald were only twenty-seven minutes back at 3:22. The Miller team was in between, three boats less than half an hour apart.

Back behind, Mike Watson was still going, as were the Goyneses. Tom said after the race, "We caught Mike around three in the morning and then ran with him until just about dawn. He said the one thing he hadn't counted on was how lonely and scary and black the river was at night, and what it could do to your mind."

Butch, my guide, agreed. "That ol' river is as black as the inside of a cow. All that little light does is poke a little hole in that big black, and you try to dive through it. And boy, does your mind go crazy. I swerved the canoe one year and my partner wanted to know what I was doing. I said I'd just saved our lives, that there'd been a GMC truck crossing the river right in front of us and if I hadn't swerved we'd've hit it. And then the year Robert and I won it, we were portaging around this mile-long logjam and he kept stopping and bending down and putting something in the canoe. He said that about every ten yards or so he was finding a new pair of tennis shoes and he couldn't pass that up."

"One year my partner and I were still out on the second night," Tom Goynes remembered, "and he suddenly pulled into the bank and ran up to a tree. I asked him what he was doing and he said he had to call his wife. He dialed a number on the tree trunk and started talking to her. I thought he was crazy until I started hearing her answering him back."

"It's amazing," John Nabors said, "what your mind will do when you get that tired. In some years, when the river is low, it can take up to forty-six hours, even for the winners, and that puts you through the second night. In 1975, when Mike Wooley and I won it, all the trees looked like cliffs with old men and monkeys scam-pering around on the top. I knew I was hallucinating, but I was hurting so bad that I just let my mind go."

Somewhere just above Cuero, Tyrone and McDonald passed the Miller team in the dark. The Miller team had gotten briefly lost in a blind cut; by the time they got back on the river the

Tyrone team had passed them. The Miller team made it to Cuero, where Doug Harrington got out of the boat. For a few minutes his partners tried to talk him out of dropping out, but he said he'd wrenched his shoulder and didn't have a thing left. Without another word they got back in the boat, two men in a three-man canoe. Quitting the race was on one level a sensible decision. Miller himself had quit the year before, but vowed he'd never do it again. "It was six months before I could look at myself in a mirror, and I'll never let that happen, not anymore."

But something else had occurred at Cuero. Tyrone and McDonald had come through just nine minutes behind the Wooley team, and the crowd went wild. Still, it was not possible for a two-man paddling team to gain ground on a sculling canoe in the lower river. The only way Tyrone and McDonald could have hoped to win was to have come out of the tricky San Marcos with a big lead and hold on until the finish.

But when they learned of the threat posed by McDonald and Tyrone, Wooley and Gore picked up the pace. "They were obviously making a super effort," Wooley said. "We couldn't believe it when our team captain told us. We were tired, but we knew they were tired too. About dawn, we began to pick up the stroke."

By Victoria they were pulling away, leading now by twenty-six minutes. We followed them in Butch's motorboat the next afternoon. When we passed Tyrone and McDonald they were still digging, but the fatigue was visible even though their stroke was still precise and rhythmic. Then we moved on up and caught the Wooley boat. Surprisingly, they looked worse. They were both glassy-eyed and slack-faced, and Mike was, as Butch said, stroking too deep. Looking at them, one began to wonder if the two teams behind them might not summon strength for another sprint before nightfall and begin to make up time again.

We stopped and waited for Tyrone to come by, timing the interval, which had lengthened to thirty-two minutes, and it began to look worse. At Swinging Bridge, Wooley and Gore were fifty minutes ahead, and later, at Tivoli, they had increased their lead to fifty-eight minutes. And night was coming on again. Ahead was the dark bay. Now it seemed that the only race left was the race Mike Wooley and Howard Gore would be running against the river and the bay and against themselves. It was too dark to see them as they came under the last wooden bridge, so we could not tell what was in their faces. But we could hear their tiredness in their sculling oars. There was nothing to do now but go and wait at the flagpole in Seadrift and see who the winners would be and if they would break the record.

Butch Hodges and Robert Chatham's record of thirty-seven hours was set in 1976. And Roy Tyrone and Scott McDonald, if they could finish, would shatter the old record for United States Canoe Association-class canoes.

The crowd of some two hundred people waited at the bay-front park Sunday night, watching anxiously across the water toward where the Guadalupe emptied into the San Antonio Bay. Occasionally a light would be spotted and someone would sing out, "There they come!"

But it would turn out to be only a fisherman or a shrimper. Then, about 9:30, a faint, flickering light was seen far across the bay. No one said a word until, as it gradually grew stronger, John Nabors said quietly, "That's them."

Now people began crowding the waterfront in earnest. Bucky Chatham had been released from the hospital after an overnight stay and he was there, though he looked weak and was wearing a bandage on his arm. His only comment had been: "They had trouble stabilizing my blood pressure."

He and Robert stood in the forefront, by the steps that led down to the water. The lights around the flagpole in the little park cast a glow some twenty feet out into the black of the bay. We could hear the canoe before we could see it. And then, suddenly, it was there, coming into the dim glow of the light.

The Chatham brothers waded out into the water to help Wooley and Gore out of the canoe; with the crowd cheering wildly, they were helped up the steps and seated in two armchairs. They looked as though they were not too sure where they were. Their wives brought them huge glasses of iced tea, then knelt and took off their shoes. Their feet were badly swollen and wrinkled. Their hands were raw and swollen. It was a long time before they could speak. They had come in at 9:40, breaking Hodges and Chatham's record by thirty-eight minutes. It was a remarkable achievement.

They sat there for an hour, not moving, while their wives put glycerine and alcohol on their feet and medicated their hands. After a time the photographers got them up for a victory handshake. They staggered drunkenly to their feet and stood there, clasping hands, swaying, speaking to each other in unnaturally high voices. After the pictures were taken, they collapsed back onto their chairs.

An hour and thirty-six minutes later, Roy Tyrone and Scott McDonald's canoe touched the side of the pier and they were officially second. They had broken the USCA record by an unbelievable three hours and twenty-six minutes. They were led up onto the ground and helped into chairs. Mike Wooley, walking as if on broken glass, came over and shook hands with Tyrone. "A hell of an effort, Roy," he said.

Doug Harrington was there, standing toward the back of the crowd. At 12:45 A.M. his two teammates, Richard Miller and Jerry Cochran, came in. If possible, they looked worse than any of the other finishers. But they'd made the last two hundred miles in a canoe that was not designed for two men. They staggered around drunkenly, grinning at each other, while chairs were brought for them. Then the first three teams to finish sat in a semicircle, hardly speaking, just looking at each other, sharing what they had done. Doug Harrington had not been able to come forward and speak to his old teammates. His wife led him away; his shoulders were shaking.

Tom and Paula Goynes were a surprising fifth. John Bugge and Bill Yonavich broke the aluminum canoe record and placed fourth. "We're pretty satisfied with that," Tom said. "Paula did exceptionally well, especially for her first time down the river." The Oregon team had a disappointing finish. When they entered the bay, they had been a strong third, but they had gotten lost and been forced to spend the night on an island until it got light enough to see. And then came the biggest surprise of all. At 11:44 A.M., with an elapsed time of fifty hours and forty-four minutes, Mike Watson, looking like one of the cadavers he'd soon be working on in med school, came paddling in. In his first attempt he had broken the one-man record by an astonishing six hours. He was unable to talk in the time I was there, but he later said in a masterpiece of understatement, "It was quite an experience."

It would be, by all admissions, at least three months before any of the racers were fully themselves again. There was no prize money involved, just trophies for those who won or placed in their class. But every finisher got a patch he could wear on his jacket. I asked John Nabors, who will be my partner in the race next year, what was the value of a trophy or a patch, since so few people knew what they meant.

He said, "Doesn't matter. You know what it means."

About seven Tuesday evening, after life had returned to normal, Robert Chatham was in a Seadrift Chamber of Commerce meeting when word was brought to him that a kayak had been sighted coming across the bay. He immediately left the meeting and was waiting at the bay front when Owen West, the last of the fifteen finishers, came coasting up to the landing, slumped in exhaustion over his tandem paddle. Robert waded out in his good clothes and helped the veteran up onto the bank.

West kept saying, "Never again. Never again."

Chatham said, "But you always say that."

As do they all.

3

Don't Look Back— You Might Be Last

I *went down to play for Del Mar Junior College during the spring semester, following a year at John Tarleton State. I stayed on for the summer because of the job that the athletic department got me and because of the weather and the general ambience of the place— including the pleasures of the Yacht Club and the girls that hung around there.*

But one day, in a fit of stupidity, I accepted a bet from Walter Lempke as to whether I could water ski from the yacht basin in Corpus Christi to Port Aransas, a distance of some 20 miles. The bet was for $15, no small amount to me in those days. But more important was my honor. I was an athlete and on the football team; so was Walter Lempke. But Walter Lempke's family was rich. His father was a doctor, and they not only had the first sunken living room I'd ever seen, they actually belonged to the Yacht Club, a thing I couldn't imagine.

To make it worse, he'd challenged me in front of a group of girls. Naturally I had to take him up on it. You didn't let challenges lie around in those days.

Now I don't know what you call them—slalom skis, I guess—those single skis you can put both feet in. Well, there weren't any of those around then. This run was going to have to be done on two recreational skis, just like your average Sunday afternoon skier.

To tell you the truth, I wasn't that worried. I was in as good a shape as I was likely to ever be, and I'd been doing a lot of water skiing. Plus, that $15 was a powerful incentive.

It looked like a piece of cake getting out of the yacht basin. For that first three or four miles it was smooth going. But then we began to hit the choppy water of the gulf as we curved north toward Port Aransas. Within five miles I was having trouble holding my skis parallel, especially the right one. It kept wanting to take off toward the east, and it was taking all my strength to hold it in place.

As mile after mile passed my thighs began to tighten up. Next came my calves, then my forearms that were holding the bar of the tow rope. It seemed that it was taking all my strength to hold my right ski in. That was quite a surprise to me since I knew my right leg was stronger than my left because I was a right-legged punter.

With about three miles to go I could no longer control my right leg, and all systems collapsed. I went into the water. In an ill humor, I was taken aboard the following boat and the bet holder gave Walter Lempke the money. He chortled. I tried, unsuccessfully, to look like a good loser.

About two weeks later an erstwhile friend told me that Walter Lempke had spent the night before my trial slowly warping my right ski over a charcoal fire. Not enough for me to notice, but just enough for it to matter.

And my wife wonders why I've played sports like a barbarian.

Walter Lempke, son of a physician, dweller in a home with a maid and a sunken living room. A man who warps my right ski for money that was pocket change to him. Junior member of the Yacht Club.

And I'm a barbarian? Hah!

My wife thinks I'm a barbarian. Why does she think so? One morning at breakfast I told her about the time I was playing third base for the Bay City (Texas) Black Cats and I hit a runner who was coming down from second base. I knocked him down with a thrown baseball to the chest instead of taking the easy out at first base.

Well, she thought that was awful. And it made no difference when I explained, as patiently as you can to a Yankee woman who doesn't know a baseball from a domino, that the guy had spiked me three innings earlier.

Of course we got the out. Buddy Barrett, who was playing shortstop and was nearly unable to run because he was laughing so hard, tagged the runner while he was laying on the ground gasping for breath.

When we got back to the dugout Coach Don Haley just said, "Good play." But my wife's comment was that she'd thought base-ball was a "clean" game. Whatever that's supposed to mean.

Well when she said that, I got slightly incensed and told her a few more barbarous details about the kind of baseball we played before millionaires of the modern game got worried about spiking each other in the stock portfolios.

I mentioned the time we were playing El Campo and a man was rounding third base with the clear intention of scoring the winning run on us. I gave him the hip and redirected him into the visiting team's dugout. That, of course, caused both teams to assemble in the middle of the infield for a spirited discussion of the sagacity of my act. And that, right there, is democracy in action, and if the rights of freedom of assembly and freedom of speech are to be attacked as barbaric, then what next? Communism, that's what.

Of course that logic was lost on her, as was my studied attempt to explain how humane it was to teach young pitchers, early in their careers, how unwise it was to throw at innocent batters who were standing at the plate with no more untoward intentions than trying to get on base.

I was of the Minnie Minoso school myself, in which a good hard swing and a loose grip could send a bat sixty feet and six inches at a pretty good rate of speed and just about knee high. I think that helped a lot of pitchers with their high jumping, and

I wouldn't be at all surprised if some of them went on to careers as dancers.

Some, like our center fielder, Tommy Morris, were advocates of bunting down the first-base line in such a fashion that the pitcher had to come over to field the ball. Naturally, your intention was to arrive where he was just as he bent over to field the ball. It was a valuable educational tool. Unfortunately, I was denied the use of this method because I wasn't a particularly accurate bunter. I was also the victim of some shortsighted umpires who considered running out of the basepath some fifteen or twenty feet illegal and not at all what the inventors of the game had had in mind.

My wife would have probably agreed with the umpires. And she'd have probably supported the attitude of a certain first baseman who played for the Wharton ballclub over a little incident in which my only intention was to keep him from injuring his glove hand. I had a little speed and was thus a pretty good threat to steal. Consequently, I drew a lot of throws to first base. Now, this first baseman had the habit of slapping me with his glove, ball enclosed for added weight, no matter how unclose the play was. Sometimes he'd slap me with that glove after I'd beaten the throw back with enough time to clean my spikes.

Well, I got to studying about that, and I concluded that if he kept slapping me with his glove he was going to do serious harm to his hand and never play the piano again. I decided I was going to have to do something to protect that boy from himself. Sure enough, as it does to all the good of heart, my chance came to help that young man. I was running hard down the first-base line, trying to beat an infield hit. The throw was high, and that first baseman had to jump for it just as I neared first base. Well, I saw my duty and I did it. I dropped my shoulder and caught him just below the hips, running right on through him. As I turned I got a glimpse of him doing a slow flip in the air and landing on portions of his head and neck and shoulders. I was impressed with his form and told him so as they were leading him back to his dugout. I even suggested he might take up diving as an alternative to playing first base. But I don't think he heard me because he was walking kind of funny and making these loud groaning noises.

But none of these carefully detailed explanations made the slightest dent in my wife's attitude. She, like all others of her ilk, are too interested in such things as not leaving empty beer cans laying around and picking up your clothes and wiping your feet and reading *House & Garden* and watching art shows on PBS and other such forms of unorganized hell.

But then I guess she's not much different from about a hundred million mothers out there who are afraid their little boys might get hurt playing "rough" sports. Well, what those mothers don't know is where the real hurt is. And that's going back into the locker room wearing a clean uniform without a bump or bruise on you.

That's what hurts. That's when you go off in a corner and undress as quickly as you can and put on your street clothes and get the hell out of the locker room as fast as you can. Most of the time without bothering to take a shower, primarily because you don't really need one, but mainly because the shower is the bump and bruise and cut panel discussion room. That's when the players stand around under the steaming spray and compare the different minor injuries they've suffered in the line of duty. They say things like—

"That ol' boy was already mad at me for robbin' him of that base hit in the second inning, so I guess he already had his mind made up he was going to take me out on that double play. Nearly chased me into center field."

Or—

"See that welt on my foot? Man, you don't ever want to top a ball down on your instep. Hurts worse than a stone bruise."

Or—

"That pitcher must have known I was going to take one for the team because he really poured it in there. Look at this lump right here on my rib cage."

Against all that there wasn't much glory in describing the pain and suffering you'd received from bench splinter scratches.

The shower room was one of the reasons I liked to play third base, especially against a team of right-handed hitters. Our main starting pitcher, Magdaleno Rico, didn't throw the ball particularly hard, and I could generally count on a good number of scorchers coming my way, which automatically made me the star of the red welt and purple bruise division. One of the reasons for that, according to Coach Haley, was that I never properly understood the function of the glove. He'd say to me, patiently for him, "Son, use your glove to stop the ball. Not your face or your chest or your knees.

You probably paid ten or twelve dollars for that glove and you ought to try and get some use out of it."

Which showed how much he knew. I'd bought that glove secondhand from a graduating senior and had only paid five bucks for it.

Of course the clean uniform curse applies to all sports—football, hockey, and maybe even basketball, though I wouldn't know about that because I was never guilty of getting anywhere near a game that came to be called "hoops." (Sounds like some sort of sucker game they'd have on a carnival midway.) It just seemed like it was more obvious in baseball. In football you could at least fall down a few times in pre-game warmups and get some grass stains on your uniform, or maybe even get muddy if it was raining. And there'd always be so many players going in and out that nobody could ever be quite sure if you'd got into the game or not. I guess the same applies to hockey, and maybe even lacrosse and soccer, though in the case of those three I'm not sure I'd care if I had played or not.

Or maybe it was Ray Noble Finch that causes me to associate the humiliation of the clean uniform so closely with baseball. I was sitting by him one day during our half of the inning and he was staring fixedly out at the field. There he was in a uniform that looked like it had just been drycleaned, and there I was, gloriously sweaty and dirty with a pretty good welt on my chest from where I'd just stopped a line drive the inning before. After a while Ray Noble said, darkly, "Somebody's coming out of there."

Well, being the thoughtful person I was I commiserated with him and tried to cheer him up by saying helpful things like, "Ray Noble, somebody's got to sit on the bench. We can't all play," and, "Like it says in the Bible, Ray Noble, some of us have got to sit and wait and inherit the earth."

But he just looked at me again and repeated himself: "Somebody's coming out of there."

Of course that somebody had nothing to do with me. Ray Noble had been beat out at catcher and at first base and, even though he was a good athlete and a fine hitter, I knew there was no way he could play my side of the infield. The only other player that had any time at third base was W.C. Gosling, and he was safely ensconced in left field. Now I will admit that I was going through what I termed a slight hitting slump. I didn't think it was all that serious even though Coach Haley, the day before, had made the uncalled-for remark that they might as well leave my name out of the box score except for the error column. Still, I thought I was safe from bench rot, never dreaming the way that man's mind worked. The next thing I knew, Ray Noble had gotten a couple of pinch hits. I was thrilled for him and told him so in the warmest terms, even repeating what he'd said to me, saying, "I'll bet somebody's coming out of there if you keep hitting like that." Which shows just what concern for your fellow man gets you. During the next game Coach Haley switched the first baseman to right field, put Ray Noble in at first, moved the right fielder to left field and, unbelievably, brought W.C. in to play third base.

I didn't even bother with the locker room after that game, much less the showers, and just went straight home in my uniform.

You notice I haven't mentioned track. That's because I'm not sure if it fits into the ruin-your-life forever clean uniform syndrome. There are no substitutes in track. If you're on the team you compete. The only thing that makes me unsure is this one little incident.

This was back before I uncovered my hidden talents and developed into the premier hurdler I was to become. We were at a little triangular meet and, for want of another warm body, the track coach stuck me in as the third entry in the mile. Now I have nothing against a mile per se. I think it's a good way to measure car speed, and it makes an excellent nickname for Denver. But I don't see much point in actually running it.

That same attitude held pretty true for me throughout that race, especially toward the end. I kept noticing that the other runners were going on ahead just like they knew what they were doing. I'd started off at a pretty good clip, not really being sure how far a mile was, but after awhile so many people kept passing me that I thought maybe I'd been mistaken about the event. Maybe I was in a relay and had missed the baton exchange. Finally, on the last lap, with the other runners growing kind of dim in the distance, I took a quick look over my shoulder to ascertain my position. I didn't see anybody, so I craned around for a better view.

I still didn't see anybody. Finally I turned around so far I lost my stride and managed to fall down, gathering up quite a few cinders with my skin as I did.

I took a shower after the meet, and even got some iodine dressing for the more severe cinder scrapes. But I discovered that there's no glory in a cinder-scarred uniform and body in a track locker room. So I don't know if the pain of a clean uniform applies to track or not. All I can do is paraphrase what Satchel Paige said: Don't ever look back. You might be last.

4

In Search of the Wild Blue Marlin

I *don't know if you could even call this sport, much less "the ultimate sport." I came closer to thinking of it as a sort of rich man's bacchanal. I should explain that by saying that I didn't actually see any of the "sportsmen" doing much sporting—at least not with the fish they were supposedly after. It sort of reminded me of going big game hunting in Africa with a guide who gets you right up next to your prey and then, if you can't make the shot, makes it for you. If the purpose is to have something to mount on your wall at home then I reckon you could call this sport. But if you've got a boat equipped with every kind of gadget imaginable, a full-time captain who knows his job depends on getting a fish on your line, and two or three mates to bait your hook and fix your drinks and give you advice. . . . well, I'm not sure what you call it.*

I didn't have a great deal to do with this story. Mostly I stayed in the air-conditioned lounge of the luxurious yacht I was on and watched TV and enjoyed a few drinks served by one of the two "hostesses" on board. There were several staterooms available that one could have used for sleeping or other purposes, but I didn't. I preferred to rough it.

The *Sukeba II* left Port O'Connor around five Friday morning, finding its way out through the dark channel with the help of radar and buoy lights. At first the other tournament-fishing boats kept pace, but the *Sukeba II* is fast, making around twenty-five knots at top speed, and it soon drew out of sight of the competition. But it wasn't out of hearing: the radio chattered incessantly as the fisherman called one another to make last-minute bets.

A sixty-five-foot custom-designed fishing boat, the *Sukeba II* is owned by millionaire oil consultant Henry Keplinger of Houston, who doesn't like his first name and prefers to be addressed by his nickname, Kep. Keplinger had come for the Poco Bueno Port O'Connor Offshore Association billfishing tournament, more commonly called the Walter Fondren tournament, after its founder, a former running back for the University of Texas and now a Houston investor. Fondren and a few fishing buddies had fished competitively against each other in a haphazard way for years. But they wanted to find out who the best fishermen truly were, so in 1968, over a bottle of Scotch, the tournament was born.

Ninety boats entered in 1980; most of them had survived a waiting list of several years, for this is *the* Gulf Coast billfishing tournament, and every sportsman willing to invest $500,000 to $1 million in a boat and crew wants to enter. They don't come just for the money, though this year it amounted to nearly half a million dollars. The true allure is that big-time billfishing may be the most exclusive sport in the world. As one of the boat owners pointed out: "Hell, nowadays anybody can belong to the country club and own a set of golf clubs. A lot of guys can afford African safaris or even a stable of polo ponies. But not many can come up with the dough to buy and maintain a true blue-water fishing boat like you'll see down here."

As the sun came up, the water began to change color. When the boats had left the Port O'Connor docks the bay had been gray; about ten miles out, the water turned green and then turquoise and then a startling cobalt blue. The *Sukeba II* was headed past the continental shelf, where the floor of the sea suddenly plunges from a depth of thirty or forty fathoms (180 to 240 feet) to eighty or a hundred fathoms. It is at the continental shelf that the big marlins and sailfish live. Kep's boat got there about eight-thirty, when the sun was already beating down.

Kep had won the tournament in 1978 and was intent on win-ning it again. So his crew had avoided the onshore activities: a dinner party every evening in a central circus-style tent, parties in private homes, parties on board the various boats. As at all rich men's tournaments, there were plenty of distractions. A party at-mosphere prevailed, created by wives, friends, and hangers-on who weren't there for the serious business of fishing but just to have a good time. Since midweek the tiny Port O'Connor airport had been crowded with private planes flying in the crowd.

The festivity peaked Thursday afternoon in an exercise called the Intercoastal Canal Olympics. This consisted of the Rope Walk, the Chair Throw, and the Ridden-Out-of-Town-on-a-Rail Race. The last event was probably the most painful, but the most demand-ing was easily the Rope Walk, which required each contestant to traverse a hawser stretched forty feet across one of the boat slips. As if walking the swaying rope with the anticipation of falling in the water wasn't difficult enough, the competitors had to drink three beers each before trying it. Fondren had set the meet record the year before by making it halfway across, but he'd retired on his laurels, claiming that the glory wasn't worth the rope burns he sustained when he fell.

But while others might have come for entertainment, Kep had come to fish. A surprisingly quiet, self-effacing man, considering his wealth and position, Kep has been chasing the wily billfish for a good ten years, during which he has owned a succession of boats, each one bigger and more elaborate than the last. If you ask him to define the fascination of game fishing he will grin and say, "Hell, I don't smoke and I don't drink. Everyone's got to have a vice; this is mine." Then he adds seriously, "I work very hard, most times four-teen to sixteen hours a day, and this is just about the only form of relaxation I have."

On board the *Sukeba II* as guests and to do a little business on the side were George Temple, a Houston oilman; Richard Adkerson, a high-powered accountant from Houston; and Tom McGreevy, a financier from Santa Fe. All had flown in on Kep's turboprop MU-2 plane. Captain Gerald Needham and his two mates, Joey Woodhead and George Overton, made up the crew. The captain and Joey are full-time crewmen; George Overton is something of an anomaly, a man of means himself but not wealthy enough either to own such a boat or prominent enough to be asked to fish on one. He had been invited simply because he was one of the most knowledgeable bill-fishermen on the Gulf Coast.

Under the rules, Kep could not begin fishing until nine, but the remaining time was well spent in cruising slowly while the captain looked for patches of floating seaweed or slick water or schools of bait fish—anything that might attract the billfish. There are three above-deck levels on the *Sukeba II*—the main deck, the flying bridge where the captain steers the boat, and finally, some twenty feet above the deck, the tuna tower. From the tower one can some-times see a big billfish swimming along just below the surface. George Overton stood there, scanning the sea for any clue to where the fish were.

The craft entered in the tournament ranged in size from forty-five-foot Bertrams and Hatterases up to custom-built boats like Kep's sixty-five-footer, the largest boat in the tournament fleet. Though these boats are intended primarily for sportfishing, they are luxurious indeed. Most can sleep eight or nine people and have air-conditioned salons, several bathrooms complete with showers, and elaborate galleys that are bigger and better appointed than the kitchen of the average apartment. Most are equipped with sonar, depth finders, bottom scanners, and the best radios available. Some even have loran (long-range navigation), a necessity for boats that sail into foreign waters for the fishing near Cuba and the Bahamas and even off the coasts of Central and South America. The *Sukeba II* houses two private staterooms and three bathrooms. There is even a color television set aboard. In fact, sitting in the air-conditioned salon drinking beer or iced tea, the crew could have easily forgotten what they had come for—to haul in the biggest and the most billfish.

Kep wasn't about to let them forget, though, and at nine they tossed out the baits. A boat the size of the *Sukeba II* trails five baits, two from outriggers, two from rods set along the side rails of the fighting cockpit, and one from a rod right in front of the fighting chair. Kep was using artificial baits, which can be skipped faster than dead bait, allowing him to troll faster and cover more water.

Patience is a necessary virtue in billfishing, which is one reason that the boats are as comfortable as possible. But after only an hour of trolling everyone jumped into action as one of the lines abruptly snapped out of the clips that held it to the outrigger—a knock-down, as it is called. The excitement soon abated, though, when George Overton reported that a lowly twenty-pound wahoo had taken the bait. Wahoos are good to eat, but they have no value in a billfishing tournament, so George Temple landed the fish. Kep was the most experienced angler on board, and he would fight the first billfish that took the bait. The three guests did take thirty-minute turns in the fighting chair, for luck and their entertainment. They kidded each other about who would be in the hot seat when a big blue marlin got on a line and how they would keep Kep from taking the rod by locking him in one of the bedrooms.

The winning catch is based on a point system. In addition to the points given for weight (one per pound), a blue marlin is worth five hundred points, a white marlin three hundred points, and a sailfish one hundred points. Obviously, the biggest prize is the blue. It is the largest, the scarcest, and the hardest to catch of all the billfish. Some blues weigh up to one thousand pounds, but these are rare and are found only in the waters off Australia. Most of the blues in Gulf Coast waters average three to four hundred pounds. They are a true fighting fish, sometimes leaping spectacu-larly out of the water as they thrash about trying to throw the hook, sometimes going to the bottom and refusing to surface for hours, sometimes even ramming the boat. Depending on the skill of the captain, the strength of the angler, and the fight in the fish, landing a blue can be an all-day ordeal. Two weeks after this tour-nament the *Chingadera*, one of the most impressive boats, caught a 672-pound blue during a tournament at Port Isabel. It required a six-hour fight to boat the fish, and Rob Terry, the angler, couldn't unclench his hands for twenty hours after the fight.

White marlin, although more abundant than the blue, run only about half as big. A very large one might weigh three hundred pounds. And sails, the most common of the billfish and therefore the least prized, average only about sixty pounds. But regardless of their size, all billfish are elusive. One expert has estimated that it takes fifty-five hours of trolling to catch one fish, which meant that the tournament entrants faced pretty long odds: they would be fishing on the waters of the Gulf for a total of only twelve hours over the two days of the contest.

As the morning wore on, Gerald Needham worked the boat back and forth over the blue sea, searching for any sign of the big fish. At one point George Overton sang out from the tuna tower that a marlin was rising for the starboard bait. The knockdown came and the line went whizzing out, making the screaming sound of huge deep-sea fishing reels. But it was just another wahoo. George came down from the tower cussing. "I swear," he said, "I saw a good marlin. That damn wahoo jumped on that bait before the marlin could hit it."

Before long, radio reports on what the others were catching started to come in. By late morning any number of boats had one sailfish on board, and the *Little Sister* and the *Teal* had each landed a white marlin. By noon the *Aquarius* had two sails and the little *Bill-Fisher* and the *Charybdis* had each caught a white. Kep was falling significantly behind. He had reckoned that of the ninety boats entered, his chief competition would be Bill Brock, Bob Byrd, and Rob Terry, joint owners of the *Chingadera*, and Walter Fondren, whose boat was the *Tsunami*. He based this judgment on their past performance, the quality of their boats, the skill of their crews, and the price they'd brought in the Calcutta.

A Calcutta is a betting pool. Each boat's chances of winning had been sold to the highest bidder and then the money was pooled. Once the tournament was over, the owners of the top eight boats would receive half the money, and the bettors on those boats would be paid the other half. (Another $45,000 in prize money came from the entry fees.) The bidding had been held on the Wednesday night before the tournament was to begin. In the big tent that had been set up close to dockside two professional auctioneers hawked the boats. Most went for $3000 to $4000 until the *Chingadera* sold for $7500. The *Tsunami* brought the highest price, $10,000. Kep's boat was second at $9000. Both Walter Fondren and Kep formed syndicates with their guests and crew members and bought their boats' own chances. A betting syndicate headed by Russell Stein, a Houston stockbroker, bought the *Chingadera*'s.

Kep had turned in for the night before they got around to bidding on the *Sukeba II*. But he left a blank check with his captain, Gerald Needham. A near-disaster occurred when the auctioneer didn't hear a bid from Needham and almost sold the boat to another bidder for $8000. The mistake finally got straightened out, though, and Needham's bid was recognized. "Hell," he laughed, "Kep would have fired me if I hadn't've got that bid in."

One o'clock came and went, and still the sea around the *Sukeba II* remained empty of tournament fish. More reports came in: by two o'clock ten sails and seven whites had been caught. The boats were now entering the dead part of the day, when the fishing would be at its poorest. "Damn," Captain Needham fretted, "I'd give a pretty penny for just one blue. Even a little one. We'd wipe out everything every other boat has got so far."

Then, at 2:20, the port inboard rod suddenly began to sing. "Knockdown!" yelled George Overton from the tuna tower. George Temple had been sitting in the fighting chair, but he quickly got out of the way as Kep came scrambling out on deck from the salon. "It's a blue," Overton reported. "I can see him."

On the flying bridge, Needham began backing the boat to make it easier for Kep to take the rod out of the railing socket and get back to the chair with it. They'd attached a safety line to the big rig, so it could be recovered if it got jerked out of his hands. Kep is not a very big person to start with, and he'd recently had an operation on his right elbow. It was all he could manage, even with the boat backing down on the line singing out, to hold the heavy rod and get to the chair. "We're losing too goddam much line!" he yelled at Needham. "Goddam, Gerald, give me some help with this boat!"

"You're all right," Overton said as he came tumbling down the ladder from the tower. He and Joey immediately began to rig the fighting harness around Kep's torso. "You got him now, baby," George said. "Just stay with him."

Now began the careful business of keeping the fish on the line as it wore itself down. Although most of this maneuvering was done with the boat, Kep decided to try to get some line back. Over four hundred yards of the 130-pound test line had already gone out, creating a terrific drag. So, in slow surges, Needham backed down on the fish while Kep tried to reel in. It was difficult, for the blue was swimming in a zigzag pattern. George Overton stood behind Kep's chair, swinging it back and forth to keep the line pointed where he thought the fish would be. "He doesn't know he's hooked yet, Kep," he said. "You better put some strain on him."

Kep was looking tense, as was everyone else. "How big you think he is, George?" he asked.

"I don't know," George said, "but I bet he'll go two hundred easy."

Then Kep noticed the crowd around him. "Some of you guys get up top," he commanded. "We don't need this many people down here. And watch those cigarettes, goddammit. One spark and this line is gone."

All of a sudden the big fish seemed to realize it was hooked. Down it went, heading for the bottom. From the flying bridge Needham yelled, "He's sounding!" The captain immediately started to back the boat down. The rod abruptly bent and the line began to scream out. Kep, who had been straining with both hands to hold on, suddenly jerked one hand loose to jam the big drag lever on the side of the reel to full drag. The line slowed, but not much.

"Gerald, dammit, we're going to lose this fish!" Kep yelled.

"You're all right," the captain called back.

Joey got some liquid detergent and squirted it on the seat of the fighting chair to allow Kep to slide back and forth more easily as he fought the fish with his shoulders and upper body, trying to re-trieve some line. Now the fish was not moving, just lying immobile on the bottom. "He's down there sulking," Overton said.

The action settled into a pattern: Kep pumping the fish, trying to bring him up, trying to gain back a little line; Needham cautiously helping him by maneuvering the boat. Then an unexpected danger appeared. A seismograph boat was bearing down on the *Sukeba II* from the port side. Behind it, on a mile of cable, the boat was pulling a barge that dangled wires and equipment almost to the bottom. If the boat crossed Kep's line it would be snapped and the fish lost for sure. Everyone began to yell at once. Needham, trying to see the name of the boat, frantically called for the binoculars. Meanwhile, Kep was shouting for someone to do something. He couldn't turn and see the seismograph boat, but he knew what it meant.

"You just fight this fish," George said as he swung the chair toward the fish's position. "Get him off the bottom."

At what seemed to be the last minute Needham reached the captain of the seismograph boat on the radio and it sheered off, taking a course that would clear Kep's line—if the fish didn't decide to run in that direction.

Kep had been fighting the blue in the broiling sun for forty-five minutes now, and the strain was beginning to tell. The crew put a towel over his shoulders and soaked it with ice water. He was still trying to move the fish, struggling to get in a few turns of line on the big reel. Then, suddenly, the reeling was much easier. Someone groaned, "We've lost him."

But George said, "No. He's coming up. Reel like hell, Kep. Don't let him get too far ahead of you."

Kep was shouting for Gerald to give him some help with the boat. But the boat was doing fine, edging forward at just about the right speed as the fish rushed toward the surface and Kep reeled frantically. Then the blue jumped, rising out of the water and turning in an arc to plunge straight back into the sea. He was about two hundred yards off the stern and he was big. "Better than two hundred pounds," George said. "Maybe two-fifty."

It was now past three o'clock and no one else had reported a blue. If Kep could boat this fish he'd be leading the tournament. As the fight went on the marlin was clearly beginning to tire. Gerald and George wanted Kep to work the fish harder, to get it in the boat as fast as possible. Kep did begin reeling harder, but he did it reluctantly, complaining that the fish still had too much fight in it to bring it in.

Then somebody yelled, "There's the double line!" The double line is two strands that connect the leader to a swivel secured to the main line. It was now just breaking water, meaning that the marlin was no more than forty feet from the boat.

George said, "Look at that swivel—it's cocked." Worried that it might snap, Kep backed off, giving the fish a little slack to take the strain off the swivel. Needham had jumped down into the fighting cockpit, where there is another set of controls, and was running the boat from there. The crew held a hurried conference about what to do, whether to bring the marlin in quickly, risking the extra stress on the metal, or to work it slowly and take a chance that the swivel might chafe the line in two. Kep wanted to play it conservatively, but Gerald and George thought it best to boat the fish right away.

"It's six of one, half a dozen of the other," they argued. "Let's try him."

Reluctantly Kep began to crank on the big reel. The fish came closer as the double line again broke water. Now they could see the marlin clearly in the water, swimming slowly behind the boat, its bill slicing the water, its dorsal fin raised. It looked big, very big.

The cockpit was cleared of everyone except the crew. Gerald grabbed the flying gaff, which works like a harpoon: the gaffer can hit the fish, leaving the gaff head embedded, and then pull it in with an attached rope. Slowly Kep worked the big fish up to the back of the boat. Joey opened the transom door, through which the fish would be pulled once it was close enough. George had gone to the controls and was keeping a slow speed ahead. Suddenly Gerald leaned over and struck the marlin behind the gills. The crew hauled it aboard, and Kep had his fish. It lay there, long and blue, iridescent, about ten feet from its tail to the tip of its bill.

"He's a good one," George said.

Everyone on board made the trip home in a state of quiet excitement. Once Gerald had reported the fish, the radio began to crackle with congratulations from the other boats. Kep, sitting back in the lounge with a diet drink in his hand, commented, "Catching a good one sure makes the trip back a lot shorter."

A large crowd was gathered around the weighing dock when the *Sukeba II* pulled in, and they cheered as the fish was unloaded. It weighed 262 pounds, which, with the 500 points for catching a blue, gave Kep 762 points and a commanding lead. Neither the *Tsunami* nor the *Chingadera* had caught anything; the smaller boats, none of which had been considered a threat, had had all the luck.

There was a dinner and a party that night, but it was not well attended—most of the crew members were now concentrating on the fishing. Kep's men were asked a lot of questions about where they'd fished. Gerald said he figured the *Sukeba II* would have more company the next day but that it didn't make any difference if others tagged along or not; one boat might get several fish, while a quarter of a mile away another boat would never get a strike.

The next morning, going out again through the dark channel, the crew was filled with anticipation. But the first indication that things might not go so well came only twenty minutes after the lines went out, when the *Mary Jane*, a forty-six-footer, reported she had hooked a blue. Then the *Spare Time* said that she was tied on to a blue. Still, Kep wasn't worried; he had all day to fish and he didn't need much besides a couple of sails or a good white to win. If he got another blue he was a sure winner.

Soon the *Mary Jane* called in that she'd boated the blue and that it would weigh at least two hundred pounds. The *Spare Time* reported that her blue was "just average." So Kep felt he was still leading—until he heard that the *Mary Jane* had boated a sail. Sounding a little worried, Kep said, "We better put something on board. We might not be ahead anymore."

Other boats were calling in steadily with reports of sails and whites, too fast to keep an accurate record of who had what. A boat whose name Gerald didn't catch reported she was tied on to a blue, but nothing more was heard, so Kep assumed she'd lost it.

Meanwhile, the *Sukeba II*'s sea yielded nothing. Gerald patiently trolled back and forth over the continental shelf, looking for grass, looking for slicks. Up in the tower George scouted for fish. Once he spotted a school of yellowfin tuna, but Gerald steered carefully around them because Kep couldn't afford the time it would take to reel one in. A little after noon the *Mary Jane* reported she had another sailfish on board. "This is getting serious," Kep said.

By now the guests were doing everything they could think of to change Kep's luck: switching brands of beer, changing shirts, varying the order of the visitors to the fighting chair, calling on all the known fishing gods. But none of it was doing any good.

And then, just before two o'clock the *Katie Ann* reported she had a good blue on board. That would go with the sail she'd caught the day before. George said, "I hope we can hold third."

Gerald replied, a little grimly, "If we *are* third." At two-thirty he blew the boat horn, sounding it four times, not for any particular reason but "just in case," he said, "the fish hadn't noticed we're here." Then everyone fell silent as the last thirty minutes—and Kep's chances of winning—slipped inexorably away.

At three o'clock Joey began reeling in the baits and storing the rods and reels in the forward compartment. After that there was nothing much to do except sit in the salon and drink beer or soft drinks.

George Temple said, "Damn, if we'd just caught at least one sail today."

But Kep just shrugged wryly and said, "That's fishing."

As the *Sukeba II* came idling up the channel in the growing dusk it passed the weighing dock. The same expectant crowd was there, the same jubilant crews unloading their catches. But this time Kep didn't stop—he had no prize to declare.

They announced the winners and handed out the money that night. The *Mary Jane*, with 1134 points, was first, winning $150,480. The *Katie Ann* barely beat Kep out, winning $75,240 for her 769 points. The *Sukeba II* was third with 762 points. Kep won $56,430. The *Chingadera* and the *Tsunami* finished out of the money.

Later, someone remarked that the cash ought to make him feel better about not winning. "Well, I suppose so," he said slowly, realizing that the speaker knew nothing of the mathematics of owning a craft like the *Sukeba II*. "I suppose if I'm very careful my share of that check will run the boat for thirty days." Then he smiled. "But if you go deep-sea fishing after prize money you shouldn't go at all. There aren't many sure things in this world, and billfishing definitely isn't one of them."

5

Still Number One in Your Hearts

---

*I*t's not mentioned in this collection of stories but, prior to receiving a long-overdue jacket from Tarleton State University, I had received a letter sweater for football from Blinn Junior College, also many years late. In looking back, it appears that I never seemed to be around for the awards banquets. I don't know why this was; some quirk in my youthful nature, I suppose.

Of the two, I treasure the jacket from Tarleton State the most for a variety of reasons. I suppose the most important was the justification it represented, as you'll read in the following story. But, more importantly, I think playing at Tarleton at the time I did and at the age I did was an important factor in what little maturing my wife thinks I still haven't done.

In the following story, you'll read about Korean veterans who'd returned from the war and gone back to school, men who tried to pick their lives up where they'd left off. I wish they'd just done that. Unfortunately, most of them returned with a lot of extra baggage, such as knowledge of hand-to-hand combat, survival, dislike for anything in their way, an intimate feel for warfare, and other elements usually missing in your basic civilian football player.

I used to look forward to the games as a rest. At least then they were venting their spleen on someone else. Practices, of course, were nothing but exercises in trying to stay alive. You couldn't say they played dirty because the word wasn't in their vocabulary. Neither was the word play. You were there, you were the enemy. And the enemy was to be eliminated.

Not too long ago my wife and I had occasion to visit an old teammate of mine, Greg McKenzie, who is now a county commissioner in Fort Stockton, Texas. My Yankee wife had heard all these stories from me about what it was like playing at John Tarleton in those days. Somehow she has developed this unwarranted idea that I am sometimes given to exaggeration. That night she got to listen to Greg talk about those practices and how a man was lucky to survive. He'd had it worse than I did. As an end and a defensive halfback I could sometimes remove myself from the worst of the action. Greg had been a linebacker, always in the thick of the action.

But all that aside, as far as I'm concerned I very easily hold the world and Olympic records for being the oldest man to receive two new letter sweater and jacket awards.

There is still more to come. Sam Houston State University may not know it right now, but they owe me a track letter from 1959. I won't count the punting I did for them.

I guess the reason I was so hungry for that football letter jacket from John Tarleton State University was to spite Coach C.B. Roland. Of course the crazy thing is that we are talking about receiving that college letter jacket thirty-seven years after I initially earned it and thirty-eight years after I got stiffed by Coach Roland, who was the head football coach at Bay City (Texas) High School. He's no longer the head coach there and hasn't been for some time. For all I know, he may well have passed on to his reward by now. Though in his case, I'm not sure passed is the proper word, because in the years I didn't play for him, or in any other years for that matter, I never knew him to actually allow the ball to get any higher than chest height except on punts and extra points, and I think those made him nervous.

Now all this, at first glance, may strike you as somewhat picayune, but then you weren't a fifteen-year-old high school boy entering his senior year with his whole social future and maybe his mental well-being riding on making the football team. I had excused myself about my junior year because I was one of those what you might call "late bloomers" and I hadn't exactly been football material that year. As a matter of fact, I had a hell of a lot more height than I needed for my weight, and I was also in short supply of muscles.

But a change had taken place in the intervening months. I'd gained weight, even more inches, and enough muscle bulk that I wasn't ashamed to go to the community swimming pool.

So I was ready. I mean I was really ready. I'd always been fast, and now that I had a little size I was going to be a handful for anyone who was going to stand in my way of being a star. I'd suffered through my junior year watching the best football players get the best girls and I'd had my time standing in the stag line. Those days were over. The only question in my mind was, because of my tallness, whether Coach Roland would let me try out for running back. From all I'd observed he seemed to favor short, squat people who, for some mistaken reason, he thought would be harder to tackle. In my heart of hearts I had the bad feeling that I'd probably end up playing end, which meant I'd have to recover a fumble to get my hands on the ball. That or go back and take it away from one of the receivers on the kickoff.

But where I played was secondary. I'd seen linemen like J.W. Watson and Ralph Hamilton doing all right in the social department, so I was willing to do a little blocking and tackling if worse came to worse. Though, truth be told, I never cared much for it. It seemed like a terrible waste of playing time and a strain on the fans who were watching you and trying to pick you out amongst the jumble of twenty-two bodies.

Came the latter part of August and time to report for football tryouts. I was in shape. In spite of my young age, I was as strong as I needed to be. I'd worked in the oil fields all summer and I'd gotten in my share of running and anything else I could think of. We didn't lift weights back in those days. Most coaches held the belief that it would make you muscle bound and might interfere with your natural physical as well as mental development. I believe the latter part of that theory was based on the fact that weights were called dumbbells. Or maybe people who lifted them were called dumbbells. Whatever the case, we didn't fool around with such stuff, even though several of my teachers must have thought I did based on some of their remarks about my scholastic ability.

That morning I was sitting on a table in the equipment room. The doctors were there and we were all waiting to take our physicals. We were all just sitting around in jockstraps making nervous talk and thinking about the two-a-days that lay ahead. Bay City is on the gulf coast of Texas and its climate was designed by a man who once ran a Turkish bath. There may have been fat people in Bay City but I had never seen any. It was even said that the only thing that didn't lose weight during a Bay City summer was a wrought-iron fence, and there was some disagreement about that.

So we were sitting around speculating on how many cases of heat stroke we'd have the first day of full pads when Coach Roland walked in. He looked around for a minute and then looked at me. He said, "What are you doing here?"

Well, that kind of took me off guard. I figured it was pretty obvious since I was dressed like the rest and looked like the rest and was sitting with the rest. But I said, "Well, coach, I'm here to try out for football." I gave a little laugh as if he was kidding, but I knew better than that. Coach C.B. Roland did not kid. He did not laugh, he did not chuckle, he did not smile, and he didn't permit it in his presence.

He'd been a guard in college and he still looked like one, although I reckon he was about forty at the time. He said, "You can't try out for football. You're ineligible."

Ineligible? Like hell I was. If there was one thing I had assiduously done it was to keep my grades up enough to make sure I'd be eligible scholastically. The valedictorian was safe, but I *knew* I had a solid C average. I told Coach Roland as much.

He said, "That ain't why you're ineligible. You're ineligible because you didn't come out for spring practice."

I was so stunned I just sat there and stared at him. Spring practice? Well, no, I hadn't come out for spring practice because I was running track and playing baseball. I thought spring practice was something you participated in on sort of an optional basis. At least I'd never heard anything to the contrary. Besides, spring was baseball and track weather. Who the hell wanted to be playing football for four weeks in April? Didn't the man know anything about the seasons? I also considered such an activity a threat to my future. I wanted to play football my senior year for female reasons. Having come of an age where the sap was rising in my trunk, I had carefully noted that it was not the track and baseball athletes who got the girls. It was the boys who played under the lights on Friday nights. I had laid my plans accordingly.

But my long-range plans were to play professional baseball for the St. Louis Cardinals or any other team that was lucky enough to get me. Consequently, I wasn't going to let any silly thing like spring practice interfere with that. I had noticed that some of our baseball players, as well as some of the track athletes, were reporting late to practice, having already put in time over on another field playing football. I thought this was just plain foolish and I was amazed that the track coach and baseball coach let them get away with it. They invariably arrived tired and sweaty, and some of them would be stove up and sore after the football team had started putting on pads. I made mention of this to Buddy Barrett, who played shortstop alongside my third base position. I said, "You are risking our chances at the district championship by what you are doing. It is affecting your throwing arm. And if you think I'm going to cover for you by cutting off those short hoppers just so you can please C.B. Roland, you are sadly mistaken."

Barrett had just given me a strange look and said, "Then I guess you ain't going to play football next year."

I said, "What are you talking about?" At the time we were taking infield practice and I'd just fielded a ground ball and sent it over to first base. The rest of the discussion got lost in practice.

But I guess I should have heard him out. As far as I know, that was the only indication that I had to go to spring practice to be eligible for football that next year. Except, of course, when C.B. Roland told me to get off that training table and get the hell out of the locker room.

It was a long year. Football season dragged on and on. I don't think I went to a single game, and I'm pretty sure I didn't have too many dates. And then, of course, basketball season came along. I have the same view toward basketball as I do toward most unpleasant things, so I more or less went into hibernation during this period.

And then came spring, a year after I lost my chance to play football. But I did get a measure of revenge against C.B. Roland. In that intervening time, I'd filled out to 195 pounds, was 6'3" tall, and I'd set an interscholastic league record for the 180-yard low hurdles. I could also run a 10-flat hundred-yard dash and I'd had a tryout with the St. Louis Cardinals.

As a matter of fact, I used to walk casually into C.B. Roland's office and remind him of those advancements in my athletic career. Ol' C.B. used to just sit back in his chair and laugh and say, "Well, that still don't make you a football player, does it?"

And then I would kind of casually mention to him that he'd gone three and six for the year that he wouldn't let me play. Naturally he always replied that if I'd been playing, their record would have been even worse.

It was a funny situation; he and I developed a sort of humorous rapport based on him having a bad record and me losing my senior year. Instead of there being any rancor on either side, it seemed that I could come by and rag him about possibly losing the best receiver he'd have ever had. Then he'd reply that it didn't make a whole lot of difference what kind of pass catcher I was since he was fundamentally against the idea of throwing the football.

Of course we did not discuss the grievous harm that his attitude toward spring practice had done to my social life. There were some things better left unsaid.

That summer I wrote off to all the colleges, offering my services as a football player. Of course the fact that I hadn't played my senior year sort of went against me. Off the whole squad that I hadn't played on, only J.W. Watson got a scholarship offer. It was, however, a pretty good one—the University of Texas. Naturally, none of this made my chances look very good. When I told Coach Roland that the only reply I'd had back from all the queries I'd sent out was from John Tarleton (at that time, a junior college), he let out a pretty good laugh.

In those days Texas junior college football was no joke. We had Korean veterans returning who still wanted to play; we had a lot of kids who were being groomed for the bigger colleges through the junior college program; and we had athletes who weren't going much further, but who could play plenty good ball at that level.

And off I was going, as a virtual walk-on, into that situation. No wonder ol' C.B. laughed.

Well, I made the ball club and got a scholarship and, pretty soon, I was starting. But it was not without pain. About three-fourths of our ball team was composed of those just-returned vets, and the only difference they knew between football and war was that you weren't allowed to carry a gun in football.

But I had a release. C.B. Roland. Every time we took a road trip I'd send him a picture postcard of the hotel we were staying in with a mark around my supposed room and the notation "I'm here."

Of course, I didn't go home that year and, just before the semester was up, I decided to transfer to Del Mar Junior College in Corpus Christi and play there. It had turned out that the John Tarleton football team was suffering from the same plague that seemed to have infected every football team in the nation—they didn't want to throw the football. And there I was with all that speed and those tricky moves going to waste while I blocked 260-pound tackles and played defense against nothing but the run.

But Del Mar had guaranteed me they'd throw the football, and they were offering me more laundry money and, hell, I couldn't turn that down.

So I left John Tarleton, and I left before the awards banquet, which is when they award you your letter jacket. At the time it didn't seem that important. They had beaches and palm trees in Corpus and girls who were tanned all year long and wore shorts. What did I need with a letter jacket?

But then came the following year and I went home to Bay City. One of the first people I went by to see was Coach Roland. I didn't say much at first, waiting expectantly for him to take notice that I'd gone upward and onward without any help from him. But nothing was forthcoming. In desperation I asked if he might not have noticed that I'd played college football this past year.

He said, "Well, I got those postcards you kept sending me, but I couldn't tell much from them. I figured you were out on the road selling shoes house to house."

Good ol' C.B. always did have a nice turn with a phrase.

I said, with hope that he might have noticed, "Listen, it was in all the papers. I played! I started!"

He said, "First I've heard about it. Wasn't in any of the papers around here." I looked at him for a long time. Then, kind of sorrowfully, I said, "C.B., you are just ashamed you made a mistake in my case. You were wrong and you know it and you just don't want to admit you let a good football player get away from you."

A second passed and then Coach Roland nodded his head toward the window. He said, "It's February out there. If you played, where is your letter jacket? How come you're not wearing that?"

I opened my mouth and then I closed it. There was nothing to say. I could have explained that I'd left before the awards banquet, but all I'd get was a laugh. I just got up and slunk out.

A little better than thirty-six years later I had occasion to talk with Ron Newsome, the athletic director at what had become the fine, four-year institution named John Tarleton State University. More as a joke than anything else, I told him the story about C.B. Roland and my missing letter jacket. The upshot was that Coach Newsome and the university president, Dr. Barry Thompson, invited me down and presented that jacket to me all those years later.

They did it. And they did it good. They did it at halftime of the Homecoming game, and it kind of touched me. They had my letter jacket and they had my jersey, number 82, with my name on the back. Ron Newsome made a very nice speech and some of the fifteen thousand fans on hand even listened. It was like one of those deals you see at halftime when an old Dallas Cowboy comes home and they retire his jersey.

They didn't exactly retire my jersey, but Coach Newsome held it up and said, "Here he is, still number 82 in your program and number one in your hearts."

I was touched. I looked up in those stands and searched for C.B. Roland's face. Naturally he wasn't there.

6

First Your Money, Then Your Clothes

*O*f course now we have pari-mutuel betting at horse tracks in
Texas. But back when I did this story for Sports Illustrated the
brush-track bookie was a very important factor in those weekend and
holiday race meets. He was colorful, he was mostly honest, and he
could carry more figures in his head than the Ford modeling agency.
I'd been trying for a number of years to do a story on one of them but,
because they were basically in an illegal profession, I could never get
one to let me see the inside.

I met the Bear in a less than fortunate way. I was in a beer joint
in Brady, Texas, when this huge, bearded man came in. He took a
place about five or six feet down the bar from me with no one in
between. After awhile I became uncomfortably aware that he was
staring at me. I knew what that meant and I broke into a light sweat.
Pretty soon he started inching down the bar. When he was close
enough he reached out and moved my beer a few feet away from my
hand. I moved it back. He moved it again. So far I hadn't looked him
in the face because I knew what I was going to see. I figured that the
only way I'd have a chance against him would be if I had a baseball
bat and an AK-47 assault rifle. Having neither, I went to the mouth.

I said, " Listen, partner, not only do I not want to fight you, but if you'll pick out somebody else in the place I'll help you whip 'em."

Fortunately that got him to laughing and we got friendly. It wasn't that the Bear was mean-spirited or a bully, it was just that he'd had a bad day and his wife had been nagging him and his girlfriend had a gripe on and I was the next biggest thing to him in the place. So he'd figured to have a little frolicsome recreation to ease his mind.

Still, I had to convince his lawyer in Dallas that I would protect his identity before he would open up to me. Curiously enough, I already knew his lawyer as the agent for a number of professional athletes who'd come out of the Southwest. I don't think I'll mention his lawyer's name, either.

The Bear, which is not his real name nor even his nickname, is a brush-track bookie. A brush-track bookie, for the uninitiated, is a gentleman who lays odds and takes bets at the countless little horse tracks, mostly in Texas, where gambling is illegal and where they certainly don't have pari-mutuel wagering.

On a Saturday afternoon, just one day short of the Fourth of July, the Bear and his partner, who we'll call Lucky, are doing business down near the paddock area at Rollie White Downs just outside of Brady, Texas. This is a three-day meet, over the Fourth of July, and one of the big meets at Rollie White Downs, just as it is for any number of other little tracks across Texas.

The Bear and his partner have come down a couple of days previous to give themselves time to hang around the horse barns, talk to trainers and jockeys and owners, and find out if there's any new horse talent running that they don't already have a line on. It is also a good time to build up their bankroll, something the Bear sorely needs to do because, since he was busted for gambling promotion in another state, he's been laying low and staying away from the tracks. As a consequence, he's come to Brady carrying, as he says, "slim to none."

The way the Bear, and other bookies, build up their roll in advance of a meet is to get into town a few days early and, while they are hanging around scouting the talent, they are also looking for an owner or trainer who's got a horse going that they are particularly proud of.

The Bear says: "What you do is, you get down there the morning of the races, say about nine or ten in the morning, when all the owners and trainers are there. Then you scout around until you find an owner who's got a horse in, say, the fifth race onward that he likes enough that he'll bet you pretty good. You give him good odds so he'll take the bet, and he hands you five or six hundred dollars, or maybe more. See, he gives you the money because the bookie always does the holding. Then right there you've got your stake for the first few races, right up until the time his horse runs. And if you can't win enough on those first four races to handle the man's bet in the fifth (even if you lose), then you ought to get out of the business. What I'm saying is, you ought to be able to go to that track with twenty cents in your pocket and if you know enough about the horses and the people, you ought to be able to go home, when the last race is done, with a pretty good payday in your pocket."

Of course no bookie is going to tell you what he considers a good payday. In fact, the one thing they don't like to talk about is how much money they've made. They'll be glad to tell you how much they've lost, but not how much they've won. But it's a good rule of thumb to know that none of them do much celebrating unless they've won three or four thousand dollars in a day's racing.

But on this particular afternoon the Bear is not happy. All the horses are running to form, and he and his colleagues are getting beat a little more than they like. A bookie likes long shots to come in because the crowds generally have enough knowledge so that they, too, have a pretty good idea who the favorites are, and even though the Bear keeps moving his line on the favorites, making them less and less desirable to bet on, the crowd still keeps taking bets at 2-3 and even 1-2 odds. And the favorites keep on winning.

The Bear growls to another bookie standing nearby, "You'd think some of these long shots would come in and give me a little relief."

The other man, a bookie nicknamed Okay, just shrugs. "That's the way it goes," he says, "first your money and then your clothes."

Of course not many of these bookies are in much danger of losing their money, much less their clothes. What it comes down to, on a slow afternoon with all the favorites running to form, is a depletion of profits. The Bear is just a touch slower than a hand calculator at figuring in his head just what odds he must give on a certain horse for a certain amount of money against what he's already got bet on other horses at money and odds. And having that talent, it is really just a question of what percentage of the total he's going to take.

It is a hot afternoon, as you'd expect in Texas in July. The track itself is a regular mile oval just as at a thoroughbred track. But here, as at most brush tracks in Texas, it is nearly always quarter horses that are raced, at distances from 330 yards up to 660 and 870 yards. A short race is always a straight ahead dash. The longer races are run around one curve, or the hook as it's called. There is a small grand-stand at the finish line, holding perhaps two thousand people. Just off to the left of the grandstand is the paddock, where the horses are saddled and led out for the race. Just past that is the jockey area. There is a good crowd out, though there will be more the next day on the Fourth. Only about half the crowd is in the grandstand; the rest are milling along the fence near the finish line or down in the open area near the paddocks where the bookies are doing business. They are obviously a western crowd—even the women are dressed in jeans and boots and western shirts and hats.

The Bear himself does not wear a hat, though he does sport $500 custom-made boots and a hand-made western shirt with two big pockets on the front. "These are my teller windows," he says, pointing to the pockets. And it is in them that he keeps his roll, paying out of one pocket and depositing in the other. He says, facetiously, "I couldn't do business without these pockets. I'd lose track of my count."

There are about ten or twelve bookies working down in the paddock area. They are distinguishable a little by the flash of their clothes and their flamboyance, but more by the rolled-up race pro-gram they have in one hand and the ball-point pen in the other. That program, race by race, is where they write the bets down. If you go up to one of them and lay a bet, say on the number-six horse, they will ask for your initials and then write down the amount of your bet and the odds, along with your monogram, beside the race in ques-tion. The curious thing about that though, is that they very seldom consult the program when the race is over. The Bear might have fifty bets on a race, twenty of which are winners, but when the race is over and the winners come to be paid, he will go in his pay-out pocket, bring out that big roll with the rubber band around it, and pay off each winning bettor the correct amount without once looking to see at what odds he made this one or that one. A man might walk up and say, "R.B., I had—"

And the Bear will say, "I know what you had on that four horse, R.B. You had three to one. Beat me out of sixty dollars. Listen, Slick, next time you got a sure thing like that, slip around here and let some of the poor folks know so they might can make a little money."

All this without ever really knowing most of the people he's betting with, except their face, their initials, how much they bet and at what odds.

But the Bear is not only in the business of knowing more about the horses than the bettors do, he is also in competition with the other bookies for the bets the crowd makes. The bookies don't work together, though they do cooperate with each other about little things such as taking some layoff money if it doesn't hurt them, or making change for each other or, to a degree, sharing information about certain horses and trainers. But other than that it's pretty cutthroat. They are usually close on the odds they'll lay, but not always, and the crowd, knowing this, shops from one bookie to another looking for better odds on the horse they like. The Bear seems to do more than his share of the business because he seems to be laying better odds on the more popular horses.

"That's because I take more chances," he says. "I *like* to take chances."

His partner, Lucky, says, "No, that ain't true. He sometimes gives better odds because he knows more about the horses than anybody else does."

Whatever the reason, the Bear is doing more business, but not necessarily more profit. And as the races reel off down to the seventeenth and last race, and one more favorite comes in, he says, as he drives out the fairgrounds gate, "Damn, you'd think these were real good horses the way they were running to form."

In fact, and as the Bear knows, they are not bad horses. Even though the average purse at most brush tracks is something like $700, some of the horses running at Brady during the July 4 meet will go on to race in major futurities and end up earning hundreds of thousands of dollars.

Of course this is no consolation for the Bear as he slumps

down in a chair and claims that he barely made expenses on the day.

Which may be true but, in the Bear's case, expenses are considerable. He drives a Cadillac, stays in the best places, and eats in the most expensive restaurants. That night, in the only private club in Brady, Texas—liquor laws being what they are—the Bear moves around, buying drinks for a trainer, picking up the dinner check for an owner or a jockey, making jokes, being a good fellow, and all the time talking about horses and listening. At first he appears to be doing all the talking, but if you watch him close, he does just enough talking to get the subject kicked off on a particular horse he's interested in. Then you'll see him do some very intent listening.

He says, "The secret to this game is knowledge. If I'm gonna make a living at it I got to know more about *all* the horses than anyone else. And there ain't no way for one man or even two, or ten, to get around to all the tracks and see all the horses. So you got to know the people who know about their horses and get your information from them."

A visitor wonders how important it is to know the trainers and jockeys well enough to be able to tap them for inside information.

The Bear doesn't even hesitate. "It's ninety-five percent of the game. Listen—" And he sweeps his arm around the dining room of the private club, "from where we're sitting I can see at least five guys who owe me money. And I don't care if they ever pay it back. In fact, I don't want them to pay me. What they can *tell* me, in the long run, will make me a whole lot more money than if they all ran up here and paid me at once."

All through the evening he will get up from his table and go over to other tables to talk quietly about horses. Or men and women will come up to his table, sometimes to bend down and whisper in his ear. When that happens he'll just nod and say, "All right, you got it. I'll see you about that tomorrow."

The Bear is somewhere between forty and fifty; he won't say exactly where. He's a big, rough-looking man with thinning hair and a very genial way of talking. He's known around the track as a man you can trust, a solid citizen who'll keep his word and always pay his bills. "That's the way it's got to be in this business," he says. "You're dealing with men who are worth millions of dollars in some cases. Try and stiff them and they'll come down on you hard.

No, around a track you've got to be straight. If you don't you'll make enemies. There may be some that can afford that, but I can't. Making enemies costs money."

The Bear has been making his living as a bookie for something like ten years. Before that he was in the contracting business and doing well, but then, one day, he just got tired of it. "Hell," he says, "I was out at the track every day anyway, so I figured I might as well try and make a living at something I liked. See, I like the excitement and I love horses. I could talk horses all day long."

A visitor wonders if he'd be just as interested in horses and horse racing if there were no betting.

"Hell no!" he says, looking at the visitor as if he's lost his mind. "And I don't know anybody else that would, either."

Which is most likely true and which makes state laws like those in Texas, which make race-track betting a crime, appear more than just a little hypocritical. It is probably safe to say that without betting there would be no horse racing.

Back at his motel the Bear says, "Look at it this way. A guy goes out and pays three or four thousand dollars for a race horse. Then he's got to invest probably that much or more in trainer's fees. Then he's got to pay to haul him to a race track somewhere, pay a motel bill and a feed bill and a stall bill and his entry fees and a jockey fee. And he's running in a race where the purse is $300. You think that ol' boy is gonna do that if he can't get a bet down? Hell no, he's not. Now he could go around and try and get a bet down with other owners or trainers, but he'd never get any odds and it might take him a day and a half to get his bets covered. Or he can come to me or somebody like me and get the business done in thirty seconds." He smiles slightly. "You might say I perform a public service."

All of the brush tracks are in small towns or small cities, where the law is or has to be very lenient. The law occasionally makes arrests, but they don't make any real effort to stop the activity. The Bear has been arrested at least eight times, as have most of the other bookies. But if the sheriff or police were interested in strict enforcement they could arrest the bookies every day there was a horse race. It's not a matter of payoffs. The Bear and other bookies swear that there is absolutely no grease, as they call it, applied to the local law.

Another bookie, Champ, says, "They just make arrests when

somebody gets on their back hard enough about it and they get scared they might lose a few votes. Of course they'd lose more if they shut us down completely. They just do it enough to keep everybody happy. You take a town like Brady. This three-day race meet is bringing in a lot of out-of-towners who'll spend a lot of money in this town. You shut down the betting and you'll shut down the racing. Then the out-of-town crowd won't come and you'll see a whole bunch of damn mad merchants and other people. You'll put a lot of jockeys and trainers and stall boys and ticket takers and parking lot attendants, and a lot of others, out of work. No sheriff wants that on his head."

The next day is July 4, and that means picnics and red-white-and-blue bunting and watermelons and county fairs and, in Brady, horse racing. Post time is one o'clock, but by noon the parking lot is already half full with a steady stream of cars arriving as fast as they can.

Over in the jockey area Roy Simmons is getting his tack ready. Brush tracks are for jockeys what the minor leagues are for ball-players; good training grounds for those on their way up and a place to make a few last paydays for those on their way down. They're also places of steady work for those who were never going to make the major leagues in the first place.

Roy Simmons is thirty-nine, though he looks older. His face and teeth show the effects of the many wrecks he's had on the race track in his career of twenty-four years. The day before he'd had fourteen mounts out of the seventeen races and halfway through the day he was so tired his hands were shaking. A jockey at Brady (and the other brush tracks) makes a $25 mount fee and ten per-cent of the purse if his horse wins. But it's no money unless you win a lot of races, because brush tracks only operate over the weekends or over three-day holidays such as the Fourth of July.

"No, of course it's no money," says Roy. "I guess I'll end up making a thousand, maybe twelve hundred over this meet. But by the time you pay your expenses and then wait for next weekend you haven't made much."

Jackie McHargh, a young jockey who is nineteen and very reckless on the track, comes over and asks Roy how he did the day before.

Roy shrugs. "I had four good horses and ten pie eaters. I won with one of the good horses and finished in the money on the other three."

Jackie whistles. "Boy, I wish I could get that many mounts."

When he's gone Roy looks after him for a second and then says, "Yeah, don't he. At his age maybe he can ride fourteen mounts in a day. People in those stands don't know what it takes out of you to ride fourteen mounts in a day. Especially quarter horses. You can rest a little when you're racing a thoroughbred at a mile, but there is no time for anything at four hundred yards except to grab a handful of mane and get to work with your stick."

Later he answers a question that is put to him. "Yes," he says reluctantly, "I've been asked to pull a horse." He gestures around the jockey area. "And I'd imagine every boy here has, too. If he's been on a good enough horse. But I never pulled one. And that's the truth."

The Bear confirms this. "Naw," he says, shaking his head, "you never fool with the jockeys. Hell, in a ten-horse race you'd have to pay off nine of them and then your sure thing would probably break his leg just before the finish. No, there are better ways to fix a race than that."

You ask him how.

"Medicine," the Bear says. "Some horses just run a lot better with the right kind of medicine in them. And at these little tracks it's pretty hard to detect. Of course you've got to know the right people to take advantage of it. You got to have knowledge. Just what I been saying." Then he smiles and winks. "You understand, I'm just telling you what I've heard. I have no first-hand knowledge myself."

The Bear is in a better mood than he was the day before. He tells Lucky, "Boy, we are gonna cut a fat hog today."

And indeed it looks that way, for a lot of long shots are coming in and the Bear is doing very little paying off. The roll in his deposit pocket is getting thicker and thicker. There is a huge crowd out, nearly double the 2,000-seat capacity of the grandstands. All of the bookies are doing business, but the Bear has a waiting line. One man takes a little too long, asking about horse after horse, and the Bear finally tells him, "Listen, this ain't a supermarket. I ain't got all day."

In the fourth race the six horse comes in without a bet on him on the Bear's racing program. The Bear makes what the bookies call a sweeper, winning all bets for that race. "That's what I like," he tells Lucky. "Makes the bookkeeping so much easier."

All through the day the betting goes on. It's a seventeen-race program and there are plenty of people who want to bet. Time after time men and women come sliding up to the Bear.

A tall man in a good western hat walks up. "What'll you give on the three horse?"

Without looking at his program the Bear says, "Give three to two."

"Give me a hundred of that."

A lady a little past sixty comes up. "What are the odds on Princess Meadows?"

"That's the four horse. Always ask about your horse by number. The odds on that horse are two to one."

"Can I bet just five dollars?"

"Indeed you can, ma'am. Just five me and give me your initials and come back and pick up your money."

After she leaves, he says, "Surprisingly enough most of my business is the five-dollar or ten- or twenty-dollar bettor. That little old lady was nervous about coming up and seeing if I'd take that small a bet. Hell, I was going to be polite to her."

But then an owner comes by and asks what the Bear will give on a certain horse. "Two to three," the Bear says.

The owner makes some remark and starts to walk away. But the Bear raises up on his toes and shouts after him. "All right, put your money where your mouth is. I'll give you even money for five hundred. No, make that a thousand."

"Hell, I'm looking for two to one," the owner says.

The Bear gestures. "Then go on up there in the stands. Maybe your mama or your wife will give you two to one."

Hearing all this, Lucky sighs. "Well, there he goes."

You ask him what that means.

"He's gone to gambling," says Lucky. "He's like a liquor-store owner sometimes. He's his own best customer. When he sticks to business you can't beat him, then sometimes he'll get a hunch and he'll take as much on a horse as he can get and won't lay off a nickel."

But for a while the Bear doesn't do that. In the sixth race, the feature race, the Bear gets heavy on one horse and walks over to another bookie, Insurance, and lays off six hundred of what he's got bet. Just before the race starts he looks at his program and does a tote board in his head. "If the four horse wins, I win $630. If the nine comes in, I make $575. If the eight comes in, all I make is $175. The rest pay around $300 because the five horse was scratched."

He makes a good payday when the nine horse comes home driving at the wire. But then he grouses to his partner, "Dammit, if I hadn't laid off I'd have won a bunch more."

"Then you'd have been gambling."

"That's what they call life, my man. Just another word for it."

Back under the stands it is cool and shady. At the concession stands they are selling hot dogs and hamburgers and doing a land-office business in cold drinks and beer.

But the Bear doesn't leave his position in the broiling sun. He does his business between the races and there's no time to run around for a beer while the race is going on.

Occasionally a friend will bring him a soft drink. Some of the bookies drink beer during the race, but the Bear never does. "This is business," he says. "I'll do my drinking later, when I get home."

But another vice bites him in the tenth race. He gets a hunch on a long shot and sends five hundred over with a friend to another bookie. If he'd done it himself he couldn't have gotten any odds because the bookie would have figured he knew something.

As it is, he didn't know anything. The horse finishes third, and in brush-track betting all they pay off on is the first nose across the line.

But in the twelfth race he bets four hundred through a friend and that bet comes through. On his own card it is nearly a sweeper, only one bettor picking the horse and that for only a sixty-dollar payoff.

The afternoon wears on, and some of the crowd is starting to leave because the feature races are over. The Bear is getting tired. Finally, it's the last race. The one horse and the two horse are the favorites, with most of the betting going to the two horse. A young lady of about thirty comes over to the Bear. She looks up at him and says, "Listen, give me a winner. I've been getting beat all day. You owe me."

The Bear gives her the barest flicker of a smile. "I don't owe you," he says, "though I know you. Bet the one horse. But don't bet him with me." He is getting very tired and looking forward to a pitcher of ice water back in his room.

She says, "You sure?"

He nods slowly. "Yeah, I'm sure. But don't take my word for it. Bet another horse."

Over in the jockey area the jockeys in the race are getting their tack ready. It's only a five-horse race. Roy Simmons has the two horse, Jackie McHargh has the four horse. A young Mexican, Oriz, has the one horse. It is a race of 660 yards around one curve. Jackie McHargh doesn't have a chance. Another jockey comes over and tells him about the mount because Jackie has never ridden the horse before and the other jockey has. The jockey says, "Don't worry, the horse will stand for you in the gate. No trouble getting out. Then just bat the horse and he's gone. He'll run, but he's a little over-matched in this race."

"Yeah," Jackie says, "just so I don't get hurt."

In the race, the one horse breaks cleanly on top with the two horse right behind him and the rest of the field stretched out. The four horse that McHargh had been reassured about came out of the gate bucking and jumping to the side.

The one horse leads until he begins blowing the hook, bearing way out on the curve into the homestretch. Roy Simmons takes the lead, but then the one horse, under good stick work by Oriz, gains slowly and, length by length, wins just at the wire.

The lady that the Bear has touted comes back to thank him for a "sure thing."

"You're quite welcome," he says, with a straight face. Then he turns to Lucky. "That's what I'd like, in horse racing, to know what a sure thing was. That woman is out of her mind."

Back at his motel room, relaxing, he takes the roll of bills out of his deposit pocket. The roll is about the diameter of a baseball, full of twenties and fifties and hundreds. He counts it and says, "Man, I feel just like a winning race horse. I did my track work and it all paid off. Right there in the winner's circle."

Someone wonders aloud if that is all it takes, hard work, practice, and diligence, to be a successful bookie at the brush tracks.

"No," he says, "you've always got to have speed." Then he points toward his temple. "Right there. Just like a race horse, there's no replacement for speed."

7
Riding High on a Bull Market

---

*T*his is an example of the type of story that Sports Illustrated used to run back in their heyday. It's what they called a Back-of-the-Book-Bonus piece, and they allowed a writer six or seven thousand words to do it. They don't run that kind of piece anymore and haven't for several years. I don't know why; maybe economics has something to do with it. All I know is that this piece on rodeo producers couldn't have been done without the freedom of that lengthy word count. It simply couldn't have been made to fit the, say, three thousand words you're normally allowed for a feature article. I'm not saying that a story about rodeo producers is that complex; it's just that there is so much to explain and there are so many people out there who don't really understand rodeo that the extra length was absolutely necessary.

The one thing I remember most vividly about this story is that I was doing a publicity tour for a book I'd just written called The Brave Men, and at the same time I was researching this story. Since I could never make airline schedules match up, about the only way I could make it from tour to rodeo and back was to rent airplanes and fly myself. Sports Illustrated didn't have any forms on their *expense reports to handle that kind of activity, but I had a wonderful lady named Pat Ryan who was my editor at SI at the time, and she made it possible. Pat is now the managing editor at Life magazine.*

Thanks, Pat.

Over in a small catch pen near the bucking chutes, bull No. 73 stood calmly, his head lowered, his jaw working on a cud. He was an old bull in his sixth season of rodeo, and he stood quietly, his only movement the slow switching of his tail and the oscillation of his jaw. The rodeo arena was empty and still, and the old bull instinctively knew that he wouldn't be wanted for several hours. It was not so with a pen of young bulls just over from No. 73. They milled about restlessly, shoving each other, working their horns against a handy side, pawing the earth. They were rookies just brought up from Tommy Steiner's ranch outside of Austin, Texas. Tommy Steiner is a rodeo stock contractor and No. 73, like all the other animals to be used at this rodeo in Waco, belonged to him.

No. 73 was a brindle Brahma, weighing almost 1,600 pounds. There were bulges and ripples of muscle under his sheen smooth coat. He appeared to be what he was, a well-conditioned athlete showing the effects of proper care and treatment. But there was almost a prehistoric cast to his huge face and the heavy blunt horns that curved sharply upward from each side of his massive head. With his eyes half closed he looked gentle and docile, but in a matter of hours he would be going one-on-one with the cowboy who had drawn him in the bull riding that night. Then, out there in the arena, he wouldn't seem so gentle. He would seem like what he was—big-time professional rodeo stock.

Outside the arena Tommy Steiner and his chute boss, John Farris, were walking down a long line of holding pens. Some of the pens held more bulls, but others contained bucking horses, both saddle broncs and bareback horses. Steiner was worrying about the mud in their pens. "Look at that stuff, John," he said. "That's no good." The mud was six inches deep and the stock was splashed and daubed with it. Steiner was worrying that standing around in the muck for long periods of time would drain the strength out of his animals, wear them down, like walking through water would a man. "We've got to get them out of this," he told Farris. "At least the ones that will be up tomorrow night. Give them twenty-four hours to rest."

For this rodeo, Steiner had shipped in eighty bulls, forty saddle broncs, forty bareback horses and a couple of hundred dogging steers and roping calves. The bulls were a problem because so many cowboys had entered the bull riding. Normally he only had to have twelve ready each night. But because of the heavy load of entrants, he was going to have to do some juggling. He never liked to buck any of his stock with less than three days' rest. Tonight, however, he would have to contest forty-five bulls, forcing him to utilize some relatively inexperienced stock he would not ordinarily put in a big-time rodeo such as Waco. This was of particular concern to Steiner because, though he is one of the top stock contractors in the country, he is best known for his fine string of bucking bulls—just like a pro football team might be known for excellent linebackers or receivers. His reputation wasn't on the line at every performance, but he did not like to put unproven stock in the arena. You never could tell what a green animal might do.

"I guess you might consider me and my stock the visiting team," he said. "That's about the way it feels, anyway. We are always on the road, always playing a strange arena. And the crowd is always pulling for the cowboys—just like in Dallas." He looked around at the muddy holding pens. "We even get the visitors' dressing room."

Bucking stock is fed a special high protein diet, trailered and hauled with care from show to show and given the amounts of rest and exercise that an athlete deserves. A bull, for instance, is fed about twenty pounds of supplemented grain a day, a carefully prepared formula that varies depending upon the season and the schedule the bull is working. Steiner finds that some of his stock bucks best with three days rest; other animals need four. "Of course you keep your stock in shape," he said. "In the first place bucking stock costs a lot of money. I guess I got upward of $300,000 invested in it. But mainly you keep them at their best because bucking is hard, demanding work. You don't want the cowboys riding everything you throw at them."

No one really knows what makes a bull or bronc buck and buck consistently and dependably. It is not necessarily just an outlaw streak in an animal, because some bucking stock is as gentle and handles as nicely as you could want—except for the eight or ten seconds that the contest with the cowboy lasts. They will stand quietly in the bucking chute, permit the cowboy to get down on them with no trouble, suffer the rigging and flank strap to be cinched, then explode as the chute gate opens, buck hard until the whistle blows, and then settle back to the docility of a milk cow.

Nor is this quality necessarily hereditary, as speed is in race-horses. Occasionally a bucking stallion will produce a short line of offspring that can make it in rodeo, but this is a rare occurrence. Steiner says, "There is no reason for it to be hereditary, any more than a guy is able to pitch a baseball because his father could. I don't know what it is myself. I only know when I find a good bull he's worth plenty of money to me."

Steiner finds his stock in a variety of ways. One method is the occasional bucking stock sales that are held around the country. These, however, operate like the waiver system used in professional football. No team is offering its best players and if any quality is to be found it is in unrecognized talent that a keen eye detects. "If a man can find one good bull or bronc at one of those sales he's done a day's work," Steiner says. "You know nobody is bringing their best stock, despite the lies they tell. You've got to look for something nobody else sees. You notice a bronc that ought to buck but doesn't for some reason. Maybe he has never been put in the chute right; or maybe he needs the flank girth a little forward. Some little something."

Steiner scouts the small amateur and independent rodeos that are held across the country almost any weekend night. "I don't get to as many of these as I should, but I've got people on the lookout. Friends of mine. Or a producer of one of these shows might bring me something. Of course, he'll have a real big idea about what the animal's worth."

A good, average bull, the kind that will buck for six or seven years and give a sound account of himself every time out of the chute, is worth around $2,000. Some go much higher, but these are the exceptions, just as an O.J. Simpson is the exception. Broncs are cheaper, though a good one will still cost at least $1,000 and a run-of-the-mill bucker around $600. The most Steiner has ever paid for

a bronc was $4,500, and be bought that animal sight unseen. Jim
Shoulders, who was the world champion cowboy five times, had
told Steiner about the bronc. "An Indian over in Oklahoma owned
him," Steiner recalls. "Had been using him in jackpot buckdowns
they were holding locally. Shoulders said he was the best bucking
horse he had ever seen, and that is a pretty good recommendation. I
got the Indian on the phone and made him an offer of $1,000 and he
took it. But then he called back an hour later and said he couldn't
sell that cheap. Said he had to have $2,000. I said all right. Next day,
just as we were hooking up a trailer to send after him, this Indian
calls again and says he's got to have $3,000. I said all right, but I went
to hurrying those boys I was sending. I wanted to get them going
before that Indian could call back. But he beat me to it. Wasn't an
hour and he was on the phone and said he had to have $5,000. That
was a lot of money. I told the Indian to wait a minute and called
Shoulders and he said the horse was cheap at the price. So I called
back and offered $4,500, and the guy took it and I just sent the
trailer on the way and left the phone off the hook. I tell you, when I
finally saw that bronc I thought, 'My God, what have I done!' He
was awful little. Didn't look like much. But we got him in shape and
started him on the major circuit right away and he turned out good.
Got voted to the National Finals Rodeo seven times and was the
bucking horse of the year two times."

Occasionally some owner will bring Steiner a good-blooded
horse that has gone sour or spoiled. "Those generally don't turn out
well," he says. "They suddenly discover they can buck and they'll
give whoever owns them hell for a while. Then I'll buy the horse, or
some other contractor, and put them to work in the rodeo. But they
don't last long. Might buck one season. Some of them go back to
being good riding or using stock. Being rodeoed don't hurt them."

Steiner has had a few notable examples of this, but there is one
significant trade that he would like to forget. "I'll tell you what
kind of horse trader I am," he says ruefully. "I bought a registered
paint horse off an old boy in Shreveport. He was a good-looking
pony, but he'd gone bad and wanted to buck. We tried him after
the show one night and he done pretty good. I gave the old boy
$400 for him. Well, we kept that pony in the string one season. He
was all right at first, but he got to letting down little by little.
Beginning of next season he wasn't doing nothing so I took him

out of the string and shipped him to the ranch. Thought we might make a riding horse out of him. I pretty well forgot about him. Then one night I called and Dad said he'd sold the paint for $600. Well, I felt pretty good about that. Got rid of a bronc wasn't doing me any good and made a little profit. But I kept hearing about that pony and running into him. Guy that bought him started taking him around to horse shows and fairs and stock shows. Next I heard he'd gone up to Fort Worth and won reserve champion in his class. Then he took him to Houston and won Grand Champion. Then I hear that the guy had sold him for $5,000. The next thing I pick up a trade paper and there's that paint. Guess who had him? The Kansas City Chiefs football team. That's the horse they ride around when they score a touchdown. War Paint they call him, or something. A horse right out of my bucking string."

Steiner keeps a chart on each of his bucking animals, noting their performance every time out of the chute. He grades them one to three, with one being tops. He was worried at Waco that he was not going to get maximum performances out of his stock. Many of his broncs had just finished performing in a rodeo at Pine Bluff, Arkansas, and had been trailered in without proper rest. He also was having to use some relatively new broncs because of the heavy demands on his stock at the end of the season. As a consequence it would be the first time in an indoor arena for a number of them and he wasn't sure how they would react. "Broncs are the most temperamental," he said, meaning saddle broncs—horses that are bucked under a saddle. Bareback horses are not called broncs— simply bareback horses. "You get some of them in a strange place and they will sull up and won't do anything," he said.

There is no set farm system for a bucking animal. Some of them break right in at major rodeos. Generally, however, an animal needs age and considerable experience. A bull usually develops around four; a horse needs to be six or seven. Most of them do not have their full strength before then, nor a consistency of tempera- ment that will ensure a dependable performance. They need to learn about chutes and the noise and routines of a rodeo. To season his animals, Steiner sometimes contests them in the smaller rodeos he produces. Occasionally he will lease out a few animals to inde- pendent producers or else season them in the rodeo schools oper- ated by some of the better cowboys. To handle a season, Steiner needs at least sixty major-league bulls and a hundred bucking horses of equivalent quality.

By the time the rodeo was under way at Waco it was obvious that Steiner's fears were being realized. The bareback riding was the first event, and the horses were slow out of the chutes and went at the bucking like they were working for low wages. Steiner stood just in front of the chutes and watched, a frown on his face. Halfway through the event not a single cowboy had been bucked down. But that was not the worst of it. The judges had already awarded three cowboys rerides because their mounts had not bucked hard enough.

A mitigating factor was the loose dirt in the arena. As a good bucking horse comes out of the chute in a jumping charge, his first important move is to plant his front feet and turn back either to the right or left, bucking as he does. If he does not get this first move in, he allows the cowboy to take a deep seat and the rider becomes hard to dislodge after that. But the horses, as they came slamming into the arena, were slipping in the shifting dirt. Some of them never quite regained their balance before the whistle would blow. For the new horses it was an excuse, one that went along with the mud in the holding pens and the strangeness of bucking under a roof.

An even better excuse was that Waco was the last rodeo of the season and the stock was tired. It had been rodeoing for ten straight months, and the miles and physical attrition were beginning to show. When the bareback riding was over not a single cowboy had been bucked down. The only bright spot had been a rookie horse, False River, that Steiner was trying. He was a big rawboned bay weighing 1,200 pounds. Already he had shown promise and tonight he had really fired out, ignoring, like the winner he looked to be, all the adverse conditions. He was the only bareback horse that Steiner had graded one.

While the calf roping was going on, Steiner stood behind the chutes, smoking a cigarette. A man came up to him. "Would you buy a mare?" he asked, without introduction.

"I don't know. How old is she?"

"Tell you the truth I've never been able to mouth her. But she'd be an honest six. I'm sure of that."

"Will she buck?"

"I've never had a saddle on her, but she acts like she wants to. I'm about half scared of her."

"How much you asking?"

"Would you give two hundred? If she bucks like you want? If she don't, you don't want her."

"I'd give two hundred. When you want to try her?"

"How about tomorrow?"

"After the show."

"I'll bring her in."

It had happened a thousand times before and Steiner was not hopeful. Very seldom did he get any worth out of such casual encounters.

The stock boys were moving the bulls up to the pen directly behind the chutes. They had no trouble with the herd of old bulls that contained No. 73, but the young bulls were still wild and excited. As they were driven along they showed how sweated up they had become and slobber ran down in long strings from their muzzles. The stock boys did not put them in with the experienced bulls, for one of the young ones might accidentally get a horn into an old warrior and then there would be trouble. Steiner watched them being driven. "Look at that," he said in disgust. "Been fidgeting all day. Won't have a thing left by this evening when they come out."

The National Finals are something like the World Series or the Super Bowl. They are held each year at Oklahoma City and the top fifteen money-winning cowboys in each event are eligible to compete. The contestants vote on the stock that is to be used. It is a high honor for a contractor to have a horse or bull voted to the finals. Through the years Steiner has had more stock at the finals than any other contractor and this year fifteen of his athletes had been selected. In the bull riding that evening he had six veteran bulls coming out. Four of these, including No. 73, had been voted to the finals.

Steiner's stock did better in the saddle-bronc riding as the first three cowboys went spinning into the dirt. Then Red Pepper, one of his top horses, came out with a young cowboy, Sammy Groves, up. Groves had his spurs in the bronc's shoulders as they broke by the judges. Red Pepper set up on the first jump, cut left, then cut right and went into a free-wheeling buck. But Groves had a good seat and, holding the long bucking rein high in his left hand, had settled back and was raking the horse rhythmically with his spurs. The contest ended with the whistle and the judges scored the ride a sixty-nine. It was a good score and, though the cowboy could be said to have won, Steiner was pleased because the crowd liked the show.

The rodeo moved along—the barrel racing, the trick riding, the steer dogging—and then Tom Hadley, the announcer, was saying: "Now rodeo fans, we come to that part of the evening you've been looking forward to. Bull riding, by far the most popular event because no other sports activity in or out of rodeo can equal it for danger and for action. . . ."

Down below they were crowding the huge bulls into the chutes. No. 73 went into Chute No. 4. He had drawn Hazy West, a good bull rider.

While the other bulls performed, No. 73 stood looking bored, his huge ears, big as quart jars, flopping down over the sides of his head. West climbed on the chute and gingerly worked his bull rope around No. 73's huge chest. Behind, a man was slipping the girth around the bull's flanks. When the gate opened this girth would be pulled tight to get the bull started. It wouldn't make him buck any harder, just make him fire out. In the case of No. 73 this was all unnecessary. John Farris, walking down the line of chutes, cautioned the flankman to go easy. "He don't really need it," he said. "Just hang it on him for show."

No. 73 was the tenth bull out of the chute. The score was bulls eight, cowboys one. Only Sammy Montgomery had stayed up, and he had drawn one of the young bulls who had put on a showy display of high leaps but had not been hard to ride.

As West eased himself down on the broad back, the old bull still didn't show much emotion, other than to snuffle and snort, the huge blasts of air stirring the dust in the bottom of the chute. Inside the arena John Farris tapped the gate of Chute No. 4 with his cattle prod and asked, "Ready here?"

"Yeah," West said lowly. He worked his legs tighter around 73's huge sides. A helper, leaning down, pulled his bull rope. West quickly took the end, made two wraps around his hand and tucked the free end up under his leg, out of the way. Then he tugged at his hat. Farris was watching him expectantly. "All right," the cowboy said in a tight voice, "lemme have him."

As if he knew what they were saying, No. 73 began to tense up. His head started a swing to the right. As it got to the apex of that swing the chute gate came rattling open. No. 73's head turned left and seemed to be following the flare of the gate. As he saw daylight he bunched, and exploded into the arena with a high, twisting leap. Even before his front feet landed, his hindquarters were coming around in a switchback and he followed that by letting his huge shoulders bunch and break to the right. With that move West lost his right spur. He began to tilt to the left as the bull began a bucking, wrenching spin right in front of the chutes. The bull spun twice, three times to the right then threw his whole weight on his massive forelegs, whipped his hindquarters around and started to the left. As he did West lost his other spur hold and came tumbling down the side. But before he could hit the ground, 73 had switched back to the right. The move flung the cowboy up and out. He hit the ground and lay a moment, stunned. One of the clowns had run over to protect him, but it was not necessary. With the weight gone 73 knew he had won and immediately stopped bucking. Now he was trotting to the corner of the arena, looking for the exit gate. It swung open and he went through, his head up, his huge horns right in the eyes of the front-row spectators. He passed down a long fence ramp, turned in through a gate a stock boy had opened, and settled into a corner of a holding pen, his night's work done.

Steiner and his wife, Beverly, sat late that evening over steak and eggs, talking about how the string had done. The life of a stock contractor is a traveling one, and it helps if your wife can come along and understand. "I thought we did all right," Steiner said. "Some of those young bulls did better than I expected. We might get four or five good ones out of that bunch.

"Not enough people really understand the contest that is going on out there between the animal and the cowboy. If they did, they would appreciate rodeo much better. But maybe that's rodeo's fault. Maybe we ought to figure out a way to make the action more obvious, like the yards gained in a football game. Because I tell you, once you understand and can appreciate, it is the best sport in the world."

Steiner flew out the next day on a hurried trip to a bucking-bull and horse sale in Ardmore, Okla. He really did not have much hope of finding anything he could use, but he was sending twelve bulls up himself and Harry Vold would be there, too. Vold is the other large contractor in the sport and is known for his string of bucking horses. He was sending thirty-two head to the auction.

A bucking sale is for stock contractors. It is not a rodeo. However, in order to attract enough cowboys to get the stock mounted and performing, the auction company offers some prize money and each ride is judged.

Most of the contractors there would be small-timers who had come to fill out their strings with the castoffs of the bigger outfits. In a few cases ranches that attempted to breed bucking stock had sent in representative herds of absolutely green animals.

Steiner and Vold instinctively sought each other out. Someone handed them a roster of the stock to be auctioned. It contained the brand numbers and descriptions of at least fifty head. "Goodness," Steiner said, looking at it, "you suppose there's a cull left in the whole country?"

Vold, who talks with a Far West accent and puts on quite a number of rodeos in Canada, said dryly, "Now that's the wrong kind of talk. I've got thirty-two head in there myself. Champions every one of them."

The sale was being held in a large covered arena with a dirt floor packed hard as concrete. There were perhaps 150 contractors on hand and some fifty cowboys to do the riding. Of course, none of the cowboys were top professionals.

Soon Vold and Steiner got down to business. Each was in the market for what the other had to sell, but each respected the level of quality the other required. They would not be so honest with others, but they knew there was no point in trying to fool each other. Steiner said, "I haven't got a thing, Harry. Couple of the bulls I brought aren't so bad to buck, but they're not showy. The cowboys don't like them and neither do the crowds. You don't want them."

Vold replied, "I got one bronc out of the whole bunch—Blue Chip, about seven years old." Vold looked over toward the crowd of riders standing in front of the chutes. "Of course I don't know if you'll be able to tell anything with that bunch of Saturday-night cowboys bucking off first jump out of the chute."

"I'll watch for him," Steiner said.

The auction got under way. A bull would be bucked out and then allowed to run loose in the arena while the auctioneer, on a high platform behind the chutes, took bids from the crowd. The

word he used most often was "prospect." He'd say, "Now any of
you producers that are trying to build yourself a good string of
bulls, here's a fine young prospect to add. He's an honest four-
year-old, been bucked only three times and the owner guarantees
this bull will give you many years of dependable performance. A
good prospect, both as a bucking bull and a crowd-pleasing fighting
bull." Or: "A fine young prospect that will be a winner for you.
Owner has just got a few more bulls than he needs so he's willing
to sacrifice a young prospect like this one. This bull turns back to
his left and spins both to his left and his right."

Steiner watched the bidding. Occasionally he would comment
to John Farris about a performance. One bull came out, bucked his
cowboy off early and then charged the clowns. To all appearances
he was a good-looking prospect and the bidding was spirited.
But Steiner said, "That bull's got quitting on his mind. He's been
bucking off amateur cowboys at some little Saturday night rodeo
and he thinks he's pretty tough. He has gotten used to bucking for
only about four seconds and that would be a hard habit to break
when you got him in against some good cowboys."

A producer who was starting a rodeo string in Illinois bought
the bull for $1,900. Steiner just shook his head. The man had
already bought several head and Steiner thought he had paid too
much each time. "Well," he said, "I expect that's the way it goes,
though. Sort of like an expansion team. You got to pay more than
the talent's worth in order to get into the game."

Later they bucked out Vold's string of broncs. Steiner waited for
Blue Chip, watched the animal perform and then bought him
for $620. "He's not a bad-looking bronc," he said. "And he ought to
buck better under the right conditions." Then he paid for the bronc,
closed his checkbook, and went to the airport and returned to the
Waco rodeo.

The man who had the mare to sell had brought her. She was
tied in a corner of one of the catch pens just behind the chutes.
Steiner glanced at her as he was getting the Grand Entry organized.
She was sweating and nervous, shifting around constantly, her
bay coat shiny with sweat. "She'll have herself wore down," Steiner
said matter-of-factly. "That fellow ought to have left her somewhere
outside."

The performance went better that night. The stock had had another day of rest after coming in off the road, and Steiner had gotten the mud situation corrected in the holding pens. It seemed to have an important effect. All of the bareback horses bucked hard and long, and there were no re-rides awarded. Even with the bull riding heavily weighted with inexperienced animals, the percentage that had been ridden was very low. Steiner was feeling good. He had expected to get torn up in this last rodeo, but it was not working out that way.

After the bull riding, after the arena had cleared, they brought up the mare and put her in a chute. Steiner had talked Sammy Montgomery into mounting out the horse for him and he had asked the pickup riders to stay on for just a few minutes.

The mare was still nervous, rearing up, chute fighting, rolling her eyes. It was an effort to get the flanking girth and bareback rigging on her. The man who owned her stood by watching. He said, nervously, "She's bucking for her life." Someone asked him what he meant and he answered, "If Tommy don't buy her I'm taking her down to Palestine." He meant the dog-food factory in Palestine, Texas, where they pay sixteen cents a pound for horseflesh.

Sammy Montgomery, standing by the chute, drawing a heavily rosined glove onto his riding hand, said, "That mare ain't going to buck."

She looked like she would. She had a mean eye and a narrow, underslung jaw. And from the way she was kicking and slamming and fighting the chute, she seemed an outlaw. But that had nothing to do with bucking.

Montgomery crawled up on the chute. The mare was jumping around so hard that he could not take a seat on her. "I'll just fly her out. Open the gate," he said. He was above her, a boot on each side of the chute. He took his handhold and as the gate opened he dropped down on her, his spurs instinctively finding their hold in her shoulders.

She did not buck. She came out squealing and jumping but not really bucking. Montgomery spurred her for a few little hops and then jumped off as one of the pickup men came alongside.

There was no need to say anything. The owner knew as well as Steiner that the animal had shown nothing. But as Steiner watched the mare being led away, he said, "Aw, I wouldn't take her to slaughter. Give her a chance. Take her down to some little rodeos. Maybe she'll learn how to buck. Give her a chance."

But the man kept on going, leading the mare out of the arena. It's a tough league to get cut in. Steiner stared after them for a second, then shrugged and turned away. "All right," he said to Farris, who was standing by for orders. "We better get the bulls rotated. Get those that are up tomorrow night on in here and let them start getting used to the place."

It would end very soon for the year and then would come the rest before the next season. The stock would be turned out to pasture, to run and roll around and shake off the fatigue and confinement of the ten-month schedule. It would be their holiday, their annual leave, and Steiner would give them almost thirty days of it before it was time to bring them in and start getting ready for the next season. They would have lost weight out on pasture, and the first move would be to beef them back up with a supplemented grain program. Then would come the testing and the tryouts; the picking of the team, the traveling squad that would go roaring off in the big cattle trucks to rodeos from one border to the other. For this selection process Steiner would hold jackpot rodeos at his ranch, attracting mostly local cowboys, but the occasional top rider would come around and this would give Steiner the chance to see the borderline cases up against the best. It would not be much different than any other tryout camp; the old veterans trying to make the team one more year, the newcomers pushing and shoving and asserting themselves.

"I get excited when we're cranking up for a new season," Steiner said. "All the stock is fresh and strong and looks so good. I think we're going to go out and put on the best rodeo ever and nobody will be able to ride my stock. Nobody." He paused and grinned. "Someday it might just happen."

8

His Head Was
Too Big for His Hat

*I*n a lot of books and nearly all movies and TV shows you'll hear a western hat referred to as a "Stetson." Of course, Stetson is a brand name, and at one time they may have been the standard for elegant Western headgear. That is no longer the case. Most cowboys today (and, as much as I hate to tell you, there ain't no real cowboys anymore, just rodeo cowboys) prefer a Resistol, especially for summer straws and for all-around wear. But the one hat that has come to take its place in prominence is the M.L. Leddy, made by the M.L. Leddy Company of Fort Worth. And of all the styles available, the one most esteemed, as you'll find out in the story, is the M.L. Leddy Supreme. That's what you call your Rolls Royce, your Babe Ruth, your Walter Payton of hats.

There is one other myth you'll see in the movies and on TV, and even hear on the street, and that's people calling a Western hat a "cowboy" hat. Little boys who get cowboy outfits for Christmas wear "cowboy" hats. Grownup little boys who are so intelligent that they decide to try and make a living riding bulls and saddle broncs wear Western hats. That's what the rules of the Professional Rodeo Cowboy

Association say: ". . . any performer or contestant appearing in the arena must be attired in a suitable Western hat."

As you'll read in the story, I finally got my M.L. Leddy Supreme. This was about 1980 and it was given to me by a friend. A few years later I began to figure that I'd outgrown the "cowboy" look. My boots weren't near as comfortable as loafers, and I wasn't driving a car (let alone a pickup) with enough headroom to allow me to wear my hat in the vehicle. So I put the boots away and carefully put that still-pure-looking M.L. Leddy Supreme away in its box.

Somewhere about 1986 I gave it away. I gave it to Pierce Holt's daddy, Les. Pierce, at that time, was playing for Angelo State University and hoping for a career in the NFL. I knew he had a career in the NFL. But one night his daddy was in town, and Pierce brought ol' Les by, I guess just so I could reassure his daddy about Pierce's chances. Well, we spent a sociable time together and, as the hours wore by, I felt more and more friendly toward Les. He was still wearing boots, still engaged in some form of agriculture, and had a ranch in New Mexico. I got to thinking about that M.L. Leddy Supreme rusting away in its box in the closet, about how the most dangerous animal I'd ridden in years was a bar stool, about what a good ol' boy ol' Les was, and how that M.L. Leddy Supreme ought to be worn by such a man.

So I gave it to him. Gave him a $350 hat that was still just like new.

Pierce Holt did indeed make it in the NFL. As a matter of fact, he's played in two Super Bowls for the San Francisco 49ers. But some time back I had occasion to need that hat for a rodeo or something, so I called Les and asked if I could borrow it back for just that brief time.

He said, "Well, sure, but I don't think you'll recognize it."

I asked him why. And he told me.

Les had pinned one side of that M.L. Leddy Supreme up in the Aussie style. He'd also had the crown reshaped and put a snakeskin hatband on it. Went and ruined a beautiful hat.

In the story that follows you'll read about a genius named J.B. Kingman. I used to think I was smarter than he. I am not so sure anymore.

S ome of y'all may recall when I told you in these pages about the days when me and four other worthless cow- boys were getting it down the road from one rodeo to another. If you do, you'll remember that we had what we called the double-barreled pickup, which we had bought on time from one of our daddies and had subse- quently converted to what was maybe the first of the two-seated pickups you see on the road today. I believe they call 'em crew-cab pickups, and it seems like they're pretty popular, but when we put ours together back in the early '50s, we had no thought of taking out a patent, else we might be wealthy men today. But that right there is a fair indication of how our luck was running, not only in contesting the bucking events in the rodeo but in just about all else.

As I said, our intention was other than commercial when we cut the cab of Player's daddy's 1948 Ford pickup in half and moved it back three feet and welded in a piece of sheet metal. If we'd known then that the idea was going to catch on, we'd have painted that piece of sheet metal and done better for a rear seat than the leatherette and chrome bench we'd stole out of the Greyhound bus station in Amarillo, Texas. God knows we took enough hoorahing about the appearance of that pickup from the cowboys who'd be standing around the contestant's gate when we'd come skidding up, late as usual, for the next rodeo. But I'm not bitter about our loss, even though Detroit stole our idea. All we were trying to do at that time was alleviate the suffering of the two of us who usually rode in the truck bed. This had been a sore spot ever since we'd all five gone rodeoing together, and it generally ended up in dispute, especially when we had to make a long haul through rainy weather or when there was a cold wind blowing that those in the truck bed claimed aggravated the cuts and bruises they'd received from being bucked off some bull or bareback horse.

But this story isn't about the double-barreled pickup. I only mentioned that to put you in touch with the general class of our outfit. This story is about rodeo cowboy hats—in particular, the hat that was the pride and joy of J.B. Kingman.

The five of us had gone rodeoing in a partnership. We were going to pool our money to pay expenses and entry fees and then split all winnings equally. Another way of putting it, given the caliber of our ability at riding bucking stock, was that misery loves company.

There was me, who, at eighteen, was an adequate-to-useless contestant on bareback horses and saddle broncs, primarily because I was too tall and generally ended up spurring myself in the heels instead of spurring the horses in the shoulder. I could've been a good bull rider because of my size and the strength in my right arm, but I was what was generally referred to as a fifty-fifty man. I had fifty percent of my mind on riding the bull and fifty percent on getting to the fence ahead of him. That isn't a combination that often goes to the pay window.

Then there was Player, whose daddy had sold us the pickup. To digress a moment from rodeo talk, in which praise is the kiss of death, Player was the best man I've ever known. He wasn't much in appearance, just a scrawny boy from East Texas with sandy hair and a crooked grin. He wasn't very much as a rodeo contestant, either; he wasn't my equal on the bulls and couldn't ride bucking horses better than me or any of the rest of the partnership. But he was our leader and I'll never know why. I've searched the souls of men ever since and never found one that could match Player's.

But, Lord, was he a joker! He once mayonnaised the sheets of my motel room bed just as I was about to tumble into it with a lady that I'd just fallen in love with and wanted to marry. But that's another story for another time.

Nor am I going to tell about the time when I'd broken my neck at the rodeo in Albuquerque and was lying in the hospital and he come in the room and give the nurse a raw calf's liver and told her it had fallen out of my body in the ambulance and ought to be replaced.

I will tell you that he got me out of that hospital by wearing one of those green doctor's smocks and without my having to pay the deductible that was due off the insurance we got from the Rodeo Cowboys Association.

Player wasn't his real name. He got it as a nickname because he was so good in the card games that were constantly going on in the rodeo clown's trailer. At twenty he already knew a good deal more about cards than the rest of us would ever learn.

We called Jack and Billy Jack the Twins because they were both from Louisiana. When me and Player had got up the partnership, we'd needed two other sources of $10 a month, and Jack and Billy Jack had been afoot and willing to put in that amount. We owed Player's daddy $50 a month for the pickup, and we figured that the best way to pay him was to have five partners at ten bucks a head. That'll reinforce your idea of just what a classy outfit we were.

But, to tell you the truth, Jack and Billy Jack weren't all that bad. As a matter of fact, Billy Jack later developed into a pretty fair saddle bronc rider. But at that time they were both kind of square built, both in the shoulders and in the head, and we treated them accordingly—especially by making them ride in the back most times.

But now to bring you to the man whom this story is about, J.B. Kingman. He was what you'd call an all-around good fellow and a wonderful chap. He was also the best rodeo contestant among us, and he never let us forget it. He'd been without transportation just like the rest of us until we'd put together the deal to buy Player's daddy's pickup, but he'd somehow forgotten that. After we'd got on the road and he'd been winning a little more than the rest of us, he'd sit up in the middle of the three of us in the front seat of the pickup and say, darkly, "I name no names, but since I'm carrying this outfit and some of us have not been winning as much as others, I ought to be riding on the outside."

I always took that personal since I had the seat by the window.

I'll give you an idea of J.B.'s loyalty to the group. As poor as we were, we'd always send in one guy to rent a motel room as a single, and then the rest of us would slip in on the sly and bunk down the best we could. J.B. once went down to the front office and complained that there weren't enough towels. Naturally we all got thrown out, but he never admitted it was his fault.

On another occasion me and Player were trying to borrow gas money from a rodeo producer. At the exact second that we were into making deep and serious assurances about our reliability, J.B. walked up and folded his arms and said, "Huh! Well just be damn sure you get enough to cover that four dollars I loaned you three days ago." Ah, yes, he was a wonderful human being.

But he did have a hell of a hat.

Now a good-looking hat, a quality hat, is a rodeo cowboy's main show-off. RCA (Rodeo Cowboys Association—now called the Professional Rodeo Cowboy Association) rules required that all cowboys in the arena be attired in a representative Western hat. We pretty much all wore the same jeans and the same shirt. And we all wore fairly cheap boots because they were going to be cut and scarred by our spurs and by the way we treated them.

But a hat was different. When we weren't getting ready to go out on a bronc or a bull, we'd all stand in the arena with our backs up to the bucking chutes and our arms folded, staring up into the crowd for any good-looking girls that might catch our eye. We figured that a good-looking, high-quality hat was the best possible advertisement for what was underneath. So you could depend on the fact that a cowboy was more careful of his good hat than he was of his mother's picture in his billfold.

And in the first (and last) year of our partnership, J.B. bought himself an M.L. Leddy Supreme. It caused a little bit of a sensation on our circuit. Now, of course, rodeo cowboys like Casey Tibbs and Jim Shoulders could afford hats like that and never turn a hair. But for brush hands like us, cowboys who found out what rodeos the good contestants were going to and then went the other way, that hat was a sharp stick in the middle of a sore eye.

We warned J.B. about it, that he was building up a lot of antagonism, but he never paid no mind; he just went on flaunting that hat. Now at that time we were eating Vienna sausage and crackers out of little roadside grocery stores and sleeping in $5-a-night motels. I wanted a Leddy Supreme, as did every other man in our outfit. In that day a Leddy Supreme, made by M.L. Leddy of Fort Worth, cost $90, and I could never get within $40 of owning one. Since that time, since I've gotten too old and belly-buckled to stand with my arms folded and look up into the grand-stands and wonder which Shiny Bright would like to take me home, a friend has given me one. It set him back $350, but still my wife wonders why I treat it with such reverence. Well, she never knew what that hat could get you.

So there we were, with that wonderful human being, mostly riding between me and Player—Player driving, me on the outside, and him with his hat on his head in the middle.

It was a beautiful hat. Some hat companies rate a hat by the amount of beaver in it, triple X or four X or even eight X. A Leddy Supreme was all beaver, 10 X, and the maker didn't have to put a symbol on it to prove it. J.B.'s was a high-crowned, pearl-gray beauty with a 4½-inch brim. He used to sit there in the pickup, being careful that it wouldn't touch the roof where the sheet metal was.

We used to eat in a lot of cheap cafés in small cattle towns. They were the kind of places where you'd walk in the door and find a little hat rack right there where you could hang your hat before you went on back to sit down at a booth or table. I guess it was one of those kind of places that gave Player the idea about J.B.'s hat.

The rodeo circuit ended up at Dallas, where they also had the Texas State Fair in conjunction with the rodeo. One day me and Player were kind of wandering around the fairgrounds when we come upon one of them booths that stitch your name or your girl friend's name or whoever's name you want on hats the booth provided. A whole bunch of hats were hung up like strings of fish from the poles around the booth. They was nothing but cheap junk, and I could see that and was about to walk on past when Player said, "Now, look here. Just wait a minute."

He was staring hard at one of them poles of hats. I couldn't see what he meant. All I saw was a bunch of cheap beaver-board imitations, the kind that would wilt if you got them out in a light fog.

But Player said, pointing, "Look at that! Don't that look like J.B.'s hat?" Then I saw what he was seeing. It was at the top of one pole. True, it was pearl gray and it had a high crown and a 4½-inch brim, but I knew it was just made out of cardboard. I said, "So what?"

But Player was already pushing through the crowd of teen-agers around the booth and taking the hat down and asking the lady how much it cost.

She told him $2 and he bought it. We walked away, him carrying that hat and me asking what the hell he wanted with it. But he had that crooked, cynical grin on his face, and he just said, "Never you mind. I'll show you later."

Well, it wasn't until we got to Weatherford, Texas, that I found out what he intended. We got out of the pickup there and went into a café to eat supper. We'd just made one of our standard drives of about three hundred miles, and we were all tired and should've been just a little cranky. We all stopped near the door and hung up our hats just like we always did. Then we went on back and found a table. That's when I should have seen something coming, for just as J.B. was about to take a seat that would have had him facing the door, Player got him by the arm and steered him around to a chair on the other side of the table. J.B. said, "Now what the hell is this?"

Player said, kind of whispering in his ear, "Listen, there's a good-looking girl sitting in the back, and I figured you'd want to sit like this so you could see her."

J.B. give him a suspicious look and said, "Now when did you ever take any interest in my pleasure or comfort?"

Player sat down by him, leaned over and said earnestly, "Well, I don't think we've been treating you fair, J.B. You've been winning the biggest part of the money we've won lately and we ought to show you more appreciation." Then he clapped J.B. on the shoulder like he was the most sincere man around.

J.B. looked at him a long time, but Player never changed his expression; he just kept sitting there looking grateful.

Finally J.B. said, "Well, if you mean it, it's been a long time in coming. I'll just tell you that—it's been a long time in coming."

And Player said, "Hell, I know that. And so do the rest of us. And to show you how appreciative we are, I think you ought to have a double order of chicken-fried steak."

This set up a squawk from Jack and Billy Jack, but Player waved his hand at them and said, "No, now look at it. J.B.'s been winnin' the money that's allowin' us to eat tonight. Hell, we got to keep him strong and healthy!" Then he clapped J.B. on the shoulder again.

After that, J.B. turned nearly impossible. He kept wanting us to pass the salt and pass the pepper and pass the butter and pass the bread. Hell, he even sent me to get the waitress to bring him some more coffee. I looked at Player, but he merely had the satisfied expression on his face that he got when things were going just as he wanted them.

Then about halfway through the meal Player suddenly remembered he'd forgot something in the pickup. I was the only one who saw him take J.B.'s hat off the rack before he went out the door.

He was gone about five minutes, and when he come back in, he hung a hat on the rack that looked a lot like J.B.'s, but that I knew for certain wasn't.

We sat around for a good while, like we always done, stretching out our meal with crackers and ketchup. Finally, when the waitress • refused to bring us any more crackers, we got up and paid and then went on over to the hat rack and got our hats and started to leave. Except J.B. just kept standing there with his hat in his hand and a funny look on his face. Player stopped and turned back to him and asked, in this real serious voice, if something was the matter.

"Hell, yes," J.B. said. "This ain't my hat!"

Player looked at it, even reached out his finger and touched it. He said, "Why sure it's your hat, J.B. Looks just like it."

"But it ain't!" J.B. said in this kind of anguished voice. "It ain't got no silk lining on the inside, and it ain't got that little tag that says it's a Leddy Supreme. Hell, it's just a damn old junk hat!"

Player put his arm around him again. "Why, it looks just like your hat, J.B."

He turned to me. "Ain't that J.B.'s hat?"

"I—I guess," I said.

"Don't it look like it?"

"Yeah," I said. "Sure does."

But J.B. said, in a voice that kind of went up and up and up and then took off from there, "But this ain't *my hat!* This is just some old junk hat."

After that J.B. went kind of crazy. He went around that café, grabbing customers and waitresses and demanding to know who had his hat. We tried to restrain him but he was like a bull on the loose, and somebody finally called the law and a deputy sheriff come in and told us in meaningful tones to quit the premises or we wouldn't have to pay for beds that night. He said, "Now I don't know what you rodeo bums are up to, but I know ain't none of you got a hat anybody would want to steal. And if you don't get out of here and quit bothering these good folks, I'm going to put you where you won't need a hat to keep the sun out of your eyes."

We got a motel room later that night, but Player had to sit up with J.B. I was in my sleeping bag over in the corner, and I could see them in dim outline sitting by the window and hear Player saying, "J.B., it's all in your mind. This is your hat."

"But it ain't!" J.B. said, and it almost sounded like he had tears in his eyes.

And Player saying, "Now, J.B., you know you been taking some hell of a lot of crashes lately on them bulls. You know they say that can mess up your eyes."

I'd asked Player on the sly if he'd been careful with J.B.'s real hat. He'd said, "Don't worry. I got it in a cellophane bag under the driver's seat of the pickup."

Things got sort of strange after that first night, because J.B. took to wearing that hat just like it was his real one. But he'd changed. It appeared that the poor quality of the hat was giving J.B. a poor opinion of himself. Nobody ever, in my hearing, actually said anything bad about his hat, but you could see cowboys giving him kind of funny looks. It appeared like it was working on his mind. He didn't stand in front of the chutes anymore with his arms folded, looking up in the stands for a Shiny Bright. And he didn't even seem to take as much personal care of himself.

But what was worse was that his contesting had gone into a dead tailspin. He was bucking off of horses and bulls that he once might have rode, and he wasn't getting us those third places that had previously formed a substantial part of our income.

I told Player one night, after the joke had run on for about two weeks, that we had to put a stop to it, that we couldn't afford it, that if he didn't give J.B.'s hat back to him and get him back on track, we weren't going to be able to make the next payment on the pickup. Player just nodded.

But I knew what he was up to. Ever once in a while I'd hear him talking quietly to J.B. He'd say, "Now, J.B., I know you're a man who is generally right. I know you was right that time you reported to the management of that little hotel in Wichita Falls that we didn't have enough towels." Or he'd say, "Now, J.B., I know that's your hat because you are not a man that makes a mistake."

Well, the next night, in Fort Smith, Arkansas, we went in a café and Player took pains to make sure that J.B. was seated with his back to the front door. Then, just as he'd done before, he made some excuse that he had to go out to the pickup. I saw him take that wreck of a hat off the rack by the front door and I saw him come back in a few minutes later and hang up J.B.'s real hat.

We left not too long after that and stopped at the rack to get our hats. J.B. took his down from where he knew he'd left it. But he just stood there, holding it in his hands and staring at it. I'd wondered what his reaction was going to be when he got his real hat back, but I hadn't counted on the way Player had been working on him.

After a long moment J.B. said, "This ain't my hat!"

Player said, "Sure it is. Look at it. Ain't it got that silk lining and that M.L. Leddy Supreme tag in it?"

"This ain't my hat!" J.B. said louder.

"Hell, yes, it's your hat."

Then J.B. said, in a loud voice, "This ain't my hat. Somebody stole my hat."

I was standing right beside him and I saw little drops of sweat suddenly come out on his forehead. Player tried to say something reassuring to J.B., but he suddenly yelled, in that high voice of his, "Some son of a bitch has stole my hat!"

There was a party of four men eating at a table pretty near the door. One of them was a pretty good-sized old boy with a bald head. J.B. suddenly launched himself at that man and began beating him over his bald head with that $90 M.L. Leddy Supreme, screaming, "You stole my hat!"

I rodeoed off and on for six years and I got my share of injuries. I had a broken neck and a broken leg and had both my collarbones broken twice and had several broken ribs and have bone chips in the elbow of my riding arm to this good day. And I'd seen a bunch of injuries that were comparable or worse. But I never saw a man as broken up as J.B. Kingman was over the recovery of his hat.

We were lucky that it happened at the end of the season, 'cause after we got J.B. out of jail, we didn't have enough money to go on rodeoing.

That was just as well. We were of too uneven a caliber to go on rodeoing as partners. Jack and Billy Jack went on and done pretty well on their own. Me and Player went on together in the partnership and then drifted off into other things. J.B. quit the rodeo that year. The last time I saw him he was driving a custom farming truck that would turn your corn, stalk and all, into silage for cattle feed. That Leddy Supreme of his had become a work hat and didn't look a hell of a lot better than the cardboard one that Player had bought him.

But he was still full of advice. Standing by his truck, he folded his arms and told me never to marry a pretty woman or buy a good hat. "Because," he said, "if you do, someone will steal them."

But that was a long time ago, when we were so young and strong that you could have thrown us against a wall and we'd have bounced right back.

And I didn't take J.B.'s advice.

.

9

Saturday's Children

This is an excerpt from a book I wrote in 1973 called Saturday's Children. I wrote about Rice University football mainly because I lived in Houston and I knew that in order to do the book properly I was going to have to become part of the team. To do that would require being on hand during those fourteen- and sixteen-hour days that college coaches put in. I guess I could have gone and gotten an apartment in Austin or Dallas or someplace like that and used the University of Texas or SMU, but I just didn't feel like it. Besides, Rice wasn't the doormat of the Southwest Conference then like it is today.

I have to say it was a hell of a year. We got blown out of a few games, but we also beat a lot of teams we weren't supposed to be able to stay with. The fun part for me was the way I was eventually accepted by the players and the coaches as just another part of the team. As a case in point, we had flown into Baton Rouge to play LSU. After we got off the plane we boarded several buses to go to the hotel. As it happened, I was on a bus with mostly players and a couple of the trainers. We were waiting for everyone to get loaded before taking off. All of a sudden a gaggle of awfully cute LSU coeds got on the bus and began going up and down the aisle teasing the players. In a matter of half a minute they managed to transform a squad of grim-faced athletes into giggling schoolboys. About that time the head coach at Rice, Bill Peterson, got on the bus. The second he saw the girls he blew his *stack. First he ran the girls off and then he ate the players out. Finally he turned on me. He said, "Coach Tippette, what the hell do you mean letting those girls on here? What the hell were you thinking about?"*

It was the first I'd heard about being a coach. I kind of liked it. Later, Peterson apologized to me. He said, "You had a chewing out coming, but I should never have done it in front of the players."

---

he evening was closing. All of the boys had been given medical examinations and most had finished their weight tests. After that would come a general team meeting, and then they would go to their assigned dorm rooms and curfew would be at ten o'clock. In the morning would come the speed tests and then lunch, and then the afternoon and the first workout. But all that was nothing. All that was just something to be done. Because after that, the next morning, would begin the two-a-day workouts, and that was something to be endured with all the will and strength and character a man could get up. It was a workout in the morning and another in the afternoon. And each was two hours under a Texas sun in August. It was two hours with your muscles failing and your breath coming in gasps and cotton in your mouth so you couldn't spit. It was two hours of hit and hit and run and hit and tackle and hit and hurt and gasp and sweat and hit and run and hurt. It was two hours with a coach yelling, "Move, dammit! Get out of there! Move! Stick your head in there! Move, move, move! Speed! Hit!"

It was two hours in the morning when all you could think of was lying down and dying. You had to go to lunch, even though you knew you couldn't eat, but you had to go because training table was mandatory. It was sitting there, trying to get something solid down, and then, finally, dragging yourself off to your bed. And lying down and finding you were too tired to sleep. Then the clock speeding by, and your roommate swinging his legs off his bed and saying, "Well, guess it's time to go get taped."

And back out in the afternoon and the little thoughts starting to enter your mind about quitting. All you had to do was walk away from the pain and the sweat and the grind. The afternoon dragging on, and the cotton and the pain and the resolve growing. You won't quit on the field. You'll finish the practice and hang it up right then. Finally, the last horn and the wind sprints and a shower and gulping water as fast as you can get it down, and then the evening training table, still unable to eat much, and then back in your room and in bed. It gets dark and you laugh softly and say to your roommate, "I don't see why they want to run a bed check." And your roommate laughs just as tiredly and answers, "They really fix it so ain't nobody going to go out for a beer."

The team meeting that first night was very low-key. With the first game a little over three weeks away there was no point in trying to fire anyone up. The head coach just stood there and talked quietly about what he expected from everyone in the room. Most of the players looked bored. They'd heard it all before. A few, the sincere ones, listened intently and made little vows within themselves.

The head coach was Bill Peterson. He was in his first year at Rice University after being lured away from Florida State by a very lucrative offer. He'd left a winning record at Florida State and he intended to establish one at Rice. But he was not feeling too hopeful about this first year. He'd inherited a group of athletes recruited by other coaches and they did not impress him. They would have impressed you or me but they did not impress his trained eye.

He looked out at them, thinking to himself that he was in for a long, hard season. With his mouth he said, "Now, I want every man in this room to believe in himself. I believe in you. The other coaches believe in you. You've got to start believing in you. You've got to think one thing—win. And you can win.

"I'm going to ask one thing of you. I'm going to ask you to think about football. See? For the next three months I want you to think about football. And nothing else. See? I want you to put that girl out of your mind, and everything else. I don't know what else you like besides girls, but give that up. Give up everything but football for the next three months. That's not so long. You do that and you can be winners." He stopped and took a cigar out of his pocket and stuck it in his mouth. For a long moment he chewed on it as he looked around the room. "You want fun? I'll give you some fun. Winning is fun. I've been a winner!" For the first time his voice rose a little. "What about you? Have you been winners?" He bore down heavily on the word. "Have you? I hear you haven't."

A few of the boys looked down at their hands.

"Well . . ." he said, letting the word hang. "You *can* be winners. If you want to. But you make up your mind what that's going to mean."

He stood up there, a big, bluff-faced man of about fifty, talking to a roomful of boys, near-men and men. He stood up there in a checkered sport coat, with a cigar in his mouth, leaning his elbows on a lectern and stabbing his finger out at them as he talked. "Every man in this room has got to play! Every man has got to reach down and get himself something to help this ball club! Now, I know how to win. Do you want to win?"

There were a few murmured assents.

Peterson's face suddenly flamed.

"What?"

"Yessir!" they said loudly.

"All right." He chewed on his cigar a moment longer. "That's all," he said. "Get to bed and get to sleep."

Their first game was going to be a classic. From across town they were going to play the University of Houston, a confrontation that Rice had avoided until Bill Peterson came to the head coaching job.

Houston was capable of inflicting embarrassment. In one game they had scored one hundred points and they had beaten opponents by more than seventy. Bill Yeoman, the head coach at Houston, was a believer in winning just as decisively as he could. And against Rice, with all the natural rivalry and prejudice to build up the hatred, it was likely there would be no quarter shown.

The speed tests had been finished that first morning and the coaches had grabbed a quick sandwich at the training table and then hurried back to the offices for a staff meeting. They met in a room containing a long conference table, with a blackboard and a player personnel chart on one wall. For a long time they all sat motionless, staring at the personnel chart, studying it, looking for changes that could be made. The chart itself was divided into offensive and defensive teams. Each player's last name was on a card opposite his position that showed him as being first team, second team, third team, and so on. One column was topped by a red cross. That was for players who were hurt too badly to practice or work out. It was still empty. Some of the players were shown at more than one position, such as Joe Buck, who had a card listing him as second-team wide receiver and third-team tight end.

Peterson was leaning back in his chair smoking a cigar. Most of the coaches were smoking, and the room was getting stuffy. Peterson brought his chair to the floor with a thump and took the cigar out of his mouth. "Damn, we're thin," he said.

No one commented. The defensive coaches were on one side of the table and the offensive coaches on the other. Peterson was sitting back from the table a little and Dr. C.A. Roberts, his administrative aide, was behind him.

In a hesitant voice Bob DeCrosta, the defensive line coach, said, "Coach Pete, I've just got to have some help."

Al Conover turned toward him quickly. "Oh no, don't start that old song again."

But Larry Peccatiello jumped in. "Why not, Al? You've got everybody now. You picked us clean in spring training. All we got is midgets. *Slow* midgets."

A football squad is not one team, it is two—the offense and the defense. They meet separately, they practice almost separately, and there is a great element of competition between both the players and the coaches. Even the game film they look at is split, with the defense watching the offensive team of the opponent they are to play next and the offense looking at the opposing defense. This competition often surfaces when the defensive and offensive coaches are each trying to get the better athletes for their squads.

"Listen," Conover said, "don't give me that old stuff, Peccatiello. You didn't give me anybody that can play."

"What about Bart Goforth? He's starting for you."

"Oh, yeah, Goforth. But he was mine anyway."

"What about Tobin Haynes? He's running second string for you." Peccatiello is an Italian from the rougher section of Newark, New Jersey. A powerful-looking man, he was a receiver at William & Mary. He is smiling, but his voice is hard and probing with the Italian-New Jersey accent getting a little pronounced as he warms up on Conover. "And how about Hershey? He could start for us."

"Oh, no," Conover said. "Don't start that old song again about Hershey. You gave me Hershey. You didn't want him!"

"Hold it," Peterson said. "Let's don't go to swapping around until we've played a little."

"Coach, I think we ought to talk about this a little," Peccatiello said after a moment or so. "We're really hurting at defensive line. I know Al doesn't want to give anybody up, but we've got to get some people that can play."

"We're hurting everywhere," Peterson said irritably. "I don't even know if I have a quarterback or not. Let's work for a while and see what we see."

"Okay," Peccatiello said resignedly. "I'm just saying that. . . ."

"We know what you're saying," Conover broke in.

They sat and looked at the board for a time longer. Peterson suddenly said, as if he had been thinking about the defense, "What is wrong with this kid Chris Hale? What's his problem?"

Behind him C.A. Roberts stirred. This was his area of interest, his problem. "We're working on it, Coach," Roberts said.

Chris Hale had been a standout in spring training at the Monster Man position. Rice played a four-deep secondary with three linebackers and a roaming Monster Man who was half linebacker, half defensive back. The position called for exceptional speed and strength. Unaccountably, Chris Hale, who had been depended on to start at the position, had not shown up. He had not even sent in word. His absence was a mystery.

Peccatiello said, "You know, that was the last kid I'd have expected to quit. I just can't figure it."

"Well, let's get something done about it," Peterson said. "I want that guy back and I don't care what we have to do to get him. Get some of the players on it." His face suddenly flared, anger showing. "Do I have to do everything myself?"

No more was said about Chris Hale, but some people in the room knew a little. The word was that Hale had gone to Las Vegas and won $12,000 at blackjack. Supposedly he had bought a motorcycle and let his hair grow and was running fast and loose. C.A. Roberts discounted the story of the $12,000. Nobody went to Vegas and did that. Especially not a college kid; though at twenty-two Hale was an old college student. It was more likely that he just didn't want any more of the drudgery of football. That happens, and often such decisions can be changed. C.A. Roberts would look into it.

After the hitting the practice began to taper off as the offense and defense split and worked at other routines. The linebackers were holding a recognition drill, and Bobby Ross was having trouble with Rodrigo Barnes.

"C'mon, Roy!" he yelled at the linebacker. "Have a little pride. For gosh sakes!"

Barnes just looked at him. Ross had the most specialized problem on the ball club. He was Barnes' coach. Peterson did not want to have any dealings with the big black because he, as head coach, could not allow himself to be pushed into a corner by Barnes. If he did he would have no alternative but to discipline him, and Barnes would not accept discipline, let alone punishment. Yet Peterson and the ball club could not afford to lose him. Barnes knew this, of course, so he constantly pushed. Ross had not been told outright, but it had been made clear to him that he must handle Barnes, keep him playing, and keep him away from Peterson.

It was all very frustrating for Ross, who was a crew-cut, fiercely dedicated young man whose whole life had been football. He did not understand Barnes, could not understand Barnes. And it was a source of the deepest personal humiliation that he had been put in such a position.

He and Barnes had reached an agreement. Ross was not to yell at Barnes on the field or to push him too hard. In return Barnes would not challenge Ross' authority—on the field. But Barnes had the habit of taking the day off about every other practice. He'd show up, all right, but he'd just go through the motions. This was so frustrating to Ross, who'd never known anything but go, go, hit, hit, that sometimes he was not able to contain himself.

Barnes got over near him, after he had hollered, and said softly, "That's one, Coach."

Ross turned away, but his face suddenly got very red.

Throughout the whole season Barnes was never to be confronted and faced down. There were incidents but, in the end, the coaches let Barnes slip out of situations that would have meant dismissal for another player. For one of the games, everyone was supposed to be aboard the bus to go to the airport at ten a.m. sharp. Peterson had roared, "That bus leaves at ten! Anybody that's not aboard gets left." At ten that morning, with everyone else in place, Barnes was spotted about three blocks up the street. Instead of hurrying he was giving it the "pro trot"—a slow, casual way of moving—as if unconcerned about how long he might make the bus wait. Everyone looked to Peterson to see what he would do. Watching Barnes, Peterson cleared his throat nervously and said, "I've got five minutes till. He better hurry." Of course, by that time it was well after ten. Barnes finally got to the bus and came aboard with an amused look on his face. Looked at solely from the view of winning, Peterson's misreading of the time was the correct thing to do. Barnes helped win the game for Rice.

Tobin Rote was getting down on Bruce Gadd, the quarterback. He didn't think Gadd had his mind on the game. During one practice Rote warned him three times about trying to pass over a linebacker; after each warning Gadd would do it again and get the ball intercepted. It was too much for the old quarterback's discipline to bear. Rote came charging up, pounding his fist in his palm. "How many times I got to tell you—you can't throw short over a linebacker! It can't be done! You can't get enough arc!"

Gadd said, "But, Coach, I'm trying to hit my primary receiver."

"Forget him!" Rote shouted. It was frustrating for Rote to try to tell a kid something he knew how to do so well himself. "Look for your secondary man! As soon as you see those linebackers dropping off, look to your right. Who's your key on Halfback Rim?"

"Mike," Gadd said.

"All right. And if Mike is dropping back, what are you going to do?"

"Go to the right to Y."

"Then why aren't you doing it?"

Gadd shook his head. "I don't know, Coach. He doesn't seem to be just dropping straight back. It looks for an instant as if he's going sideways."

"Oooooh!" Rote said in disgust. "All right. On the ball! Let's get over the ball and run it again."

There was another key on Halfback Rim. As the tight end left the line of scrimmage he was to look and see if the linebackers were blitzing. If they were he was to cut immediately to his inside and yell, "Hot, hot, hot!" Then the quarterback was to dump the ball off quickly to him.

Consistently, Gadd was getting confused and taking too long to release the ball. It finally brought Bill Peterson storming down

out of the stands. He came stalking up and read off the linemen for
not blocking, the receivers for not running the proper routes and
the quarterbacks for holding the ball too long. "You've got to
throw it!" he yelled, his eyes wide and angry. "You can't complete a
pass until you *throw* the ball! Are you scairt to turn *loose* of it?"

The formal scrimmage was very bad. Or at least it was very bad
from Peterson's viewpoint, which was the offensive viewpoint. The
first-team offense could not move the ball against the second-team
defense, and the first-team defense completely overwhelmed the
second-team offense. The only bright spots were Stahle Vincent's
running—which he did almost singlehandedly—and the play of
Larry Caldwell. Caldwell several times caught short passes and
turned them into long gains with superb moves downfield. He'd
catch the ball, then, holding it with one hand, he'd slide back from
a tackle by a linebacker, cut away from the smashing charge of a
cornerback and, twisting and turning, dance his way downfield for
fifteen or twenty yards before he would finally be hemmed in by
more men than he could get away from. The way he was playing
reinforced Bill Peterson's thinking about running the Z-up for
their first offensive play against Houston. He was already starting
to call it the Houston Special.

For the past week the offensive staff had been meeting late
every night to discuss strategy and settle on a game plan.

"Won't work," Conover said.

"Rote looked around. "Why not?"

"Because the guard can't make that block on Willie, that's why
not," Conover said.

Rote dusted his hands off and laid the chalk down. "Al, you've
got your flow going the other way. That'll freeze him. Then your
guard gets through there before the quarterback ever rolls back to
the right."

"Oh, hell, Tobin," Al exclaimed disgustedly, "Willie's ten yards
outside him. By the time the guard gets through and goes for a
block the linebacker is already in our backfield."

Rote came back and sat down. "I'll tell you this. I stood over
centers for fifteen years in pro football and if a guard can't make
that block he's got no business on a football field."

Conover suddenly hurled himself to his feet and rushed to the
blackboard and began pounding it with his fist. "Listen, *dammit,*

I'm telling you that block can't be made! You know so damn much!"
He hit the board again. "I'm about to get tired of your big-time
noise! Just how many linemen have you ever coached?"

Rote cleared his throat.

Conover hit the board and whirled around. "I'm just about tired
of all your garbage! You understand me?" Conover took a step toward Rote, and Rote stood up and took off his glasses.

Peterson had been sitting by, smoking his cigar. Now he said
quietly, "All right you two. That's enough."

The two big men stood there for another second, glaring at
each other, but finally Conover sat down and Rote put his glasses
back on.

Peterson heaved himself up. "We better call it a night." He
yawned. "There's not much more we can do. Let's all go get some
sleep."

The morning of the game, Bruce Gadd was lying in bed running through the plays in his mind. All of a sudden he went into a
panic as he realized he couldn't think what to do on certain plays.
"Philip!" he asked his roommate urgently. "Which way do I turn
on Lead Draw?"

"To the left," Wood said. Then he laughed softly. "Don't
worry, you're just having a nerve or two. It'll be all right after the
kickoff."

Across town Chris Hale was home in his apartment trying to
decide if he should go to the game or not. All during the summer
he'd had every intention of playing his senior year. He had done
his running and weight lifting and sent in his progress cards with
regularity. Then, just a couple of weeks before time to report, he
had taken off from his job and gone to Vegas. Incredibly, he had
somehow run a few hundred dollars into $12,000. And there, amid
all that air conditioning and pretty girls and easy living, had come
his first doubts about the logic of playing football. Back in Houston
he had bought himself a motorcycle and fallen in with a couple of
guys who seemed to know what life was about. He had rented an
apartment and they had moved in with him. He had not contacted
his parents or any of the coaches because he was confused. But
his two friends were not confused. They said anybody that played
football was a clown. They said why go out there and sweat your
tail off when you can lie around and drink and smoke a little pot

and enjoy things. They said he was just a tool of the coaches and the frumps who sat up in the stands hoping to see him get his head knocked off. What did he want to be, they asked him, some kind of idiot gladiator?

So he had let his hair grow and ridden his motorcycle and they had made all the swinging places. He was paying most of the bills, but that was only natural—$12,000 was a lot of money and there was no way to spend it all.

Except lately he had been wondering if most of his friends' reasoning had not come from the fact that if he played football, he would have to give up the apartment and move back in the dorm and they would no longer have a free ride. But what was hurting worst was to read the sports pages and get that old feeling again, that old game feeling. And there was the guilt. Rice was hurting and it looked like Houston was going to massacre them. He saw where Bill Latourette would be starting in his position, and he worried about that. Bill was a great guy and a good football player, but Hale did not think he had the speed or the football sense to handle that Houston run-pass Veer attack. But how could he go back out now after he had missed the two-a-days? The guys would resent him missing the real hard work. And the coaches probably would not let him come back anyway.

So he lay there and worried about going to the game. Most likely he would not even be able to buy a ticket. That would be ironic—that he could not even buy his way into the stadium. And then there was the danger he would see someone he knew. What would he say to them?

No, he should stay at home and listen to the game on the radio.

One of his friends came in just then. "Hey man," the friend said. "Big news. They got a new group down at the Cellar. Let's get some chicks and go down there tonight."

"No," Chris said.

"Why not, man?"

"I'm going to stay home and listen to the game on radio."

His friend looked incredulous. "Have you lost your reason, man? Listen, football is nothing but. . . ."

"Shut your mouth," Chris Hale said.

Houston came out on the field after Rice. The two squads stole quick curious looks at each other. This close it was easy to see how much bigger the Houston players were. They were better-looking athletes, too; tall and rangy, with flashes of speed as the lines of receivers went out for passes. Rice was a fourteen-point underdog. With reason.

The Rice captains, Stahle Vincent and Dale Grounds, went out to midfield and won the toss for Rice, and then all the players were gathering around Peterson and he was saying something, but the noise was so loud that none of them could hear. This did not matter, though. They did not need to be told anything at this point. And then they were breaking out and the receiving team was running onto the field as Houston prepared to kick off.

Tommy Clanton and Eddie Collins were deep for Rice. The crowd rose as the Houston kicker advanced on the ball and hit it and sent it tumbling high in the air. It went end over end, short, and Tommy Clanton took it at the 13 and came up the left sideline. He was hit at the 25, spun away, turned toward the center of the field, fought off one tackler with an outstretched hand, and then ran into a knot of blockers and tacklers and went down on the 32. It was good field position. It was a good place to try the Houston Special.

Peterson had Gadd by the arm on the sideline. "Run it," he said urgently. "Go to the Special."

Gadd nodded and trotted out on the field buckling on his chin strap. He was so nervous and tense he had trouble running. He got to the huddle and leaned in. "Houston Special," he said, his mouth dry as cotton. "On hut. Break!"

The players broke out of the huddle with a single handclap and rushed up to the line. Gadd walked deliberately to the center, looking to the left and right, supposedly looking over the Houston defense. But he was so tight and so scared that he was seeing nothing. He was just going through the motions. He crouched behind Wright Moody and stuck in his hands. "Blue!" he yelled, "76, 55, 22, hut, hut. . . ."

The ball hit his hands on the first hut and he whirled, feeling it slipping even as he turned. Behind him he could hear the impact as the two lines met. But all he was aware of was the ball hitting the ground at his feet and bouncing backward. He chased it, one step, two steps, and leaped and smothered it with his chest. Immediately he felt crushing weights come piling in as the Houston players tried to knock him loose from the ball.

He had fumbled and lost three yards. He got up feeling very bad and still very scared. Stahle Vincent touched him on the arm. "Shake it off, man. That don't make no difference."

On the sidelines Peterson spit out the cigar he was chewing with a violent sound.

Midway through the second quarter the Houston bench was beginning to look worried. The offense had moved well, driving deep into Rice territory on several occasions, but each time the drive sputtered and two field goal attempts had failed. So it was still a scoreless game as Rice took over on its own 30. Stahle Vincent went over right guard for twelve yards, pulling two tacklers along for three yards before they could bring him down. Something was becoming apparent. The Houston defense was tiring. Even with all their depth they were beginning to drag. From the 42 Stahle again went into the line and made five more yards. In the press box Tobin Rote was studying the Houston defense. He suddenly said into the phone, "Coach Pete, they're going to be in Five Short. The Special will go right now."

Gadd came rolling out with the snap while a flurry of receivers went short. Eddie Collins did a hesitation fake and then turned on his speed down the sideline. He caught the Houston defensive back going the wrong way, got by him, and gathered in the pass on the Houston 15. But the back, running hard, slanted in and knocked Collins out of bounds at the eight-yard line.

The Rice fans were yelling and screaming, and Rice called time-out with a minute and fifty-seven seconds to go before halftime. Gadd trotted over to the sideline. Rote, from his position in the press box high above the field, was talking frantically in Peterson's ear. "Let's stay on the ground, Coach. Stay on the ground. Try Stahle on 17 Lead."

The Rice bench was silent as their team lined up over the ball. Perhaps it was because they did not really believe they could score. They had been fired up, but they had never actually thought of beating Houston. Or even leading them. Now they had held them scoreless for almost a full half and here they were on the eight-yard line with four downs to run at it.

When Guard Randy Lee lifted from his stance and charged to
block his man, he felt his left knee, the bad one, give. But he had
made contact and he kept driving, trying to take his man straight
backward. Beside him he felt something brush past and he knew it
was Mike Phillips leading Stahle through the hole. Then he felt
shocks and blows and violent contact as the Houston defense
moved in to meet Vincent.

Vincent was hit at the line of scrimmage by the defensive end,
but he jerked away from him and put his head down and pushed
and shoved as tackler after tackler hit him. For the last yard he was
carrying five men. They finally got him down, but only after he
had made four yards.

"How you feel, Stahle?" Gadd asked him in the huddle. The
play had just come in and it was a sweep to the right with Stahle
carrying the ball. Stahle just nodded at the question. He did not
have enough breath to speak.

The play made three yards. Stahle tried to dive for the flag at
the corner, but was knocked out of bounds just two feet short.
On the next play, Mike Phillips went over the top of a huge pile at
the line of scrimmage and the referee raised his hands. The Rice
bench erupted. Before anyone could stop them they had charged
out on the field and were jumping around hugging their teammates. It took the referees a few moments to restore order, and
then Alan Pringle came in and kicked the extra point and Rice
led 7 to 0. It was beyond belief, beyond understanding. And it did
not last.

Across town, Chris Hale was listening on the radio and smoking
a cigarette as the third quarter began. He heard the announcer say,
"Mullins rolls right, fakes to Newhouse, rolling straight back. He's
going to pass. He's looking long. Stanley! Stanley is around Latourette! Mullins to throw! Stanley is behind Latourette! He's got it!
It's a footrace and Stanley is drawing away! He's at the 50, the 40, the
20, nobody's going to catch him! Touchdown, Houston!"

As he listened, Hale slowly brought his head up to attention.
The hand holding the cigarette fell down across his thigh. "No," he
kept saying. "Don't let him, Bill."

When the runner scored, Hale flung the cigarette across the
room. He felt personally guilty for the touchdown. "Oh, you bastard!" he said of himself. At that moment he resolved to see if they

would take him back; to see if they would give him a chance to redeem himself. Which, of course, they would—and did.

It was a very bad third quarter. Houston kicked off after taking a 14-7 lead and Tommy Clanton, unsure of where he was, caught the ball and then lost his balance and stepped out on the one-foot line. He came to the bench saying, "Oh, let them get it out of there! Please, let them get it out of there!"

But on the first play, Mike Phillips was hit at the line of scrimmage and lost the ball. Phillips scrambled backward and recovered his own fumble, but he was in the end zone and Houston had two points on the safety. It was now Houston 16, Rice 7.

Rice rallied in the fourth quarter to make it 16-14, but Houston came back, Mullins scoring on a quarterback sneak. After the kick it was 23-14. Three minutes remained on the clock, and Houston drew a fifteen-yard penalty on the kickoff for unsportsmanlike conduct. Houston was winning, but not winning the way it had wanted to, and a lot of the red-shirted players were angry.

Houston now gave ground very grudgingly. Too many times it came up third down and long. Somehow Rice managed each time to get a new first down, but the clock was ticking away. Then came a sudden Rice touchdown on a long pass from Gadd to Eddie Collins. The Houston Special, but too late. Only seconds remained on the clock. Rice was beaten, 23-21.

The crowd behaved very curiously. While the tired players were trooping off the field, the people simply sat. They should have been getting up and rushing for the exits, but they continued sitting for a long time. They were either wanting more football or too overwhelmed by the unexpected things they had seen to be willing to quit the place where it all had occurred.

The Houston players and the Rice players went up the ramp together. A few handshakes were exchanged and a few "Nice game" murmurs, but not many. Mostly the players just seemed tired. Rice had been defeated, but it had won something. Houston had won, but somehow seemed defeated.

The players were very slow in getting undressed and showering. There were apples and sandwiches and ice-cream bars piled up on a big table, but no one seemed to want anything.

Outside the gates at the top of the ramp a crowd of people had gathered waiting for the players. They were friends and family and the curious, but they were going to have a long wait. Bart Goforth had taken off his shoulder pads, but he had not undressed any further than that. Periodically he would pick up the pads and smash them down on the floor. Joe Buck, who had not played much, was helping Stahle Vincent undress. Buck was doing most of it, because Stahle was so exhausted he could do nothing but stare straight ahead. "Raise your arm," Buck said, as he tried to work the shoulder pad over Vincent's head. "C'mon, Stahle, raise your arm. Man, help me a little. Just a little." It was like trying to undress a drunk.

Peterson was a long time letting the press in. Finally he went into the little office where the other coaches were assembled and nodded to the student manager at the door. He did not really feel like talking, but talking was part of his job. He would do it, though all he really felt like was sitting down and not thinking for a long, long time. It had been incredible, he was thinking, how close they had come, 23-21, when they were not supposed to have come close at all. It seemed, he thought, that coming that close they should have won. It seemed like it ought to have been that way. He knew he was going to have a hard time getting this game off his mind. And the season had hardly begun.

Rice was to finish its year 3-7-1. Chris Hale rejoined the team and was soon starting again in the defensive secondary. At season's end, Bill Peterson resigned to become head coach of the Houston Oilers, taking Larry Peccatiello with him. Rice named Al Conover to replace Peterson, whereupon Tobin Rote quit. Rodrigo Barnes is now with the Dallas Cowboys, where he has proved to be a promising linebacker.

10

Picked Last for the Last Time

I don't know that any story I ever wrote in my twenty-some-odd years of sportswriting brought back an incident more clearly than what you are about to read in the next few pages. Later in life I would often hear the expression, "Many are called but few are chosen." I never knew where the quote came from or exactly what it meant, but I'm pretty sure it had something to do with sandlot football and waiting on the sidelines. They say that children's games are the cruelest. That's probably true, but it's even more true if you don't get to play. That's the cruelest cut of all; that's even crueler than being cut by the Chicago Bears the day before they get the roster down to the 45-man limit.

I came to write this story in a rather strange way. I was living in Mason, Texas, at the time and I felt a great need for white beaches and cobalt blue sea and balmy breezes, so I said to my wife, "What say we up and go to the Bahamas for a quick vacation?"

It was about ten degrees outside at the time with a cold wind blowing, but my wife immediately said, "Oh, no. No deal. We can't afford it."

I said, "Okay, what if I call my editor at Sports Illustrated and pitch them an idea and they buy it and I write it and they pay us. Then can we go?"

She said, somewhat severely I thought, "No, you've pulled that number on me before. If you've got an idea for a story then do it and get paid and we'll throw the money away frivolously on such things as groceries and house payments and silly things like that."

Women will take such views, why I've never understood. But she'd cast the gauntlet down and I had no other recourse than to pick up the phone and call my editor at SI, Linda Verigan.

Now the terrible part about the dilemma I was in was that I didn't have the slightest idea for a story. I'd just been trying to talk my wife into a vacation I badly needed, whether we could afford it or not. The story idea was just bait.

I made the call without the vaguest notion of what I was going to say, more or less hoping Linda wouldn't be available and that my bluff wouldn't be immediately called.

But she was there. For some odd reason, the minute I started talking the remembrance of all those old sandlot games came into my head. I guess I hadn't thought of them in thirty years. But as soon as I started talking the whole scene came back with such a rush that I practically told Linda the whole story over the phone. If she'd been recording the conversation I would never have had to type it out. I finished and I waited. Then I said, "Well?"

Linda said, "Are you crazy? This is November. I'm up to my ears in football stories, all the way from college to professional to high school. And you want to pitch me some story about a bunch of kids playing touch on somebody's vacant lot? Get real."

"It was tackle," I said a little stiffly. "And it wasn't just anyone's vacant lot. It was hallowed ground. It was where I began my athletic career."

She said, "That's another good reason not to buy it."

I said, a little desperately, "Listen, Linda, this story is heart wrenching, it's poignant, and it's a story your average American can identify with. We all played sandlot football. But how many of us went on to the pros?"

I could hear her thinking.

In the pause I said, "And, besides, I think I can parlay it into a trip to the Caribbean."

With what I thought was a bit frostier tone than necessary she said, "We don't buy stories so writers can go scuba diving. But I'm going to buy this one. Not to send you to the Caribbean but because it had better be heart wrenching and poignant and all that other guff you said. It had also better be somewhat funny."

My wife maintained her position about the Bahamas, but I don't think that need concern you about what follows. It still doesn't matter who gets called, it's who gets chosen.

I n my near-adequate athletic career, what with rodeoing and track and baseball and a little college football, I had, well-spaced though they were, my few moments of glory. Nothing spectacular, you understand, but, still, enough to stay with you for a lifetime.

So it might seem strange that my greatest moment— and the greatest accolade I ever received as an athlete—came on Dr. Simon's vacant lot in Bay City, Texas, in 1946.

I don't know who your heroes were back in the mid-'40s, maybe Sid Luckman or Doc Blanchard or the immortal Frankie Sinkwich, but mine were Al Blaylock and Dee Dee Pollard and Steve Long. I'm talking giants now. Two even played on the high school team.

I was about twelve years old, and, since we played sandlot football all year long, in the off-season I was occasionally afforded the chance to play with them.

The games always ended the same: just about dark, with someone's mother stepping out on the front porch and calling, "Yoo hoo! Charles (or Bill or Mack or Morris), it's time to come in to supper!"

Now we grammar school kids, "small fry," as the big boys called us, didn't always get to play. Sometimes the sides were even, and we simply stood around on the sidelines hoping we'd somehow get into the game. We played Saturdays and Sundays and a few times after school, but mostly it was those Saturday afternoons when the Big Games occurred. And it was at the end of one of those Big Game days that my greatest moment came.

Getting into a game depended on how uneven the sides were among the high school boys or just how benevolent they were feeling that day. Actually, though, the most dreaded thing was being picked last. When it came to us sideliners, there were few feelings spared. One of the captains would say, "Well, I'll take Fred and Guy. You can have that other kid."

And the other captain would say, "You kidding me? He couldn't catch a pass in a washtub."

"So what, you ain't going to throw to him anyway."

"Yeah, but them two you want might get in somebody's way as blockers."

And when all the arguing was done, somebody might notice you standing there all by yourself and he'd say, "Oh, you can have him."

"Naw, you take him."

And then, when you were the last one picked, you'd run over to your team, your head down, your whole body flushed with shame and embarrassment. That's the way it felt to be the last picked.

Al Blaylock was my special hero for several reasons. One was that he was a starter on the Bay City Black Cats football team. Another was that when he was a captain in the game on Dr. Simon's lot, he'd see that I wasn't the last one picked.

There was a third reason, too. I had fallen off a garage one time and broken my nose and collarbone. Because of this my mother had expressly forbidden me to go on the roof of our garage or that of any other garage.

Well, what my mother didn't know was that I wasn't playing on the roofs of garages; I was conducting aeronautical research. I was looking for a roof with the perfect slope and enough runway to launch the glider I was building.

And one day it occurred to me that the Blaylock garage might be perfect. It was a shedlike affair with a high front that fell off to a low back and appeared to have enough runway to give me air speed.

But I needed a closer look. So one day I shinnied to the top, made some quick calculations that convinced me it would work and then started to get off at the low end. But just as I was sliding over the edge, I slipped and managed to snag a ring that my grand-mother had given me on a protruding nail.

And there I hung, about two feet from the ground, unable to pull myself back up enough to get the ring off the nail.

Just then Al came out the back door of his house and immediately saw my trouble. He lifted me up by the legs so I could free myself, set me on the ground and promised never to tell my mother.

And he didn't. You don't forget a thing like that when you're making up your list of heroes.

I don't know exactly how long Dr. Simon's lot was, maybe a hundred yards, but only about sixty yards of that was playable because of the trees at either end. But we used them as goal-line markers, and, as a matter of fact, it was two of those very trees that helped me to make probably the greatest play of my life and win that accolade I've referred to.

The boundary on one side was the curb of the street, so it was a pretty good idea not to get knocked out of bounds there. The other sideline was the demarcation between Dr. Simon's lot and old man Oates's. Simon's lot was always mowed, but Oates's wasn't, so the sideline there was sort of like the difference between fairway and rough.

We didn't have a first-down marker. We usually considered two completed passes in a row, of some vague distance, or a run of an equally arbitrary distance, as constituting a first down.

Or at least it did if you won the inevitable argument.

The day of the play, the play that still sticks out in my memory, began like any other. It was a Saturday, and it was getting late. Once again, even though I was on Al's team, I had been chosen last. Perhaps he'd overlooked me, or perhaps he'd had other things on his mind. But, nevertheless, I'd still had to trot to my team's huddle with my head down and that feeling of third-rateness running through me.

We'd been playing for hours, and dark was descending. I don't remember what the score was; all I knew was that we needed one more touchdown to win.

We were on about the other team's 10-yard line and had to score on that drive. We were well inside the sun's two-minute warning. In the huddle Al called a pass play, telling his main receivers where he wanted them to go. I didn't get any special instruction.

But I ran out on what I guess you could call a fly pattern, without much expectation of seeing the ball since the big guys seldom threw to us minor-leaguers, certainly never in critical situations.

But as I ran down the right sideline, nearing the goal-line trees, I looked back and saw Al scrambling, frantically looking for an open receiver, any receiver.

It was in that instant that I heard the call. I put on a burst of speed and, using the righthand goal-line tree, put a perfect pick (and I didn't even know what a pick was then) on my defender and cut left. Just as he was going down, Al saw me and threw.

He'd led me a little too much, but I stretched and stretched and caught the ball on my fingertips. I clutched it to my chest, wrapping my arms around it.

In that second I also ran headlong into the other goal-line tree. It was a sycamore, I think.

When I came to, I was on my back, over the goal line, still holding the ball.

Somebody on my team said, "Hell, we win."

I heard that, but what I really remember was that as we were walking off the field, Al Blaylock put his arm around me and said, "Well, boy, after that catch I don't think you'll ever have to worry about being picked last again."

My supreme moment.

I'd never have to worry about being picked last again . . . at least not on Dr. Simon's vacant lot.

11

If You Haven't Got the Horses, You Can't Win the Race

I was very glad when Sports Illustrated asked me to do this story because it gave me the chance to pay back Nat Sawyer with a little ink for all the favors he'd done me. Nat had helped me through a couple of difficult track events and given me training and moral assistance. In return I think I gave him quite a few laughs, though he could have had those anyway.

Ink is more important to an assistant coach than it is to a head coach or an athlete. If the athlete performs he's going to get the publicity; that's automatic. And a head coach can be judged in his job performance by his won and lost record. But the assistant coach just sits in the background, doing most of the work, but mostly going unnoticed and unheralded. It is very often a thankless, underpaid, and tenuous job. All of them do it for the love of the game.

There are thousands of assistant coaches out there striving for that next step up the ladder that I could have written about. I just happen to know and like Nat Sawyer.

Covering football for as many years as I have, I couldn't help noticing that about 95 percent of the college players I came into contact with were planning on becoming football coaches.

That's about like 95 percent of every graduating class deciding to go on and be lawyers.

Which, by the way, may be the case.

But I was still struck by the imbalance between supply and demand. I don't have any idea of how many football programs there are in this country; junior high, high school, junior college, college, semi-professional, professional.

But I do know that just about every college in this country, all the way from NAIA schools to the big powerhouses in the Division I class of the NCAA, are turning out a whole slew of new coaches.

And that's year after year after year.

Will they all have an equal shot at becoming the new Bo Schembechler or Lou Holtz, the new Don Shula or Paul Brown? Will their quality and ability automatically float them to the top like the running talent of a Walter Payton or the passing arm of a John Elway?

Back in the early 1970s when he was still the head coach at the University of Texas, I casually asked that question of Darrell Royal. He said, "Hell, no." He said, "I figure we've got to be turning out about five thousand football coaches a year and I don't have any idea where they're going. Maybe the lucky ones are landing a job right away as an assistant on some junior high program, but I think there's a bunch going into real estate or insurance and waiting for somebody to die or retire."

I asked him again about the ability factor. He said, "Look, there's so damn much more to it." We were sitting in his suite in a hotel in Houston, Texas, and took a moment to have a sip of coffee and look off into the distance. I think he was quickly reliving his own rise to the top and just how many might-not-have-beens he'd avoided. He said, "There's so damn much luck involved. It isn't that you've just got to know the right people, you've got to know them at the right time. They've not only got to want you, but you've got to be able to move at that instant and that's not always possible. Listen," he said, "coaching is not that hard. I mean the X's and the O's of coaching aren't that hard. But there's so much more to it. There's the organization, the motivation, the recruiting, the handshaking, the—"

He just stopped and shook his head as if thinking about all of it was getting to be too much. But, in response to my prodding, he said, "I'll tell you . . . . Most of these kids coming out of college today have about as much chance of making it to the top job at a major college as all those kids out there taking piano lessons have of making it to Carnegie Hall. And I don't mean as an usher. Now you figure the odds."

None of this meant very much to me until I became friendly with a young assistant coach, Nat Sawyer, at a 4A high school in West Texas. His head coach, Jim Slaughter, had just been offered a plum job at Corpus Christi Carrol, a 5A school, the highest-ranking division in Texas. Slaughter wanted Nat Sawyer to go with him as his defensive coordinator.

Nat couldn't, and for some reasons that had absolutely nothing to do with football. That's when Darrell Royal's words came back to me, ". . . got to be able to move at that instant and that's not always possible."

Sawyer's major problem was his house. In a depressed housing market he had the choice of continuing to make payments on a house he wouldn't be living in and that might be a year or better in selling, or simply walking away from his equity. Either move would have cost him many more thousands of dollars than he could afford.

It makes you wonder if Amos Alonzo Stagg or Knute Rockne would have become legends if they'd been faced with the same problem.

But there was an even worse alternative for Nat. If he stayed where he was he would probably be giving up any chance to move up. Lake View High, where Nat coaches, is in an economically depressed area and that sort of an environment does not turn out big, strong athletes.

Nat says, "You know, sometimes the only good meal these kids get is off our lunch program. I've gone into my own pocket to feed some of these kids and I know you don't get big, aggressive players off that kind of nutrition."

Jim Slaughter had told me the same thing.

But Jim Slaughter had been a miracle worker. He'd somehow managed to get those undersized, scrawny kids to play so far over their heads that they'd compiled a record that should never have been. He'd gone 53-23 in his tenure there.

But now Jim Slaughter was gone.

Larry Peccatiello, now the defensive coordinator of the Washington Redskins, had once told me when I'd asked him why he'd moved from the Houston Oilers to the Seattle Seahawks, "Hey, you don't move up from a losing team. You coach for a losing team and they figure you're a losing coach."

Nat Sawyer knows he's on a loser and that his career may well be at a dead end if something doesn't happen. He's thirty-one years old and he doesn't much expect the Lake View team to go much better than 3-7 in the coming season. And that's if they're lucky. He says, "You can motivate these kind of less-than-average players to go above their heads for maybe two games. More than that you can't expect."

Meanwhile, Jim Slaughter has gone down to Corpus Christi Carrol and turned their program completely around. From four straight nothing seasons he has, in two years, built a record of 23-2.

Nat Sawyer fiddles with a beer can and admits, "Yeah, I should have forgotten about the house and gone with Jim. Right now I'm just so damn frustrated I don't know what to do. We don't have a kid coming back that can run under a five-flat forty. And that includes our running backs."

Mark Gesch inherited Jim Slaughter's head coaching job, but Nat doesn't resent his success even though they were on equal terms as assistants when Slaughter left. He does, however, resent the disparity in salary. Sawyer makes a little over $30,000 a year. Gesch makes around $50,000. But Gesch, or any other head football coach in a high school, doesn't have to do anything but coach football. Sawyer has to teach three hours of American History and coach the track team. In addition, he's on the road to at least ten coaching clinics a year trying to learn about new defensive schemes or better ways to stop the offenses he faces with those scrawny little kids.

He says, "I don't know that it makes much difference. If you haven't got the horses, you can't win the race. But it's our job to try."

He works, year round, about 120 hours a week and he hopes

that no one will ever figure out what that comes out to an hour. He says, "Probably the same price a fry cook gets down at Burger King."

He's had thoughts about entering what he calls the "private sector." I think that's what Darrell Royal meant when he told me about all those would-be coaches going out and becoming insurance or real estate salesmen.

Sawyer knows that the road to the big time doesn't lie just through those X's and O's. He knows there has got to be a lot of glad-handing and patting the right backs and learning all the other tricks of the trade that get a football coach to the top. Now, in the offseason, with what little time he has, he's trying to develop those skills. He came out of a student coaching job at a university and immediately landed the head coaching job at a 2A school. It didn't work out because he thought all you had to do was draw those plays on the blackboard.

Of course that's about one tenth of it.

So he'd gone to work for Jim Slaughter at Lake View. He learned a lot under Slaughter, but he didn't learn quite enough. Else he'd have said the hell with that house and the equity and gone with a winner. But that's hindsight.

Naturally this story is going on all over the country. Even as you read this there are assistant coaches in every school in this country agonizing over career decisions. They're talking to their wives and friends and family about what they ought to do.

None of them know.

If you want to get down to the truth it's still the old buddy system. You better know the right buddy at the right time and you better be able to make a move and you better have what he needs.

Or else you are going to end up in the "private sector."

Because most of the people who hire head coaches don't know the first thing about football. They hire on your charisma and your PR abilities and other intangibles that don't count.

Just like Nat says, certain assistant coaches get hired because of their academic background. He says, "I know guys, because they can teach math or a science, not that they're better coaches, but just because of that, get hired. History teachers are a dime a dozen. You go in for an interview and they don't ask you about your coaching, they ask you what you're certified to teach."

What is Joe Paterno certified to teach?

I ask Nat a question. "There are a hundred thousand high school athletes out there praying for a four-year football scholarship. You got one. Which was harder, getting that scholarship or succeeding in coaching?"

He doesn't even hesitate. He says, "Coaching, of course. When you were an athlete, a player, you knew all you had to do was take care of yourself, be in shape, be willing to hit, and learn your play book. But coaching. . . ."

His voice trails off and he shakes his head. "There's all of this other stuff, stuff you don't have any control over." He looks away. "You go to all these coaching clinics and all you hear about is guys · trying to cut deals. 'If you make it, you hire me. If I make it, I'll hire you.'"

He shakes his head. "That's a bitch, ain't it?"

No, sounds like a crap shoot to me.

Still, Nat can't conceive of being anything but a football coach. About the only thing he says he'd change would be renting instead of buying a house. "That," he says, "or get me one of those mobile homes."

12

A Birdie in the Hand Is Worth Two in the Dark

*B*efore the pollen drove me and my allergies out of town, I used to live in Brenham, Texas, not too long ago. I lived out in the country on two acres of ground completely surrounded by fields and fields of coastal bermuda hay. As near as I can tell I bought one of the local allergists a new house and maybe sent his son through medical college. But all that money spent was to no avail. Nothing helped. The good doctor finally gave me the advice that made it all worthwhile. He said, "Get out of town." And to think I only spent two years and God knows how many thousands of dollars just to hear him say that.

During those awful days of itchy eyes and running sinuses and total lassitude I used to watch the farmers out in their fields around me making hay and pitching up those awful clouds of pollen that were making my life a little less than a dream. I had a Ruger 30-30 carbine back in the bedroom closet, and I used to look out at those farmers on their tractors and think longingly of what beautiful targets they made. But I'd already checked with the local sheriff and found

129

out that it was a misdemeanor to shoot a farmer off his tractor, even if he was causing you to nearly want to turn the gun on yourself. Such thinking on the part of lawmakers is one of the reasons that, even today, I'm a staunch anarchist.

But as bad as I hated those farmers, and as much as I begrudged the money I was paying the allergist, it was nothing to what I felt about being Larry Squier's pigeon. Because of the lack of oxygen occasioned by my allergies, all I could do was play golf—from a cart. I couldn't play tennis, I couldn't enter any Masters Track Meets, I couldn't even bowl (as if I would think of such a thing).

All I could do was show up about mid-morning every day and play golf with Larry Squier. He was the pro at the local club, but that time of the morning was his to play with whoever he wished. Larry and I were good friends so I guess that's the reason he chose to play with me.

That and the diabolical pleasure it gave him.

He didn't nick me for much money; that never was the point. But it didn't seem to matter how we arranged the handicap, Larry always arranged to beat me. Somehow. Either I choked or he pulled one of those shots out of his bag that only pros can pull.

It was the frustration of being beaten so consistently and so narrowly that caused me to come up with the plan that you'll read about in the following story. I understand that night-glo golf balls are fairly common now, but they weren't then.

I don't think I've ever taken greater satisfaction out of a victory.

Now if only I could have shot one of those hay farmers off his tractor. . . .

Anyone can be pushed too far, even a golfer with an 18 handicap who tends to swallow the apple on crucial two-foot putts. I don't say this in apology for what I allegedly did, or even as an excuse for what some people might call an excessive reaction to imagined abuse. I offer it only as a bit of advice to those who might be tempted to push the little man a shade too close to the brink.

I make specific reference to Larry Squier, who is the golf professional at the country club in Brenham, Texas. Now, Larry is my friend. But there was a time when the mention of his name would make me grit my teeth. Like after one of our matches. Sometimes during.

I used to play a lot of golf with Larry. I had plenty of free time and we used to squeeze a considerable number of nine-hole matches in between his duties as the pro. Naturally we had a bit of change riding on these matches, usually in varying combination of bets. Obviously, Larry being a professional and me being an 18 handicapper, a good deal of consideration was given to the difference in our play. Larry seemed very generous in allowing for my handicap (though he was fond of saying that my handicap was my swing). I say seemed to be generous because, no matter what he gave me, it never seemed to be enough.

I never won a match. I never won a dollar. I never won anything.

Larry was from the East and I think it was from playing with those sharks up there that he developed his surgeon's eye for just how close to the bone a sucker could be sliced up. He always just managed to win, just managed on the vital hole to pull off the exact shot he needed.

Or help me make an equally impossible bad shot so that I could manage to salvage defeat from sure victory.

Because Larry was a past master at the subtle Gotcha, that spoken or unspoken distraction that can have you thinking on your back swing, pulling a one-foot putt, shanking a five iron, or blading a wedge. He did nothing overt, nothing you could write down and say, "Look here, see what he did to me?" Nothing like that. Just little subtle things. I could be down over a two-foot putt and glance up and see him with that New Jersey grin on his face. Then that grin would somehow get imprinted all over the ball and I'd either push it or pull it or even bounce it over the hole. And even when I didn't look at him I knew that grin was there and the effect was the same.

All right, all right. You're correct. It is part of the game and I'm a crybaby to mention it. But the worst part about it was that he gloated. And rubbed my nose in it. Not demonstratively; just little things like saying to some other members, in my presence, "Gee, as small as number nine green is, I wouldn't think anybody could four putt it." Then he'd grin that New Jersey grin at me.

He even started telling his women's golf group about some of my shots. Oh, not mentioning me by name, of course. But my wife was a member of the class and she'd come home and tell me that Larry had told the funniest story about a shot some golfer had made. The shot was mine, naturally.

Me and the camel's back broke at the same time. It happened when I was in the process of telling Larry I had to find some way to beat him. I'd said that my health was suffering, my work was deteriorating, that my nerves were in such bad shape I couldn't even eat a bowl of soup without spilling it. He just said, "Forget it. You couldn't beat me if I played blindfolded. You're my pigeon, fella!"

Well, I blew up. I exploded. I said, at the top of my voice, "Oh, yeah? Oh, yeah! You let me pick the conditions and I don't even want any strokes."

He wanted to know what conditions. I said, "In the dead of the night. When it's dark."

He sounded bored. "You can't see the golf ball after dark."

I said, "Maybe you can't, but I'm part Cherokee Indian and Indians can see in the dark. You said any conditions. It's not my fault you couldn't see the Manhattan skyline from the east bank of the Hudson."

He said, "Even Indians can't find golf balls at night. We'd lose a hundred balls on the first hole."

I thought wildly. I said, "No we won't. I've got a degree in chemistry, something you didn't know. I'll get some chemicals and doctor up the golf balls so they'll glow in the dark. That is, unless you want to back out."

He just shrugged. "Why should I back out? Your swing won't be any better at night than it is in the daylight."

I do have a degree in chemistry, even though I've never practiced as a chemist. But that didn't daunt me. I still knew enough to converse with an agent of a chemical supply house and get what I needed. I figured to treat about six golf balls each. Surely, if the results were what I expected, we would not lose more than that over the nine holes we'd agreed to play.

I first tried luminol powder mixed in a carrier of liquid dimethyl sulfide, applying it to a golf ball that had been sprayed with yellow day-glo paint so that the mixture would stick. It stuck all right and it glowed a little, but it glowed blue. Not a good color to pick out against a night sky. And it wasn't anywhere near bright enough. I needed a long-term chemical reaction. To get that I mixed some potassium hydroxide into my luminol-DMSO compound. I got a chemical reaction and a much brighter glow, but it was still blue. I took a couple of the treated golf balls out in my front yard and knocked them around at night. I didn't find one of them until the next day.

What I needed was a distinctive color. I got some fluorescein dye and threw that in with the rest of the conglomerate and the result was something my wife said would look very nice on a Christmas tree. The golf balls had a blue, glowing background sprinkled all over with bright, luminous flecks of yellow. They looked sort of like an inverted planetarium. I treated twelve balls and notified Larry that the match was on. The stakes were set, the conditions (medal play) agreed to, and the time (ten o'clock the following night) fixed. He laughed, but he said he'd show up.

As a last measure, to make sure the chemical reaction that was producing the glow would last through the match, I irradiated all of the golf balls with a black light just before I set out for the course.

I was nervous. The stakes were heavy, more than I'd ever played for in my life. I was also not quite as certain about my night vision as I had been. I had checked it the night before and the results were not as positive as I'd expected. I know you grow shorter the older you get, but it seemed as if some of my Indian blood had leaked out, also.

Larry was a good deal surprised by the golf balls when we met at the country club course. He said, "You made a mistake, fella. This is going to be like playing in the daytime. You'll need strokes, but it's too late."

Well, it wasn't like playing in the daylight, especially with a waning moon. I made a mistake on the first hole, a par four. Without thinking I used my driver and hit a fade that found the tree line and bushes on the right side of the fairway. Larry snickered and drove straight down the middle with a four iron. The reason it was not like daylight was that you could see the ball all right, but the darkness of the ground below gave your depth perception fits. It was even worse hitting off a tee, since the ball seemed to be floating in the air. That was why I'd hit a slice instead of my customary smothered hook.

I lost a ball and two strokes on the first hole. Larry made bogey 5 and I had a 7. Matters did not improve on the second hole, a par three. Actually we were both on in two, but Larry two putted while it took me three strokes to get down. He snickered and said, "You're consistent. Putt the same day or night."

On the next hole, a par five, I followed Larry's example and used an iron off the tee. There was water on the hole. On my second shot I very carefully hit what I thought would be a layup, leaving me a pitch to the green. But distances at night are very deceptive and I mutely watched as one of my few dead straight shots sailed vividly into the middle of the little lake.

Larry said, conversationally, "Doesn't the golf ball look pretty up there against the sky? Looks like a shooting star. It just goes and goes and then *plop!* It disappears in the nice water."

Let me say that Larry is an affable, generous, likable person. He is an excellent and popular teaching pro. He is very nearly civilized. He knows about chairs and wiping his feet and mostly uses a knife and fork when he eats. He can even be trusted in mixed company. Why is it then, that on a golf course, I have this insane compulsion to cause him physical harm?

We had a pretty good moon that night but if anything, it only made it worse. Moon shadows blended in so well with the ground that you couldn't tell where one began and the other left off. The greens were much harder to read and, on some shots, what you thought was a mound or depression on the fairway would turn out to be a moon shadow created by a nearby tree. The result was either a topped ball or a bent shaft from sticking the head of the club directly into the ground.

An interesting phenomenon was occurring. Some of the chemical compound was rubbing off onto our clubs and, during a swing, it would look like two giant fireflies hurtling toward a head-on collision. It didn't hurt my game, but it didn't help either. And I was beginning to need help badly. After only three holes Larry had four strokes on me.

He was also beginning to make little war whoops and say, "How's your eyes, chief? Seen any palefaces?"

Surprisingly, I didn't lose any ground over the fourth and fifth hole. Larry managed to hit into the rough on two occasions and lost a ball. The balls themselves weren't so hard to find—if you could get close enough to look for them. The biggest danger in the rough, where it was really dark, was getting tangled with the bushes or walking into a tree.

Then came the sixth hole, a dogleg to the right with water and impenetrable rough at the top of the dogleg. I thought, since I had been slicing, and since the distance to the top of the dogleg was not that far, I'd take a chance and hit my driver. I had to gain some ground somewhere.

This was not the place to do it. My ball took off like a shooting star, bent to the right, kept bending, bent some more, and finally, just before starting back toward the tee, disappeared into the thick of the rough, fifty yards from the fairway. Behind me Larry was about to choke trying to keep from laughing out loud. I said, "Shut up." The ball was obviously out of bounds.

He said, "Darn, guy, I didn't know Indians knew about boomerangs. Was that a trick shot?"

I was so unnerved that I promptly shanked my next shot, a safety with a five iron, into the water.

Larry said, "You better be careful, Little Beaver. Your quiver is getting empty."

He was right. I was down to two balls. I hadn't counted on such attrition. Larry had only lost one ball.

I finally got off the tee and nursed the ball down the fairway and around the dogleg. I set up for my next shot. I was very nervous. My knees and my hands were shaking. The ground was shaking. The golf ball was shaking.

There was a gulley to the right of the green. I don't know how deep it was because I'd never been to the bottom. No one else had, either. For all I know it may be one of the last unexplored pieces of territory in the world. Prehistoric man may be living there today. If he does he has a hell of a stock of golf balls. Mine added one more to his collection.

I walked slowly to the seventh tee, refusing to ride in the cart with Larry. He had begun asking my why didn't I do a rain dance and maybe get a delay. He asked me why I didn't take up archery. He said I must be some poor example of an Indian because I'd gotten the scalping part backwards. He said he'd heard about Indians counting coup, and did that mean they could count strokes, also? Because if it did I was twelve behind.

Just for my information, you understand. Nothing malicious intended. Yeah, and you can't get mugged in Passaic.

We got to the seventh tee and Larry bent over to tee his ball up. I watched him, thinking. I needed something. I needed something big. Huge. Enormous. Dirty. Diabolic. Deplorable. I cleared my throat and said, sounding a little anxious, "Oh, hell!"

He looked up. "What?"

"Uh—" Then I shook my head. "Oh, nothing, I guess. Probably too late anyway."

"What are you talking about?"

I acted hesitant. "Oh . . . Larry, I honestly think, you'd feel better if you didn't know."

I had his attention. He stood there holding his golf ball. It glowed in his hand. He said, "Know what? What are you talking about?"

I still acted reluctant. Finally I kind of sighed and said, "Now, don't blame me. It was an honest mistake. I just forgot, that's all."

"Forgot what?"

I said, "Well, I forgot to give you some of that lead oxide cream to rub on your hands. Like I did."

He looked confused. "Lead oxide cream? What in the hell are you talking about? What's that stuff for?"

I shrugged. "Well, you know, it acts as a radiation screen. Especially since we're handling the balls."

He almost jumped up in the air. "Radiation screen! What radiation? What are you talking about?"

I made my voice soothing. "Just a simple little precaution. It probably doesn't matter. The effects should be pretty mild. I don't think you'll get very sick at all. Maybe a little hair will fall out, but that's to be expected."

He was almost shouting. I was enjoying myself immensely. "What radiation? What hair falling out?"

I said, "Well, you know the only materials that glow in the dark are radioactive. Like—"

He yelled, "What!"

"Like radium or uranium or any of their various isotopes. I thought you realized that was what was making the golf balls glow in the dark."

He looked down at the ball in his hand and his eyes got bigger and bigger. Then he dropped the ball as if it had suddenly caught fire. "You—" he said. "You, you—"

"Larry, listen," I said, "you're overreacting to this. No pun intended. Of course, they said the atomic bomb was overreactive. Seriously, you won't have any really long-term effects. It's just a little radium sulfide."

But I didn't get to finish. He'd jumped in the cart and gone tearing off, screaming back threats and curses at me. I yelled after him, "You have forfeited the match! You lost!"

I stood there in great satisfaction. It was the ultimate Gotcha. After that he couldn't have hit a golf ball with a tennis racquet.

When I got home my wife woke up to tell me that Larry had called. She said, "He really sounded upset. What happened?"

"Nothing." I said. "It's late. Go back to sleep." Then I carefully unplugged all the phones.

The phones started ringing the next day as soon as my wife reconnected them. I took the same tone as I had the night before, soothing, reassuring, sympathetic, snide.

He called three times before I finally told my wife what happened. I had planned to milk him for about two or three days, wringing every Gotcha he'd ever used on me completely out of his system. But my wife finally made me tell him. She said I was being mean.

Mean? After the things he'd done to me? The mind is swept away by such logic.

So, the next time he called I told him the truth. I did take some satisfaction in the fact that he didn't believe me at first, but then I gave him a list of the chemicals I'd used and told him to go ask somebody at the local college. They'd confirm that none of the chemicals were radioactive. Either that or go buy a Geiger counter.

I expected him to be grateful when he called back, but he wasn't, which kind of hurt my feelings. Here I was, throwing away a perfectly good two or three days of watching him writhe and worry and what did I get for my troubles? Nothing, not even a thank you. As a matter of fact he was even madder than he had been, which proves there is just no pleasing some people. He claimed I'd broken nearly every law in the USGA rule book and ought to be barred from every golf course in the world. In addition to that, he said I was probably in violation of any number of Atomic Energy Commission rules and ought to be thrown in jail. He finished up by claiming the match.

"Like hell." I said. "You forfeited."

"No, you were disqualified. You can't win a match by a criminal action. You might as well have pulled a gun on me."

I was astounded. "What criminal action?"

He said, "What do you call threatening a man with spare parts from an atomic bomb?"

It did no good to protest, to point out that the chemicals were harmless, that any injury was done to his mind. He just said, "I have made a ruling. You lost. Pay up."

The match had been too important to be played for mere money. Our wager had been that, if I won, Mr. Squier was to caddy for me in full view of the membership. If I lost I was to let it be known to one and all that, day or night, I was still his pigeon.

I have taken my own sweet time about paying up, first, because I think I won that match by a TKO with my world- and Olympic-class Gotcha, and, secondly, because of what Mr. Squier said when I mildly suggested that he ought to pay for half of the cost of the chemicals.

Some people just have no sense of humor.

13

Watch Out,
Waldo Pepper

I always wanted to go air racing like you used to see in old movies.
You know, harrowing, breathtaking thrills as plane after plane ma-
neuvered around the pylons and flew wing tip to wing tip as they
roared toward the finish line. I never quite got to do that. I did get an
exhibition hop over the course described in the following story, but
that was more a courtesy to me as a writer than as a pilot. They
wouldn't even let anyone in the air at the same time as me, much less
let them race me.

The only air race I ever participated in was a race between
Kerrville, Texas, and Lakeside, Texas, a distance of about two hundred miles. I was racing a pilot friend of mine named Chuck Matson
and we were both flying Cessna 150s. Now a Cessna 150 is not a
racing plane. As a matter of fact there were trucks going down Inter-
state 10 that got to the Houston area before Chuck and I did. Chuck
won, but I think he cheated. A 150 is such a kite that a difference in
pilot weight can make a difference of three or four miles an hour. I
outweighed Chuck by forty pounds, so we agreed he'd carry a forty-
pound can of water onboard to even matters out. When we got to

Lakeside that can of water was empty. Chuck said it didn't matter because he'd gotten so thirsty en route that he'd drunk it.

A ir racing is alive and as well as can be expected for a sport that almost died of neglect back in the early 1960s. In fact, the recent Texas National Air Races, sixth and final stop on this year's tour, were staged in a fitting sort of Old Home Week atmosphere: the sport came back to the pastureland where it got its start, when pilots often used a couple of handy barns as pylons.

This time the racers assembled on a ranch a few miles from Graham, Texas, and the pylons were set along the floor of a small valley, a perfect amphitheater that could have held many more than the four thousand or so enthusiasts who showed up. Still, many of the spectators had demonstrated laudable expertise and courage themselves by flying in through the drizzle and low ceilings. Their main interest was in the event that would decide the national championship in the T-6 class. The leader was Bill Turnbull, who had won at Reno earlier, closely followed by John Mosby and Roy McClain. Unfortunately, Mosby had come up with equipment trouble and couldn't make it. But Turnbull, from Lewisville, Texas, and McClain, from Eufaula, Alabama, were in good shape.

There are four basic classes of airplanes in racing. Formula I (midgets), Unlimited, Sports Biplane and the T-6. Many experts insist that the T-6 class has to be the most exciting since the other three invariably produce a wide degree of performance among the various aircraft, which makes for some dull races. The T-6, however, is a basic stock model in a sense and only so much can be done to it. That means the best pilot usually wins—and that is the way air racing ought to be. The T-6 is the old Army AT-6 or Navy-Marine Corps SNJ, the trainer in which so many World War II pilots learned to fly. A lot of the critters were produced and a lot were sold as surplus aircraft to civilians. And any time you get enough of anything that's fast and can be steered, you're going to end up with races—and that's how the T-6 class came to be. As a bird it is sturdy, with one of those enduring designs, and it packs a lot of horsepower. For those who don't know much about aircraft, the T-6 is the plane Errol Flynn was always flying in all those cadet movies when he was winning his wings. Occasionally it would become a Japanese Zero simply by adding meatballs to the fuselage and wings.

It is further fitting that the T-6 should have found its last home in racing, because it was from racing that it sprung. When the war came along, the fighter and training planes that were produced came directly from racing technology developed during the '20s and '30s. The T-6 was as much a primary design as any plane in the war and looks like a lengthened version of the little, sturdy low-winged monoplanes that ate up the competition back in the days when pilots wore riding breeches and white silk scarves.

When the racing began, Turnbull won his elimination heat easily, but McClain threw a prop spinner on the fifth lap of his six-lap heat. The effect on McClain was minimal, since he had such a large lead—but the incident almost cost second place for Jim Mott, known affectionately as the Black Knight of Carson, California. Mott had been dueling hot and heavy with Cal Earley of Houston and, flying the high groove on top, he had spotted the object flying off McClain's craft. He got right on his mike and yelled, "Hey, Twenty-Five, something just fell off your plane! You better get that thing on the ground!"

But McClain had realized what had happened and, other than cutting back on power to reduce vibration, he never paused as he screamed through the last lap. Unfortunately, Mott had been turning a pylon when his attention had been diverted—and he yawed so widely that Earley was able to take back second spot temporarily.

The racing course at Graham was three and one-half miles around, offering six pylons set in a sort of oblong pattern. The pylons were fifty feet high and a judge lay under each, sighting up to see if any part of a plane cut inside. Such an infraction brings a penalty of a full lap, which is the same as finishing last. The planes compete at speeds of 215 to 220 mph and when they're barreling around the pylons, cocked up in eighty- or ninety-degree banks, the low wing of the airplane is sometimes only ten or fifteen feet off the ground. It seems an invitation to tear up an airplane and to prove just how really fragile is human flesh. The only thing that makes it possible is the supreme skill of the pilots. A T-6 is a large, heavy thing. It weighs around 7,500 pounds and if one then takes that very same large thing and installs an engine so that it will go 200 mph and then starts flying it around in a tight circle just a few feet off the ground, one has got a dangerous pastime. Now add five more of these things on the merry-go-round and you've got a ridiculous situation. Race cars are involved with only two dimensions of movement; side to side and front to back. In air racing one has a third dimension, up and down, and there is as likely to be another plane above or below you as one by your side. Nearly all of the racers are professional pilots of one form or another; many are airline pilots, many are crop dusters, all have an immense number of air hours in aerobatics and precision flying.

All the pilots belong to the Professional Race Pilots Association. It would seem to be professional only by degree, since no one can presently make a living off the tour. The victor at Graham, if he also won his elimination heat, would get only about $2,500. The purses at the Reno and Mojave races had been only slightly higher. This isn't nearly enough considering the cost of the airplane (about $20,000), maintenance, travel and crew expenses. But Jack Lowers, the PRPA vice-president, says, "I think the day is coming when a pilot can make it racing. I wouldn't have believed this four years ago, or even two, but I can see the interest picking up. We had 35,000 people out one of the days at the meet in Reno. The word has just got to get around that air racing is back. People will come. It's a great show."

Meanwhile, they used the air-start at Graham. In this form, a pace plane brings the contestants down to the start/finish in a parallel line. When he thinks they are even, the pace pilot says, "You have a race"—and then pulls sharply upward. When the starter turned loose the finalists at Graham, McClain got his throttle firewalled an instant before Turnbull and that—combined with his pole position—allowed him to take a half a plane lead as they screamed in on the first pylon. There, Ralph Rina got around Turnbull, which dropped Turnbull to third, with Ralph Twombly holding fourth, Bob Metcalfe fifth and Jim Mott in last place. They held this stance for one lap, roaring down the straight, their engines taking on different tones as they flung the aircraft into the severe banks around the pylons. At the No. 1 pylon on the second lap, Turnbull passed Rina at the same spot where Rina had passed him before. This put Rina back in third. At almost the same time, Metcalfe passed Twombly, who was now in fifth, ahead of Mott. But Mott, using his accustomed high groove, inched his nose forward over the tail of Twombly and was calculating moving into fifth position coming off the pylon before the backstretch. Up front, Metcalfe had got around Rina to take third. But McClain and Turnbull seemed locked together as they flew down the straights and swept around the pylons, Turnbull just above and a few feet outside of his rival.

Looking up, McClain could see the underbelly of Turnbull's silver plane, seemingly close enough to touch. He was hoping he could creep forward just a few feet more. If he could, his prop wash would slow Turnbull down and force him to either go higher or fall in farther behind.

Back of them, Mott could tell he was gaining on the leaders, though he knew he was really too far back to do much. Still, he did have about ten feet of altitude on the field, which could be used for extra speed when he came down the final straight.

As they went through the fifth lap, Turnbull, who had been waiting for McClain to make a mistake, thought he'd finally caught one. It appeared that McClain was getting in tight on the straights and the effect was to slingshot him wide on the turns. Turnbull let his own plane edge outward a little, sensing that a time would come when he might dip inside as they banked past a pylon.

In the back, Mott had gotten ahead of Twombly and Rina and was taking aim on Metcalfe. And he still had his altitude. Gripping the stick with a feathery touch, he put the nose over ever so gently. He was going to use his altitude now to catch Metcalfe. Realistically, third was all he could hope for.

Then Turnbull finally found his chance. McClain had gotten in too tight, and as they came up to pylon No. 1 on lap seven his momentum was carrying him out too wide. Kicking his plane into a dipping bank, Turnbull dropped neatly into the empty space, forcing McClain even farther out. When they came level McClain was behind and out.

As for Mott, the dive from the extra ten feet of altitude had given him an added five or six mph. He used it to simply dive under Metcalfe, and when he pulled up he was in third place. Turnbull came flashing down the straight .07 of a second ahead of McClain and took the checkered flag from the judge at the base of the home pylon. On the hillside, the crowd was jumping and applauding. Later, Turnbull said, "You know, you do this thing mostly for the thrill. I wish we could hear the crowd when we come dobbing it down the straight with a win." He smiled. "But them big engines just make too damn much noise."

Those who don't go to air races may represent a generation of people who have completely missed out on the romance and thrills of flying. For most folks flying now means walking down a long corridor, being seated by a young lady, eating a steak and drinking a cocktail while the plane climbs on course, flies to the destination and descends on course. There is about as much sensation of flying as riding in an elevator. Air racing, if it makes a comeback, might be able to lend us some of the real feeling.

14

I Never Get Seasick

I originally did this piece for Yachting magazine through the auspices of the Hobbins mentioned herein. As I recall, the original thrust that the editors asked for was that the story center around the convenience and comfort and adaptability and whatever else of the deep sea fishing boat. I think I was chosen because of my total inconvenience, discomfort, unadaptability, and whatever else for occupancy of such a vessel. Obviously, as you will read, the story did not come off as programmed.

The curious part is that, a few years later, I actually went back to Port Aransas, chartered Captain Rick's boat on my own, and went fishing. I had a hell of a good time. I got a number of strikes, lost several good fish (which made Captain Rick stiffen his upper lip) and finally landed a 180-pound sailfish. My only regret was that the magnificent fish had gotten the hook caught in its throat and we couldn't release it totally unharmed. I hope it made it all right.

The last I heard, Mr. and Mrs. Hobbin had gone into sponsoring dirt-track stock car racers. I guess there's no accounting for tastes.

I was going to catch a billfish, in a tournament no less. Oh, maybe not an eight-hundred-pound blue marlin, but at least a swordfish or a sailfish. And a good-sized one, too, the kind you see mounted behind the bar in restaurants in Florida and Tahiti and places like that.

Of course, I wasn't leaving from places like that. In fact I was going out of Port Aransas, Texas, a place not quite on a par with Key West or Hawaii or some of your similar paradises, but it was a fishing port and it was a tournament and people had been known to leave Port Aransas in a boat and return with some sort of billfish.

Now this wasn't exactly a real billfishing tournament, not the kind that offers hundreds of thousands of dollars in prize money and features fishermen who own banks as a hobby and fish from sixty-foot yachts with a crew of however many they want, some of whom aren't knockout-looking girls.

But it was a tournament and there was a category, among the many, for the biggest billfish. And that was what I was after.

I had never actually been deep sea fishing before, for billfish or any other kind of fish, but I didn't regard that as a major handicap. I'd talked about it a lot and I'd seen movies where deep sea fishing was involved and I had done the obligatory reading of Hemingway and Zane Grey (a lot of people don't know that Zane Grey wrote a lot about fishing—they only think of *Riders of the Purple Sage* when they hear his name) so I felt I was pretty well prepared. What, after all, could be so different between the different types of fishing? You used a line and you used a pole and you used a hook and you used bait. Anybody that could catch a perch or a catfish could catch a blue marlin.

Oh, of course I'd read all the stories about a guy sitting in the fishing chair, battling some fish for eight or ten hours, sweat pouring off him, his hands blistering, pain evident in his face, his aides pouring buckets of water over him, someone rubbing his back, someone else reviving him from time to time with swift gulps of rum, a beautiful woman in an unfinished bikini kneeling by his side and begging him to cut the line, give up the fight, save himself. Yeah, I'd seen all that in the movies and I considered it a trifle overdone. A little overkill for the paying public. Hell, *you* were in the boat, not the fish. If worse came to worse you could run the beast down. All the odds were on your side. What could be so hard?

Besides, having played most sports, I was a little tired of hearing people rant over the rigors and deprivations of a sedentary activity out on the bounding main. Hell, I'd been an athlete and I figured anything you did sitting in a chair couldn't be all that traumatic physically.

Still, I went into the activity with an open mind. I've always prided myself on that quality: taking nothing for granted and giving the other fellow his due. After all, sport is sport whether you're pitching horseshoes or riding bulls. Some may be a little more demanding, but they all require a certain amount of skill.

Of course I was a little amused about all the preparations that were being made. Judging from the size of the rods and reels I figured we were setting out after elephant and might have said so if I hadn't had such good manners and the good sense to not jeopardize my standing on the boat as a nonpaying contestant. That was being arranged by a Mr. and Mrs. Hobbin of Houston, who wanted an account taken of their adventure with an eye toward publication. He was in computer rentals and she was in abject fear of being seasick.

A condition I gave no thought to. True, my water experiences consisted of a little lake fishing and a Mediterranean cruise, but I'd never suffered from motion sickness of any kind and wasn't about to give in to the idea of sticking some silly patch behind my ear or swallowing Dramamine twenty-four hours in advance.

The only thing that was bothering me in the slightest was the name of our boat, the *SeaRay II*. Admittedly I didn't know anything about boats, but if you've got a two, then it follows that you must have had a one, which brings up the immediate question, "If this is all so safe, what happened to *SeaRay I?*"

I thought about asking our boat skipper/owner, Captain Rick, but decided not to. He didn't look like the type that would think much of such a question and would probably give me an odd look. Personally, I thought he'd seen too many Errol Flynn movies. He was a middle-aged man with a clipped, precise mustache who was tanned well beyond the point of the Surgeon General's warning. He also wore his captain's cap, which was appropriately salt-whitened and worn, at a jaunty angle. I've never much trusted or liked people who wear any type of headgear at a jaunty angle.

But, numerals aside, the *SeaRay* looked like a fine vessel. She was a sleek forty-footer and she had the flying bridge and the fighting chair and a head and a galley and a lounge that did double duty as a small dining room. She was obviously a day tripper because she'd been stripped of her bunks. I was told she had a good record. I didn't know what that meant, but I took it under advisement and tried to look wise about the whole affair.

The mate, who I was told would handle all the fishing chores, including baiting the lines and doing the gaffing and all other such stuff, was a lady of lower middle age named Doreen. Off season, I was told, she drove a truck and did odd jobs around the small fishing town. I was going to tell her there was a career waiting for her out there as a circus roustabout, but I thought better of it and just contented myself with losing two beers to her arm wrestling. One thing for sure, she'd never fit into a size eight again.

But, all in all, I was fairly content and expectant. That is, until Captain Rick informed me what time we'd be voyaging out the next morning.

Four A.M. In the morning. Four hours after midnight. Eight hours before noon.

Try playing baseball or going rodeoing at that hour.

All of a sudden I wasn't so eager to catch a fish, not even a billfish, not even an eight-hundred-pound blue marlin.

But it was carefully explained to me that, in order to get into sporting waters, we had to go way out, way out until we got to where the big fish roamed. Some sixty or seventy miles out. And to do that, to be in position at first light so as to benefit from a full fishing day, we had to leave early. All this was explained to me by Captain Rick in his clipped tones from under his carefully clipped mustache. He said it in such a way with such regal disdain that I was mighty sorry I'd asked. I was also beginning to lose all interest in going out and hunting something I couldn't see, couldn't hook, couldn't catch, and probably couldn't eat. But Mr. and Mrs. Hobbin were counting on me to immortalize the sport further (or at least immortalize their part in it) and so I couldn't very well shuck off their hospitality without being rude.

If I'd known, then, what later events were to bring, I would've gone ahead and been rude. In fact I would've been downright hostile and uncooperative.

We left the dock in dark so black you could have cut it with a knife. Captain Rick was up on the flying bridge steering us out through the channel to open water. I could see the little lights atop the buoys marking our route but I was damned if I could make any sense out of them. I only hoped that Captain Rick could, though, at that moment I would have just as soon run aground. The Hospitality Committee had had a party the night before, and some of the less wiser souls had gone off the deep end, and I am not referring to the dock. One of those less wiser souls was sitting in the cramped dining quarters listening to Mr. and Mrs. Hobbin chatter gleefully about the adventure ahead. Being shallow water drinkers, they thought it was just peachy to get up before the day started and get on an unstable vessel and go romping off into the black void. But that wasn't what was bothering me. Tugboat Annie was in the galley, about a foot and a half away, fixing breakfast. There are a lot of things I don't want to smell at four-thirty in the morning and fish and potatoes being fried in what had to be cod liver oil is very definitely one of them.

Besides, the whole adventure was boring. It was too early to drink a beer, you can only drink so much hot chocolate, and I was not at all interested in breakfast.

So we motored along the channel at a good five miles an hour. Every so often, out the lounge's windows, another boat's running lights would become visible, but that was rare. Not many of the tournament's entrants were fishing for billfish and, consequently, they'd be leaving at a later hour. The next batch after us would be the snapper fishermen heading for the banks some forty miles out. Then would come the trout and ling and other assorted fishers who would be just barely venturing out in the gulf. Then finally would come the boats, one of which I should have been on, that would be fishing the bay. As far as I was concerned they were the only ones with any sense.

At some point just before Mrs. Hobbin's cheerful chatter drove me overboard we finally broke out of the channel and Captain Rick plunged the throttles forward. I felt the surge of the boat breaking through the swell, felt the G forces slinging me aft, and said, "Well this is more like it! We're flying!"

Only to have Tugboat Annie, busy at her propane grill, say, "Are you nuts? This turkey boat only makes about twenty-five miles an hour. I could pass this thing in a rowboat."

But what kind of cheery news could you expect from a female longshoreman (longshorewoman? longshoreperson?) frying fish for breakfast? I made comment on the unusual choice for the morning meal. Mrs. Hobbin hastened to explain that it was tradition. She didn't say what kind of tradition. Setting fire to witches had once been a tradition. So had having more than one wife. Or wearing beanie caps your freshman year.

Fish for breakfast, fried fish, made about as much sense.

After we were going good I went out the back door and sat down in the aft section that contained the fighting chair and the ice chests and the bait lockers. The sky was as black as the sea, all the stars with any sense having retired. Occasionally there was the dim light of another boat hurrying out in the hopes of ruining the day for some poor, unsuspecting fish. Occasionally there would be the flash of some phosphorescent fish leaping about. At least the air was considerably fresher, not counting the bait locker, than it had been in the dining room/lounge.

Mrs. Hobbin came out. I thought at first she'd gone slightly off color, but then I realized it was just a reflection from our port running light, which was green, shining on her face. But I asked how she was doing anyway. The boat was costing them six hundred bucks a day and I figured I could make the big gesture. She fanned herself with a tackle brochure and said she was just fine, that she'd taken all her pills before going to bed and that her husband had assured her she would be fine.

Which must have been great reassurance since she'd told me she'd been out with her husband about ten times before and all ten times she'd gotten sick. I'd asked her why she kept going out and she'd said that, well, they liked to share things. She didn't say if that included the seasickness.

But Mrs. Hobbin was a nice lady in her early fifties with a kind of nervous frailness about her that sort of made you feel protective. I felt like I ought not to say anything that might sound critical of her husband.

Which was good because Mr. Hobbin came out. He was a short little man with a balding head hid under one of those caps with a bill on it like Pinocchio's nose. He reminded me of somebody's accountant.

But he was beaming and breathing deep and stretching out his arms and proclaiming what a great morning it was. He'd left the salon door open behind him and a strong, warm blast of fried fish had followed on his heels. I got up and shut it as fast as I could. Mr. Hobbin, however, opened it back up saying that, uh, maybe the galley and lounge could do with a bit of airing.

That made me smirk. Nothing would have pleased me more than to have heard the old salt say it was getting a little close inside for him. But just as I was about to open my mouth the former lady wrestler turned chef called out "Chow!" I couldn't say for certain that there was the slightest hint of hesitation on the part of the Hobbins, but they didn't exactly make a mad dash to get at the vittles.

Tradition, however, had to be maintained at whatever the cost. Mr. Hobbin paused just long enough to ask me if I wasn't coming in. I said that, no, I'd just stay on the fantail and smoke cigarettes and drink warm beer and maybe eat some of the bait if I felt the need for something solid. Mr. Hobbin looked disapproving. Mrs. Hobbin just looked distressed. He said that I ought to have something substantial in my stomach, that the surest way to *mal de mer* was to sail on an empty stomach.

I assured him that's the way I'd always done it, and they disappeared into the grease pit of Long John Silver's. I wasn't sure, but I thought I caught a desperate look backwards by Mrs. Hobbin as she ventured toward the fried mullet and sponge potatoes sauteed in diesel fuel.

I sat there thinking the trip might not be so bad after all. The air was pleasant and the smell of the water not all that bad. I couldn't see its color, but I figured we were still in the bay. Mr. Hobbin had told me the water would stay gray until we reached some sort of oceanic shelf and then we'd be in the gulf and the water would automatically turn a startling blue.

I could see Captain Rick up on the flying bridge, looking intrepid in shorts and a tank top and his captain's hat, steering by the soft glow of his compass. I guess he was up on the bridge so he could see further, but I couldn't figure out what he was trying to see. I couldn't figure out anything to look at.

The formidable Doreen came out of the lounge and said, "This here's the last call. You eat it now or I'm gonna throw it overboard."

"Commend it to the deeps," I told her.

The time ran on. The sea seemed very gentle. Not glassy, mind you, as I've heard it described, but we seemed to be splitting our way through it without any undue effort. Off in the general direction of the east I could see a low glow on the horizon. I figured either an oil tanker was on fire or the sun was coming up. Underneath my feet the deck of the fantail vibrated to the pulse of the twin inboard engines that were lodged somewhere "down below."

Wherever that was. Probably had something to do with the bilges.

Not too long after that Doreen came out with a mass of rods and line and God knows what all. She laid her load down on the deck and opened the bait locker. I immediately got to my feet and moved to the other side of the boat. She switched on a light mounted on the aft wall of the lounge and illuminated the whole cockpit area.

The smell was reminiscent of the galley while under the siege of her cooking. I said, "You're not getting out some more fish to fry, are you?"

She'd pulled over a canvas deck chair and was sorting through the contents of the fish locker. She gave me a disgusted look. "What's the matter with you, buster? This here is bait, not eatin' fish."

Going just on smell, I couldn't tell the difference.

She said, "I'm fixin' to sew this bait on the hooks."

"Oh, of course," I said. "I knew that. Sew it, you say?"

"Hell yes, sew it. What'd you think?"

Well, I thought you did it like any other bait, impaled it on the hook. But this bait was going to get the seamstress treatment.

I started to say something else, but just then Doreen raised her head and said, "Uh oh!"

I jumped. I don't like people saying "Uh oh!" in ominous tones. I damn sure didn't care for it with only a flimsy hull and the dauntless Captain Rick between me and a bottomless pit. I said, "What?"

She said, tensely, "Lissen 'at starboard engine."

I looked around wildly. I didn't really know what she was talking about. She tapped her foot on the deck. "Not out there. Hell! Down here. The starboard engine."

I looked at the deck but couldn't see anything. It was becoming lighter and lighter and I could see out across the sea. A light mist was forming. I said, nervously, "What am I looking for?"

She gave me a look. "Lissen, I said. You ain't lookin' fer nuthin'. 'At sonbitchin' starboard engine is missin'."

My eyes got big. "Gone?"

She said, "Sssh!" In one hand she was holding a hook of a size that was last seen on a pirate and in the other she had a small frozen fish she was about to feed the hook to. But her attention was all on the sound of the engines below deck. She said, "That engine ain't raight. Ain't runnin' raight. Missin'."

As if he'd been listening, Captain Rick suddenly pulled back on both engines and we began losing speed in a big hurry. With the engines quieted to idle and the boat barely moving forward I could hear the water washing up against our stern. Captain Rick came down the ladder from the flying bridge. He looked jaunty, but he also looked unhappy. He said, to Doreen, "Let's get the bilge boards up."

I didn't like the sound of that, but I got out of the way as fast as I could. Which was just as well because he and Doreen proceeded to pull up most of the floor of the cockpit. I found myself balancing on the stern railing with my feet on the seat of the fighting chair. Mr. and Mrs. Hobbin were peering out the door of the lounge.

While we watched, Captain Rick somehow lowered himself into the depths of the boat, flashlight in hand, and disappeared. We could hear him clanking around, swearing occasionally, and now and then giving Doreen unintelligible orders. Once she went to the throttles that were in the cockpit and revved the engines with the propeller in neutral.

It was all very mysterious and fascinating. Off in the east the glow had turned out to be the sun instead of a burning tanker and it was getting light fast. After a time Captain Rick came up wiping his hands on an oily rag. I watched him, admiring the man. He'd gone down into that black, nasty bilge in pressed, starched white shorts and shirt and come back without a spot on him. I reckoned not even Errol Flynn could have done that.

But he got back up on deck and he and Doreen held a whispered conference. I overheard a few words, but couldn't make much sense out of them. Finally he turned to the Hobbins and said something that sounded like, "The inkflinger on the oil force feed is overriding the automatic watering system and I'm afraid the sync meter is going to outflange the bumper sticker and overheat."

Then he said, "So what it means is I'm going to have to shut down that starboard engine." He looked out across the water. "We're about fifteen to twenty miles from blue water, but our speed will be considerably decreased. It's up to you folks. Do you want to go on with one engine or turn back? I think we're safe enough, but it will make it a long ride home. What do you say?"

He was looking at the Hobbins. He didn't ask me. If he had I could have given him a right quick answer.

Mr. Hobbin said something nautical like, "Well, of course you're the captain and if you say it's all shipshape we'd as soon press on."

Or something like that.

Mrs. Hobbin looked like I felt. The trip was going to be long enough as it was without us trying to limp along on one leg. I murmured something about taking a vote but no one paid me any attention.

Captain Rick said, "You understand if we get into a big one I won't be able to maneuver as well. Might not be able to help you as much."

Mr. Hobbin said, "That's fishing, Captain Rick. The luck of the sea."

Where had the man learned to talk like that? Did he rent computers that talked like that?

"All right!" Captain Rick shouted. "Then fishing it is!"

And he bounded back up the ladder to the flying bridge just like a man who was enjoying himself.

"What happened?" I asked Doreen.

She said the same thing Captain Rick had said. Then she went back to tormenting the dead fish with her enormous hooks. I leaned over the side and stared at the gray water, waiting for it to turn blue.

About an hour later we discontinued the tournament and bill-fishing phase of our trip and entered the survival segment. This part had not been mentioned in the tournament brochures or by either Mr. or Mrs. Hobbin when they'd invited me along on this excursion. Instinctively I knew I wasn't going to care much for it.

What happened was that the only engine we still had operating gradually gave out. First it slowed down, then it spitted and sputterd a little and then it quit.

Running.

Captain Rick came down from the flying bridge, only now he didn't look like Errol Flynn. He looked like Errol Flynn with a red face and a mouthful of cuss words.

Our generator had broken. After that the engine had used the batteries to draw power to fire its spark plugs. At least it had until the batteries had run down. After that we were just there.

Captain Rick came up from the bilges and gave us the bad news. He said, "I'm afraid we're without power."

Boy, that was an understatement.

Mr. Hobbin said, "Luck of the sailor, Captain Rick. Can't be helped."

I just sat there, sitting on the side of the cockpit, waiting for someone to do something. No one did. I finally cleared my throat. I said, "Uh, hadn't we better do something?"

Captain Rick looked around at me. "What would you suggest?"

I said, "Hell, I don't know. Something. Call somebody. Don't boats have something like the Automobile Club? Call them."

Captain Rick said, "We can't call anyone. The radio won't work. The batteries are dead."

Off in the distance I could see boats cutting through the waves, throwing up white bow spray, heading for where we were supposed to be. I said, "Hell, let's signal somebody. Get a tow."

Captain Rick said, "They wouldn't stop. They're going fishing."

I said, not without some heat, "The hell with their fishing! We need a tow."

Mr. Hobbin said, "Not sporting, man. We're in no danger. Just an inconvenience."

"Inconvenience—" I was seriously thinking of doing Mr. Hobbin in. I said, "What are we supposed to do?"

Captain Rick said, "Wait. There'll be some early boats coming back this afternoon. We'll get a tow or get them to notify the Coast Guard."

"This afternoon? Man, are you talking about *this* afternoon? Ten hours from now? Out here on this boat?"

They were. And we did.

Sit there.

After about fifteen minutes, with nothing else to occupy my mind, I became aware of the motion of the boat. The sea, which had seemed so smooth and solid, had suddenly become unreliable. The boat was rocking. I don't mean violently, but first the front end would rise up and then the back. Then one side would get higher and then the other. It wasn't bothering me, of course, because I don't get any kind of motion sickness, but I was hoping it wasn't having any bad effect on Mrs. Hobbin. I didn't figure she would enjoy that fried fish twice.

Up on the flying bridge Captain Rick was running a flag up the high pole, one that boats traditionally used to display the pennant for the kind of fish they'd caught, either a marlin or a sail or whatever. Captain Rick was running up a red distress flag. He did not look happy.

Mrs. Hobbin came out of the lounge looking brave. She indicated the sprawl of tackle and gear on the deck. Doreen had just finished baiting a couple of lines before the generator had packed it in. She said, with what I thought was false cheer, "We could fish while we're waiting. You sit in the fighting chair and I'll hand you a rod and reel."

I sat in the chair but I didn't like it. It reminded me too much of a dentist's chair. Mrs. Hobbin handed me a rod and reel with a dead fish on the end. The reel was about the size of an oatmeal box and I could have pole vaulted with the rod. The dead bait smelled like breakfast.

Doreen was watching. She said, "Shoot! You can't fish for bills from a dead boat. You got to troll."

I said, "Just watch this."

I stood up and, imitating the motion I'd seen surf casters use, I swung the rod and meant to sling the bait out about a hundred and fifty yards. Unfortunately the drag was on and all I did was knock Mrs. Hobbin's big, broad-brimmed hat off and snap the bait back and hit myself in the chest with it.

Doreen went, "Har, har, har."

Mrs. Hobbin helped me get the drag off, but that still didn't quite seem to handle the problem. I made a couple more attempts, succeeding only in getting a pretty good backlash worked into the line on the reel. That got more laughs from Doreen. Finally I just picked up the bait and threw it. I'd had a pretty good arm in my days as a third baseman and I made a throw that would have done credit to anyone throwing a dead fish. You can't get much spin on one and the line tended to add some drag.

But I got it out there. I sat down in the chair. I could see the bait bobbing around between swells. Doreen just said, "Gawd!" and went off to do whatever it was a mate did on a distressed boat.

It wasn't long before it came to be hot. Mrs. Hobbin sat by me with her big straw hat on and tried to look interested. Back behind me I could see Captain Rick sitting at the controls on the flying bridge. I don't know why he was up there. I think he was sulking. Mr. Hobbin and Doreen were in the lounge. They were probably exchanging views on important subjects.

The boat kept rocking, swaying and rocking up and down, up and down, up and down. I tried not to notice the horizon.

My bait was floating on top of the water. It was still visible, but it had floated off around fifty yards away. I couldn't imagine a big fish finding it very interesting, much less appetizing. Every once in a while I gave the rod tip a little jerk to try to get some action on the bait, but the drag was off and the line was running free so mostly all I did was strip more line off the reel.

Mrs. Hobbin was beginning to undergo a facial color change and it wasn't from the sun. She tried to keep a brave smile on her face, but I could see her going a distinct yellow and she was doing a lot of swallowing like someone manning the pumps as the bilges overflowed.

I was feeling fine myself. I never got motion sickness of any kind.

I dozed off. Or at least I lapsed into some sort of torpor from the morning sun and the motion of the boat. I became aware that Mrs. Hobbin was talking, or at least making some sort of noise. I turned to my right to see her. She did not quite look the same. Her face had either gone deathly white or green. It was hard to tell because she kept ducking her head so that the wide brim of her straw hat hid her face. But there was no mistaking the sounds she was making. She was just turning toward the rail as I said, "Mrs. Hobbin!"

I was not wearing the harness you hooked the rod in, just holding it sort of loosely in my lap. I laid it on the deck in front of me and gallantly rose to go to the aid of the stricken lady when I heard somebody yell, "Fish! Fish! Dammit, you've got a fish!"

"What?" I stopped and looked around. Then I looked up. Captain Rick was jumping up and down on the flying bridge pointing out toward the sea. I turned around and looked. As I did Mr. Hobbin and Doreen came pouring out of the lounge door hollering, "Fish, fish, fish!"

Mrs. Hobbin just made very unpleasant noises.

I looked aft and, just as I did, I saw a blue-and-white shining fork-tailed fish with a long bill come leaping out of the water. I did not immediately connect him with our boat, just stood there admiring the sight. Then I heard the sound of the reel at my feet as the line went singing out to sea.

"Hit him!" somebody said.

"Hit him?" It took a minute for it to sink in. Then I jerked up the rod and gave it a good yank. All that happened was that a few yards of line running out from the boat lifted into the air. I could still see the fish jumping. It appeared to have my bait in its mouth. Or at least something brown was hanging out the side.

"The brake, dammit! Use the brake!"

The real had more gadgets on it than a sports car. Mr. Hobbin and Doreen were at my side. A half dozen fingers were fumbling with the workings of the reel. I jerked again. It felt a little more solid.

"Hit him again!"

I did. Now it definitely felt like I was into something solid. I stumbled backwards into the chair. I still hadn't hooked up the harness.

"The brake! Take the goddam brake off before the line breaks."

More fumbling and then the line really began to sing.

"Put on a little drag! Hurry up! You're losing too much line!"

I did, but my mind was still on Mrs. Hobbin. Also, I was looking at the horizon, a thing I'd carefully kept myself from doing. But now, because of the fish, I had no choice. I said, "Mrs. Hobbin—" But no one was paying her the slightest bit of attention. Even above the hubbub that Mr. Hobbin and Doreen and Captain Rick were making I could still hear her at the rail. Hear her all too clear.

Doreen said, "Gawd, it's a big one. Sail. What you thank, Rick?"

"Two hundred pounds," he said. "Easy. A very big one."

"We caught a fish off a floating bait," Mr. Hobbin said, marveling. "The luck of the sea. Can you imagine that?"

I would have said something to the effect that the fish wasn't caught and if he did get caught it wasn't going to be "we," but for some reason I didn't feel like talking. A lot of saliva was suddenly flooding into my mouth and I was acutely conscious of every motion of the boat in relation to the horizon. I tried to take my eyes off the horizon, but nothing seemed to help. Mrs. Hobbin had subsided into a sort of quiet moaning. Even though the fish was pulling strongly on the line I snuck a quick glance over at her. She was draped over the rail like a load of wet wash. Nobody was paying her the slightest bit of attention.

"Reel in! Try to get some line in!"

I tried, imitating the style I'd seen in the movies, jerking the rod back and then reeling and then jerking the rod back again and reeling some more. I did that, but my heart was not really in it. For a minute or two I'd been real excited about hooking the fish, but now I didn't seem to care about anything. A sort of gray haze was obscuring my vision. My stomach was moving around to different parts of my body. My mouth couldn't keep up with the demand put on it by my saliva glands. Lights were dancing in front of my eyes. All of a sudden it seemed very important that I go to Mrs. Hobbin's side and offer her what comfort I could. I was smelling fried fish and fried potatoes; I was smelling every greasy fried food I'd ever smelled in my life. I was experiencing tastes that did not exist. I was not feeling very well.

I still had not attached the harness. I thought, being considerate, that the people who really liked to fish ought to have a go at this fish. There was probably a good seven or eight hours of fight left in him. Maybe I'd come back later. Right then I wasn't feeling all that interested. In the interests of cooperation I hurriedly jammed on the brake, the same thing you would do with a car if you were about to turn it over to someone else, and then sort of haphazardly handed the rod to the hazy figures at my side. "Here," I said. "I don't think—"

I was in the process of standing up. I felt a sudden jerk. The rod flew out of my hand. I dimly saw it splash into the water some ten yards aft of the boat. I sort of mumbled, "Sorry," and then went quickly to join Mrs. Hobbin.

It was kind of a long day after that. No one said much to me. Some eating went on and some beer drinking, but most of the company seemed to shun my company. Only Mrs. Hobbin had given me a little consoling pat. I think she'd wanted to say a few words, but her husband had hustled her into the lounge.

Only Captain Rick had offered me a complete sentence. He'd said, "That rig cost $400."

Which I thought a bit excessive. But then, I didn't feel in a position to argue.

Late that afternoon a boat stopped and gave us a tow. They were flying a pennant showing they'd caught a blue marlin. I heard their skipper call to Captain Rick about our luck. Captain Rick turned and pointed at me. He said, "You're looking at him."

Which just goes to prove my point that getting too serious about sport takes all the fun out of it. I've said that after I've struck out with the bases loaded, I've said that when I've fallen down with a clear field between me and the goal line, I've said that when I've missed a two-foot putt for the money, and I've said that when I've tripped over the last hurdle with a clear lead. I even tried to tell that to my fellow fishermen. Only Mr. Hobbin replied. He said, stiffly, "It's no good fooling around with tradition, you know."

I still insist I didn't get seasick. It was just a natural reaction to all that tension and yelling and people getting too excited. People should show a little more control. Fishing is supposed to be relaxing. You get all tensed up, you're liable to get sick.

Which, of course, is not the same thing as getting seasick.

But I'll always wonder if Mr. Hobbin paid Captain Rick for that rod and reel that he so carelessly lost overboard.

15

You Are Now Leaving Fat City

On the surface this may seem like a silly story, full of guesses and half truths and speculation and more than a little weird thinking. You might think that because of one of two reasons; either you are terribly naive, or you are one of the participants mentioned herein.

All I will say is that, yes, there was some couch-sitting thinking that went into it and that, yes, I might have taken off a little too far on a hunch here or there, but, basically, I've got my facts straight. I've been around sports far too long not to have noticed what has been going on in the athletic community and long ago it led me to search for answers that I believe this story reveals. In a sense it is a mystery story and, because of that, should not be included in this collection. But I view it as a mystery story that explains a number of unanswered questions that do involve sport. And where sports are concerned I am a relentless pursuer. I have always vowed to take my reader behind the scenes. Sometimes into the locker room, sometimes on the turf of the arena, sometimes into the personal life of the athlete. To do that you've got to ignore boundaries. Sometimes it's exciting, sometimes it's sad, sometimes it's uplifting, and sometimes it's exhilarating, like the clean

crisp sound of a football game on a fall afternoon. Sometimes it's as
sordid as dirty socks.
  Sometimes it's fat city.

I made the mistake, at my age, of entering a track meet. That was the first mistake. The second was getting a groin pull. That put me on the couch for some three weeks with nothing else to do but watch television. I was hurt so bad that I couldn't even get out to the kitchen to make myself a glass of iced tea. And my wife, having the attitude she does, wouldn't bring me any. All she kept saying was, "Well, you brought it on yourself, didn't you?"

Is that a universal trait among wives?

But the end result was that I was laid up on the couch with no diversions except that remote control in my hand. Normally I would have read, but, by the first week, I'd read everything in the house and I wasn't about to trust my wife's taste at the library. She runs to movie star biographies and the British royalty and such. Not exactly my glass of tea.

But it was a lucky break because I got on to something I think is an important discovery. In fact, I think it's right up there with the discovery of penicillin and sliced peaches.

I began to notice that most of the ads on TV were for fat-reducing plans. All of them intended to take those "unwanted" pounds and inches off of you.

You know the kind, the ones that have "Linda R. of Syracuse" saying, "I lost 62 pounds in three weeks with the Vita X diet program. And, would you believe it, I ate all the foods I wanted including hot fudge sundaes."

Or, "Vivian B. from White Plains" saying, "Gosh, it's so wonderful to date again. And all thanks to Doctor Charlie's wonderful pecan and sawdust diet, I'm 89 pounds lighter and have rediscovered that person I always knew was in there."

Then, on another channel, would come this knock-out woman climbing out of a hypo-thermal bath saying, "Would you believe it, I used to be a size 24. But now, thanks to the All-World Health Spas, I'm a perfect size 8. You too can lose those unwanted pounds and inches. Just call the toll-free number and. . . ."

Inevitably, there would come another commercial featuring a lady using a machine that would show her doing nothing more than you could gain by ordinary situps. But the voice-over would say: "With Coach Zelmo's revolutionary Hom-izer, you too can lose those unwanted pounds and inches. It's packable, it's portable, it's yours to use whenever you want. Just send. . . ."

It just kept running on. All those unwanted pounds. This lady lost 18 pounds, this one 45, this one 62, this one 180.

It finally got to me and I began to do some simple calculations. I began by figuring that there were 220 million people in the United States—forget the foreign countries; that will wait for a later report.

But what I finally figured out scared me. I got off the couch and limped into the kitchen where my wife was. I said: "Listen, I don't want to alarm you, but something is greatly amiss here. I've been watching the diet commercials."

She said: "So what?"

I almost whispered it. I said: "You may not realize it, but, according to my calculations, thousands and thousands of people are disappearing every day."

She gave me a kind of calculating look. She said: "What are you talking about?"

I said: "You haven't been watching the TV commercials. Books, diets, spas. Every one of them is claiming 40, 60, 120 pounds weight loss. And every one of them is claiming thousands of clients. Go ahead and multiply it. That is the equivalent of thousands of people disappearing every day! Where are they going? Tell me that!"

She just said: "Go back and sit on the couch."

In a sort of desperation I said: "Look, matter doesn't simply disappear into thin air. You take a lady that once weighed 240 and is now down to 120, then you tell me where that 120 pounds went!"

Well, I went back and sat on the couch, but I brooded about it. I'd been to college and I knew all about photosynthesis, but it did not relate to the present case. I was onto something and I resolved to pursue it to its end.

I have scattered clues. I hope you have picked them up because we are now in relentless pursuit of the solution of this mystery.

The phase "unwanted" pounds kept pounding in my head.

All the commercials said the same thing: "Lose those unwanted pounds."

Unwanted. Unwanted.

The mystery began to unravel about a week later when I was watching a sports show. The interviewer was talking to a wrestler who had moved up in weight class and the wrestler said: "Yeah, I wanted to gain about 20 more pounds to fit my frame so I went through a weight program and here I am."

Notice he said he "wanted" to gain 20 more pounds.

The opposite of unwanted.

Weight program my foot. It started me thinking. I'd been a jock back in the 1950s but we didn't have any guys around, as they do today, whose necks started at the end of their shoulders. We had barbells and other forms of weight program equipment, but we weren't producing the kind of specimens you see today. Even then we had our own form of Nautilus equipment. I know, because I'd once clipped an ad out of the back of a comic book and sent off for the Charles Atlas course on "dynamic tension" which is, when you really break it down, all that most of these expensive aids come down to.

As a sportswriter, I've been in a lot of locker rooms. It was in the late 1960s that I began to see a change in the athletes. Of course they'd always been big and strong, but now I was seeing guys with muscles that made their veins stand out in their calves and biceps and, sometimes, if I asked the wrong questions, in their foreheads.

I saw this trend continue into the '70s and the '80s and I guess, except for my debilitating injury, I would have been like you; I would have gone on believing what I read in the newspapers about steroids and Human Growth Hormones and so on and so on. And let it go at that.

Except I now knew that something was wrong somewhere and I knew I was onto the answer. I was like Mike Hammer where he says "two plus two doesn't come to five."

I wasn't going to take five for my answer. I considered calling trainers for National Football League clubs, but I knew that all I'd get would be evasive answers or hang-ups.

I finally went to two professional sources I knew I could trust. The first was a druggist, Bill O'Banion, who does a ravishing business in diet pills. I explained my theory to him, but he proved to be a disappointment. All he said was: "I thought you'd quit drinking." And hung up.

The next was Dr. Willard Aubrey, who'd cleaned my teeth for me a couple of times and even filled a cavity. But, most importantly, I'd noticed his weight fluctuating some 50 pounds.

He didn't hesitate once he knew I was onto the system. He said: "It's like giving blood. We send it off and get money back."

I said: "How? Is it shipped by ambulance? Parcel Post? UPS?

He said: "That I won't tell you." And hung up on me.

I now leave it to you. Here are the final pieces of the puzzle. Fit them in as you dare.

(1) Muscle tissue weighs approximately three times more than fat tissue. Therefore, if Jane L. in California loses 60 pounds and Mike R. in Atlanta suddenly gains 20 pounds of muscle, where did that come from? And don't tell me better diet or lifting weights or steroids or any of that other nonsense. We had all that back when I was playing.

(2) Women athletes suddenly emerged into the spotlight in the late 1960s. Think I'm wrong? Did you see any women on TV running track or playing tennis or golf or volleyball prior to that? Of course not. And, just coincidentally, that's about the same time that male athletes started getting all this muscle bulk. Happenstance? Heck no! A deal was struck.

I'm not going to go so far as to say it had anything to do with women's lib, but I defy you to find me one serious athlete, where muscle bulk is concerned, who is not in favor of women's lib.

(3) Now, since the '70s and the '80s, women are getting slimmer and the athletes are getting bigger and stronger. Again, coincidence? Of course not.

I still don't know how they are transferring this tissue material from place to place, but I know they are doing it. It is a dark conspiracy, my male friends.

Weaker sex? Ha Ha.

Write me if you know anything.

I rest my case.

No, I don't. I've got one final point. You ever notice it's always women in those TV ads? With few exceptions you never see or hear men talking about weight loss. How long has it been since your male friend or neighbor said: "Well, I've finally lost those 20 'unwanted' pounds I've been after."

Never, that's how long.

Male athletes quietly encouraged the already growing clamor to bring female athletes into prominence. That set up a role model chain reaction that caused millions of women across the United States to begin losing weight. The pay-off for the male athletes was tons and tons of "unwanted" fat tissue they could convert into muscle bulk.

I tell you, the various sanctioning bodies are testing for the wrong substances. What they need to do is start talking tissue cultures. I bet, if you were to culture the biceps of some 280-pound tackle who's suddenly gained 40 pounds, you'd find traces of Adam's rib in there.

I still don't know how they are transferring the stuff, but I have my guesses on that. Let me put this bug in your ear. Do you think it's coincidence that we've had this sudden upsurge in overnight express mail services?

Think about it.

Now I do rest my case.

Though I may get back to you later as other facts come to light.

16

We're Old Cowhands . . . from the Meadowlands

I used to have a friend named Harry Wills who could get almost
apoplectic about the public's general misinformation where rodeo
was concerned. If he saw a movie or a TV show about rodeo he'd sit
there mumbling and cussing saying, "No, that ain't right." "No,
dammit, that's not the way it is." "Goddammit, why can't they get it
right!" "Why in hell don't those smart-aleck Hollywood producers hire
somebody to tell them how it is!"

And on and on ad infinitum.

He was the worst, but most rodeo cowboys, to a greater or lesser
degree, tend to get upset about the public's misconception of their
sport. As far as I'm concerned they have only themselves to blame. I
know of no other sport that has done less self-promoting or been as
incestuous as rodeo. It's almost as if everyone in rodeo were saying,
"This is a private club and you not only can't belong, you can't even
know any of our little secrets." I largely blame the Professional Rodeo
Cowboy Association (PRCA) for this, but every rodeo contestant is

*equally guilty. What usually happens, informationwise, is that about
a week before a rodeo is in a town the PRCA sends out a press kit to
the local newspapers. Then some reporter, whose knowledge of real
rodeo extends to the fact that he's vaguely heard of Larry Mahan or
Casey Tibbs, is assigned to do the story. And they wonder why almost
nobody knows about 'em.*

*Of course part of the problem lies with the public. There's a
general belief among the populace that anyone who's actually ever
seen a horse or a bull, or who knows someone who has, is automatically an expert on a very complex sport. This is a shame because
rodeo is the only sport that can truly be said to be American in origin
and continuity.*

*In the last twenty years I think I've written every rodeo piece ever
published in Sports Illustrated. They didn't particularly want this
one, as I remember. But it was during the summer and they had an
issue top heavy with baseball stories so, for the purpose of their "mix,"
my editor called and asked me to write her a rodeo story. This is the
one I did. I hope Harry Wills read it. If he did, I think he would have
been nodding and saying, "Damn right! And about time, too!"*

There's a good deal of misunderstanding on the public's part about rodeo. I say this as a former rodeo
cowboy who has enjoyed both the triumphs and the
vicissitudes of that sport. Surely, some of you have
read in these pages about the days when me and four
other worthless cowboys were getting it on down
the road, from one rodeo to another, in a double-
barreled pickup. Well, that partnership split up because of general
ineptitude by all concerned and sent us each out on his own. That
worked out pretty good for me on one hand, but kind of bad on
another. The bad was that I wasn't sharing in the winnings of any
partners. The good was that it gave me plenty of time to be alone
and reflective.

And, Lord, did I have time to reflect. I recall once in Corpus
Christi when I didn't have money enough for a motel. So I went
to an all-night movie. On the bill was a rodeo movie. I guess the
theater was showing it in honor of the rodeo being in town. But if
anything could have been more inappropriate I couldn't have

imagined it. There was the hero, looking like Mr. New York Broadway, who'd probably never been closer to a head of bucking stock than leaning over the fence. And he was wearing a bandanna around his neck! I wouldn't want to be the cowboy who showed up in a rodeo arena with a bandanna around his neck. Not if I wanted out with my life. But I guess I have a special resentment toward that movie because it kept waking me up, and the images on the screen kept reminding me of the sorry plight I was in.

I still don't think there has ever been a good, remotely accurate movie or TV show about rodeo. For one thing, the plot usually turns on the hero *winning* the big rodeo. Well, a rodeo isn't a Ping-Pong match or a horse race; you do not *win* a rodeo. There's no grand prize or jackpot. On the men's side, there are three bucking events—saddle bronc, bareback horse and bull riding. The other two men's events are steer wrestling and calf roping, which require a trained horse as part of the competition. All events pay pretty much the same, except the calf roping, which has better prizes only because there are usually more entrants. For the most part, the cowboys' winnings come from their entry fees, with very little "added" money, except at the bigger shows. As I say, there's no grand prize.

But there's invariably a scene in the rodeo movie or TV show that goes something like this: Breathless heroine, a knockout in a gingham dress that took nine seamstresses hours to get tight in just the right places, says, "Oh, Mother, Jim and I are going to get married!"

Mother: "But Carrie Lee, Jim hasn't got a penny. He's just a broke cowboy. What would your father say?"

Carrie Lee: "Oh, Mother, Mother, Jim's going to win the big rodeo tonight. And the grand prize is $5,000! Five thousand dollars, Mother! We'll be rich! And then we're going to buy a big ranch and raise whiteface Herefords an', an', an' . . . young'uns!"

Even William Inge was guilty of such foolishness in *Bus Stop*. The hero had won the grand prize at some rodeo or other and felt that gave him the right to court Cherie. I'm not knocking artistic license. Lord knows that has been my only excuse over the years for some of the liberties I've taken in my writing. But too often the license taken with rodeo is, as the cowboy said about a bull that hooked him twice, "a damn sight more than was necessary."

Inge made another mistake: He allowed the hero to tell of competing in both the roping event and the bucking events. That almost never happens, because bucking-event cowboys and roping cowboys—"horse draggers"—are about as alike as quarterbacks and linebackers. Bucking-event cowboys, except for a few famous names, are like border bullfighters, working two and even three rodeos a week, racing pell-mell from one to the other either by flying or by driving at breakneck speeds. They are usually broke, hurt or about to get hurt. And most of them have to quit the circuit from time to time to work at an honest job long enough to make the money they need so they can go back and lose it on the circuit.

The horse draggers, on the other hand, are among the landed gentry, being either ranchers or the sons of ranchers. They have to be a good deal better than broke, too, because a good roping or dogging horse can cost anywhere up to $50,000. Besides, a horse dragger has the expense of caring for his animal as well as the cost of a trailer and a first-class vehicle to haul it around. The bucking-event cowboy carries practically everything he owns in his rigging bag.

Bucking-event cowboys aren't really cowboys in the sense of knowing much about the care of cattle. They are athletes doing a balancing act on the back of a beast that outweighs them by twelve or fifteen to one. The horse draggers, with their ranch-life backgrounds, know something about cattle, but there was never any steer dogging done on ranches or anywhere else, and now there's very little roping done. It runs too much weight off a head of beef.

And certainly, bull riding was never a part of ranch life. Can you imagine a cowboy getting up from the breakfast fire and saying, "Well, reckon I better go on out there and ride a few bulls and get them in shape." I bet there's not a hundred bucking-event cowboys who could sit a working cattle horse all day without getting sore, and I bet there are even less who know how to milk a cow. Lord, today there are even rodeo cowboys from *New Jersey!*

Bucking-event cowboys don't get in fights—at least not very often. All the movie and TV shows illustrate them doing exactly that, but it's not correct. Oh, they might fight someone from the town where the rodeo is being held or, very occasionally, a horse dragger, but they seldom fight with each other. There's no percentage in it. If you whip a bucking-event cowboy tonight, he's going to fight you again the next time he sees you. A man who makes his living getting on the back of a beast that doesn't smoke or drink, eats and sleeps well, gets plenty of exercise, has two horns for offensive purposes and outweighs the man by 1,800 pounds isn't about to be afraid of another 170-pound human who's only sporting two fists.

The ideal ending to a fight between two bucking-event cowboys is a draw. That's where both stand there panting, glaring at each other, having knocked each other down about nine times, and you say, "Well, you had enough?"

And he says, "If you have, but I ain't going to say it first."

"Well, neither am I. But you had enough?"

"If you have."

"Well, I ain't going to say it first."

If you're lucky, at that point mutual friends intercede and help you save face by saying, "Ah, hell, both of you have had enough. Let's drink a beer and forget about it."

I once had a running fight with another bull rider that lasted more than a year and a half. It was over a disagreement about who had won the attentions of a particularly good-looking Shiny Bright, as rodeo groupies are known. I won the first several fights in pretty good style, but that didn't make any difference. Every time I saw him, it was fight on sight. Then he got to whipping me, and I didn't have any better sense than to drop my rigging bag and charge him the minute he came into view, never mind the time or place or circumstance.

But we were fair about it. One time I showed up at a rodeo in El Paso having spent my last dollar to get there and pay my entry fees. But I was in luck; I had drawn a bull that, if I could ride him, was good enough to put me in the money. As I came in behind the chutes my rival saw me and started my way. I held up my hand and said, "Claude, wait a minute. I'm broke and I've drawed a money bull for tonight. He's tough enough without me trying to get down with a broken jaw and all beat up."

He stopped and considered. "Which bull you drawed?"

"Eighty-seven."

He thought about that a minute, and said, "Yeah, that's a money bull. I'll just see you later."

Well, I put a pretty good ride on that bull and ended up taking second money. Claude was waiting for me behind the chutes when

I came back. He put out his right hand to shake and said, "Nice going, cowboy. Hell of a ride."

I took his hand and shook it and said, "Thanks."

Then he hit me with his left.

Our running battle finally ended a few months later in the parking lot outside the fairgrounds in Amarillo. We were reduced to panting at each other on all fours.

Gasping for breath, I said, "Say, what the hell was her name?"

He said, his head down. "Whose name?"

"Who, hell! The name of the girl we're fighting about."

He thought for a long minute and then slowly shook his head. "Be damned if I know."

I said: "Neither do I. So I'll say I've had enough if you will."

"I will, but I ain't going to say it first."

I think we ended up by saying it together on the count of three.

But I guess the greatest misconception about rodeos has come from humane societies, who regard them as form of cruelty to animals. Well, all I can say about that is, if I'm reincarnated, I would like to come back as a head of bucking stock. Short of those guys with lucrative contracts in the NBA or whatever league, bucking stock are as well taken care of as any pro athlete. They get the best care and the best food and are usually rested for several days between events.

Not the least of the reasons for such royal treatment is that a good head of bucking stock can cost anywhere from $1,500 to $18,000. Choice bucking stock is bred for its role, just as a show horse or a race horse is. You can't teach a horse or a bull to buck at the level required in professional rodeo any more than a coach can teach a halfback how to run. It's talent. And no rodeo producer is going to misuse a valuable animal anymore than Calumet Farm is about to set a prize three-year-old to delivering milk.

In a dark period of my rodeo career, I found myself unable to sustain myself on my winnings, and I went to work for Tommy Steiner as a stock boy. Then and now Steiner was one of the preeminent producers, having more head of stock at the rodeo finals than any other producer. But this particular time, we were at a rodeo in Baton Rouge and the local humane society had sent out three ladies to investigate the reports of cruelty to animals. They were ladies of the old school. This was in the early '60s, as were the three ladies. They came picking their way through the mud and dirt behind the chutes to accost Tommy. Their chief complaint was over the flank girths used on the bucking horses.

A flank girth is a strap that goes around the flanks of a horse, just in front of its hind legs. While the horse is standing in the chute the strap hangs loose, but when the cowboy is down on the horse and as the gate opens, a helper standing on a platform behind the chute pulls the strap tight. The intention is to make the horse start bucking immediately, because there is nothing more dangerous to a rodeo cowboy than a horse that won't "fire" as the gate opens. The rider is tensed up, expecting that first jolting charge. If it doesn't come immediately, he tends to relax. Then, if the horse starts bucking unexpectedly, the cowboy can be seriously hurt.

These three ladies didn't know that and didn't understand that a flank girth doesn't hurt a horse. That area on a horse is sensitive in the same way we are under our arms. If anything, it's ticklish.

I was standing nearby as they came up to Tommy. From the looks of them I didn't figure any of them had been any nearer a rodeo horse or knew much more about bucking stock than Elizabeth Taylor. But they immediately began haranguing Tommy about his cruelty to animals, particularly in reference to the girth. Tommy is a patient and courteous man, and he tried to explain the use of the girth and why it wasn't inhumane.

But that wouldn't do. The lady in the middle, all lavender and lace, said in a strong voice, "That's easy enough for you to say, Mister Steiner. But I'd like to know how you'd feel if *you* had your testicles bound up in a leather strap."

And Tommy, twirling his cigar in his mouth, said: "Ma'am, I don't think you understand. All the bucking horses we use are geldings."

And the lady, drawing her head back, said, "Sir, I don't care what *color* the horses are, it's still inhumane."

And that, my friends, is the truth.

17
The Turk

*T*his is a vintage story of mine, but it's one that I like very much because it's still current and illustrates the profound uncertainty most NFL prospects face when they go to training camp for a professional football team. Of course, this story doesn't apply to those high draft choices who report to camp with big signing bonuses and bigger contracts with no-cut clauses. They know who The Turk is, but they also know they'll never hear him at their door. Not at the beginning of their career, anyway.

No, the players who listen for those dreaded footsteps in the middle of the night are the lower draft choices, the guys picked up on waivers, the older players trying to hang on for just one more season. They don't talk about him, but they know well who The Turk is and they know that any night might be the night he comes for them.

Most of the dollar figures in this piece are now well out of date, but the tradition of The Turk and his methods remain the same. A knock on your door late at night. The fateful words, "Coach wants to see you. Bring your key and your playbook."

They call him the Turk because he carries a sword, a scimitar, to use for the purpose of cutting you adrift.

Phil Abraira is in another training camp, only this one is different. He's in the Xerox training camp for beginning salesmen. He's back in Florida now, Fort Lauderdale, where it all started for him. He says it feels strange to be back there, not far from where his football career began. It didn't end there, but the end is there, and he finds it ironic that he should be sent to that particular camp. Certainly he didn't ask for it and, maybe, would have preferred not to have gone.

After the Oilers cut him he laid around Houston for a while until his money began to get low. He didn't call any of the other pro teams for a tryout—he knew that would be futile—and he didn't exactly hope that one might call him. But he found himself being never far from the phone, found himself staying in touch with the Oilers, casually though, in some kind of remote, subconscious hope that the enormous error that had been made might suddenly be discovered and rectified. Of course it didn't happen, nothing happened. He just laid around, finding what solace he could in the girls he met. That, at least, was one arena he could score in. No cuts in the female league.

But, finally, it came time to do something, to reorganize, to make some sort of life game plan. He began going around to employment agencies and that was very painful. First, his past career didn't exactly fit the application forms. The little boxes that asked: LAST PLACE OF EMPLOYMENT, BEGINNING SALARY, DUTIES, ANNUAL SALES FIGURES, etc., were not designed to handle a haphazard career in pro football. But what was most painful was the interest and awe of the people when they found he'd been in pro football. "No kidding!" they'd say, "You were with the Chicago Bears! And the Oilers! My God, we never had anyone in the office like that!" It was painful because it produced the cry of what might have been. If they could be that full of admiration and pleasure at the little he'd done, how sweet, oh how sweet, it might have been if he'd made it. After a while he got to where he hated to even tell anyone and he tried to think of reasons he could use to cover those three years since he'd been out of college. He thought of saying: "Oh, I've been writing a book," or "Been on an extended camping trip," or "Worked as a volunteer for a losing politician." But that wouldn't work and he had to go through with the continuing process of dredging out his old life and dreams and trying to find a whole new set to substitute.

And then there was the business of missing football so badly. He could stand to watch the college games because he'd succeeded there. But Sunday's were bad, very bad. Occasionally the Oilers would be playing in town and once, just once, he called Dan Henning for a ticket and went to the game. But he left at the half and didn't go back. Sundays he'd try to find someplace that didn't have a TV tuned in to the football game. "You know," he said, "that's the damnedest thing. You can't go anywhere on Sunday afternoon where they haven't got the TV turned on some game. Maybe out in the woods. But then some sonofabitch would probably come along with a portable." He finally developed the habit of just sleeping all Sunday afternoon.

* * *

I don't know where the term "The Turk" comes from. The Turk, of course, is the guy who goes around knocking on unlucky players' doors and saying, "Coach wants to see you, bring your playbook and key." The name probably comes from the image of some cat hanging around with a scimitar, ready to lop off the heads of the players who are cut from the pro squads. But it's not the head he gets; what he cuts off is the dreams and the hopes and the football careers of a lot of young men who may or may not have any business playing pro football. Of course whether they have any business playing is academic, a dream is a dream, whatever the qualifications. And a snatched-away dream is just as snatched whether you're a free agent or someone as high up the ladder as a seventh- or eighth-round draft choice.

Everyone who comes to pro camp comes with the idea that he is going to make the ball club, even in the face of all adverse logic. There are forty spots open on a pro squad and most of those are already occupied by returning vets or high draft choices with no-cut contracts. But, at every pro camp in creation, there will be ninety or one hundred or more players showing up, half of whom don't have a chance.

In high school you were THE stud; in college you were one of the main ones, pitying those unfortunate souls who sat on the bench and never got into a game until it was decided. And now here comes a man telling you that you can't even make the ball club! Can this be you, you wonder? But, yes, it really is you the man is talking to. Your roommate lies on his bunk, a startled mixture of relief and sympathy on his face. You look around and then you look back at the door. The man is still there, the Turk, beckoning. "Coach wants to see you. Bring your key and playbook."

"Now?" You still don't believe it. Failure is a dose they don't give penicillin shots for; failure is a disease whose symptoms you're not even familiar with.

"Yes, now."

"Now, huh?"

"Now."

Of course it's not such a shock to a lot of the players because they've been that route before. Some have been cut several times in one season; failing with one ball club, then catching on with another only to relive the experience. But that doesn't really make it any easier because they've had a preconditioned life of athletic success and, anyway, hope rises—it always rises—especially in early camp.

Phil Abraira, a receiver, was one of those who'd seen the Turk's fez at his door before. After a successful career at Florida State he'd been drafted twelfth by the Chicago Bears only to be cut after the third exhibition game. When the shock and the righteous indignation at such professional stupidity had worn down a little he'd gone off to play for the Pottstown Firebirds in the Continental League, vowing to show the Bears. But the Firebirds' front office had the unhandy habit of not having the cash ready come payday and Abraira had packed his gear and gone off to look for a straight job, totally through with this thing football. That resolution lasted until the next season when he thought they might be more sensible in Canada. Calgary beckoned, even giving him a nice little bonus, and he went up there to try his hand at the twelve-man brand. He might have made it, too, except he pulled a hamstring muscle on the first day of practice—at a showy player introduction held for the season ticket holders, of all things. By the time he got well and got back to full speed it was time for Calgary to make their final cut and he was one of the Americans who went.

Now he was through. He went to Miami and got himself a job teaching math and coaching the freshman football team at a high school there. He was through with football except he'd never quite let himself go. He kept noticing how careful he was about his health, how in-shape he stayed. He kept discovering himself running wind sprints and working on his moves. A math teacher doesn't have to be in shape; neither does he need to know how to fake out a free safety.

Then Bill Peterson, his old coach from Florida State, got the Houston Oiler head job and he called up and asked for a tryout and got it and was invited to camp.

One more try. One more chance. And, just like the ninety-eight other players, he arrived with the sure feeling that this time he'd make it.

I went up to the Oiler camp after they'd been working out for about three weeks. They were up at Schreiner Institute, up in Kerrville, in the dry air of the Texas hill country. Of the original number the Oilers were now down to sixty-five players with a cut to sixty to come in a few days. I watched a hard practice and then watched Peterson make the players run fourteen forty-yard dashes after they were through. They went off dragging to shower and dress. Then, a half hour later, I saw a guy who could only be a professional football player, playing tennis with some girl. I went over and asked Rusty McDearman of SMU, a tight end, who the crazy man was.

"Oh," he said, "that's Phil Abraira, he never gets tired."

Later in the evening I saw him talking to some girls' camp counselors who were always hanging around the Oilers. I went over and got talking and we sat under a tree and drank a beer and smoked a cigarette. He was very cheerful and optimistic about his chances. "Hell," he said, "they've got to carry six receivers and that's all we got in camp right now." He talked about the two years he'd failed and the jobs he'd worked at, especially teaching school. "I don't think I could go back to that," he said thoughtfully. "Football's been my whole life and I miss it too much when I'm not playing. But I'm not worried," he'd added confidently. "I know I'll at least taxi."

But I had other information. I was hanging around with the Oiler coaches and they were mostly talking personnel because of the impending cut. Abraira's name kept coming up. Because of a series of unfortunate injuries and contract problems, they were hurting for big linemen. This meant they might have to be deeper at these positions than ordinarily because of a lack of quality.

Dan Henning, who coached the receivers, thought Abraira was a good football player, but that didn't mean much. Larry Peccatiello explained it by saying: "Listen, there's a very fine line that separates those that make it from those that don't." He measured off a quarter of an inch with his thumb and forefinger to show just how fine a line it is.

But, then, they say football is a game of inches. In all ways.

I'd see Abraira around the camp and he never looked like a man who might have part of this future decided for him in the next day or two. I asked him what he'd do if he was cut, would he try to catch on with some other team? "No," he answered, "I'd hang them up. If I cleared waivers that would be it. But," he added, "I feel pretty good about my chances."

Cutting a player is not as simple as telling him goodbye. Everyone that comes to camp signs a contract. Most are the standard NFL contracts that call for $12,500 a year if they make the ball club. Football players are paid by the game during the regular season; fourteen divided into whatever their contract is for. During camp and the exhibition season they get thirteen bucks a day plus game pay depending on their playing experience. Rookies get nothing per game and a man is a rookie until he's played in three regular season games in one year. For this $13 a day a player belongs to the ball club from six in the morning until eleven at night. The rest of the time he can sleep if he wants to.

Before a man can be cut he must be put on waivers twenty-four hours prior. Often a player will be waived after the afternoon workout, then blissfully go through the two the next day, while all the other clubs turn him down, only to find out that his day's work has been in vain. He might have been sensational that practice, but it's too late. His bags have already been packed for him and that great catch and run he made have gone unnoticed because the coaches have already cut him. He just doesn't know it yet.

A player is cut on paragraph six (of the Standard NFL contract), the performance clause. What it says in legal language is later interpreted by the head coach when the Turk brings the player in his office. The coach says: "Well, we just got three guys better than you," or, "The staff just doesn't feel you have the speed," or, "I'll tell you, as a man interested in your welfare, that you just don't have it. Why not be thinking of something else?"

You don't have it; you're not good enough. That's what it finally comes down to.

The Oilers went up and played the World Champion Dallas Cowboys in an exhibition game that was billed as something called the Texas Super Bowl. Abraira didn't get in the game for a single play. It didn't hurt his confidence. He consoled himself with the thought that the coaches were having a look at the questionable players. After the game he saw Ron Sellers, whom he'd played with at Florida State. Sellers said he felt confident of beating Lance Alworth out of the starting job and Abraira replied he felt good about his chances of hanging on with Houston.

He survived the next cut, though not entirely on his own prowess. They were having contract problems with Gene Ferguson so they put him on the suspended list. Also, Walt Suggs' injured knee wasn't coming around fast enough so he went on injured reserve. In the end they only had to cut three players and Abraira was not one of them.

Then, Thursday, they went into Houston to play the Chicago Bears. Paul Magalski, a running back and a former teammate, sat in Abraira's room and talked about being cut. Speaking slowly and choosing his words with painful deliberateness, he said: "The thing is, you get used to being taken care of. You made the team in college and there was always someone to take care of you and see that you were all right. You didn't have to worry about nothin'. And up here, if you make it, there'll be someone to take care of you. You'll be taken care of. But if you don't make it . . . He stopped and looked over at Phil Abraira. Abraira didn't say anything. "Well, you just don't know what to do. You're not ready to look out for yourself. You know."

Abraira got in one play in the Chicago game, on the kickoff team. The next week his confidence began to erode. Neither Henning, nor any of the coaches, seemed to have anything to say to him. He was used very sparingly in the practice scrimmages, and then only when a warm body was needed. No longer was any one correcting his form or his moves. They just left him alone.

But he said, "They still got to carry six receivers. So long as they don't pick someone up on waivers I'm all right."

Of course that wasn't much further. Every day the Oiler coaches were scanning the waiver list looking for help in the line.

Since they were down to the required sixty players, anyone they brought in would mean that someone was going to have to go. And Abraira was at the top of the list.

The Turk is very often a member of the scouting staff. This is so because the scouts have little association with the players in camp and this helps keep the whole business on a colder, more impersonal plane. They like to have it that way. Pro football, they say, is a cold, cruel business. The people involved say that a lot, as if saying it somehow makes it seem less so. Of course it's a cruel business. Anything is cold and cruel where some will succeed and others fail. It just seems a little hypocritical to go around saying it all the time. As hypocritical and cruel as a pro coach giving the camp squad the old team spirit speech. How can half the squad feel the old team spirit when they're going to get cut? That's like the halftime speech the coach makes. What he's saying is really directed at just twenty-five or thirty players, but that fourth-string running back, who won't get in the game, hears it just the same. What's he supposed to do with all that psyched-up feeling he's got built up—go run through walls?

On a Wednesday, after being in camp for thirty-seven days, Phil Abraira was standing in his room about noonday, trying to decide if he wanted to each lunch or go see a girl he knew in Kerrville. The day before, all without his knowing it, he'd cleared waivers. He'd gone through the two-a-days that Peterson had angrily put back in after the team had lost to Chicago. He might as well have not been there. He was no more visible than a ghost. The only attention the coaches paid him was to carefully keep him out of any contact or rough work where he might get hurt. When the knock came he turned and looked at the door, not moving his body, just his eyes. He had a good idea who it was. No one ever knocked at doors in training camp, not a buddy coming to visit, anyway.

The day before the Oilers had been awarded three players off waivers. They'd arrived in camp that night. Abraira hadn't seem him, but, that morning at breakfast, he'd heard some of the players talking about a receiver named Quinn who'd just come in. But that wasn't what had suddenly made him expendable, it was the two big linemen the Oilers needed. One of these was taking his spot on the roster.

The knock came again.

"Come in," he said.

It was Bruce Kebric, one of the Oiler scouts. The players all called him Brucie Baby. He opened the door, looking embarrassed.

"Yeah?" Phil said, knowing what he wanted.

"Uh," Bruce said, looking more embarrassed, "Uh, coach wants to see you."

Abraira grinned slowly. "And bring my key and playbook?"

"Yeah," Kebric said. "I guess so."

"You want the playbook now?"

"Yeah," Kebric said. He still hadn't come in the room, just stood there in the door looking uncomfortable.

The room key and the playbook are not of equal value. They figure the playbook is worth a $500 fine, but the key is only $2.50. They deduct that from your final check if you don't turn it in.

Kebric had come for Abraira because there were three players to be cut that morning and Schlinkman had divided the work between himself and his assistant. They wanted to get them gathered up with as much neatness and dispatch as possible. As they'd started out, Schlinkman told Kebric to take one side of the hall and he'd get the other. As he'd approached the first door, Walt had thought how appropriate his last name was. Schlink, in German, meant "noose." Noose-man. Hangman. The Turk.

Abraira's interview with Peterson was very brief. The coach didn't even invite him into his office. Instead he came out in the hall, looking uncomfortable, his hands jammed down in his pockets, the stump of a cigar clenched in his teeth. "We just didn't think you had enough speed, Phil," he said unhappily.

Abraira asked him, "I guess I cleared waivers?"

"Yeah," Peterson said gruffly.

"Nobody wanted me?"

"Not right now," Peterson answered. He looked nervous. Peterson did not like the task of cutting players. Sometimes, to the ill of both himself and the player, he tried to soften the blow. "Why don't you go back to Houston," he said, "and get yourself a job? If something happened we might could reactivate you."

"Yeah?" Abraira said. He wasn't feeling much of anything yet, just a certain numbness. The straw floated by without his reaching to clutch.

"No, I mean it," Peterson said. "See John Breen about it. Maybe we can help you get a job. Tell him I said so."

"Yeah," Abraira said.

They all went down together in the station wagon with Walt Schlinkman for their physicals. Besides Abraira there was Glenn Chmelar, a free agent defensive tackle from Baylor, and Elmer Allen, a boy who'd received a nice bonus but hadn't worked out. They were quiet on the ride. Occasionally one would crack an appropriate joke and they'd all laugh nervously. Schlinkman said: "You guys shouldn't feel bad; this is something that happens to everyone. Don't take it too hard."

Abraira said, dryly: "Thanks for making us feel better, coach." There was nothing that could make them feel better. They had failed and they felt very much out of it and very alone. Where, only a few hours ago, they had belonged to something, a football team, they were now unbelonging. In a little while they'd be going their separate ways. Chmelar was going back to Baylor to study for his master's. Allen was going home to his parent's farm.

They paid Abraira for the four days per diem he had coming plus the price of an airplane ticket to Miami. He went to Houston. He had enough money to last him for a few weeks. He didn't know if he was going to see Breen about the job or not. He didn't know what he was going to do.

On Saturday the Oilers came into Houston to play the Green Bay Packers. Abraira found it ironic that, only the Saturday before, he'd been up in the hotel, a part of the team. Now he'd have to buy a ticket to get in the stadium. He cringed from going to the hotel to visit his old, brief teammates.

He said: "I don't know what I'm going to do. I keep thinking I've got football out of my system, but then I see I haven't. I'd like to think I'm going to get a straight job and settle down, but I don't know." He sighed. "I wish I could say I hadn't been given a fair shot. But I can't say that. Maybe, if I can get a job traveling, I won't think about it so much."

* * *

One day he'll get out of training camp and then he'll be on the road, peddling electronic equipment. He's going to get his desire to travel, which he hopes will make it easier to avoid and disregard pro football. Meanwhile he's on a determined program to smoke and drink himself completely out of shape. "I got a rigid schedule," he says, "And I stick to it. I was always good at training and this is just another kind. I'm going to get myself so out of shape that there won't be the slightest chance for the bug to get me when next season rolls around." He paused. "I'm glad I'm out of it." Then he paused again and said, slowly, "But, God, do I miss it."

18
The Harder They Fall

Bill Broyles *of* Texas Monthly *asked me to do the following story. I said I didn't want to do it because I'd already done a story on rodeo producers ("Riding High On a Bull Market") and Tommy Steiner was in it. Bill said, "No, no, no. I don't want a story on rodeo producers, I want a story on Tommy Steiner and the Steiner family and what they've meant to rodeo."*

I still said I didn't want to do it. I said, "Tommy and I are too close and every time we get out on the rodeo circuit together he does something to me that gets me in trouble."

Bill said, "Well, okay, if your mind is made up. Why don't you go find an empty office to kill a few minutes in and then we'll go to lunch."

Well, one thing that has never been said about me is that I've turned down a free lunch. So I went off to wait for Bill to finish some little dabble of work. About thirty minutes later Tommy Steiner walked in. That conniving Bill Broyles had sent for him.

Now Steiner is and has been one of my best friends. I can't speak of his opinion of me because I don't repeat such language. But, anyway, Tommy and I went off to lunch leaving the Machiavellian

Broyles behind. Once we got settled Tommy asked me what I thought about the story. I said I thought it was a bunch of bull, pun intended. He told me confidentially that he thought the same and that we ought not to do it. Or at least he didn't want to do it. I said I didn't want to do it more than he didn't want to have it done. He said he doubted that because if I wrote the story it would mean he'd have to put up with me hanging around for ten days or two weeks and he already had enough aggravation in his life. I said that that went double for me and I wasn't about to try and take on the job of making him look even half human. He said that was good because I ought not to write the story on account of the only thing I knew about rodeo was that I'd never been any good at it and the sport didn't need any more bad publicity.

Rodeo people very often engage in such brilliant repartee as that.

During the two weeks I was out on the circuit with Steiner he did a lot of horrible things to me, some of which I cannot mention. One that I will, though, happened when I left to go back home to write the story. At the time I was married to my first wife, a jealous woman without any noticeable sense of humor. Steiner somehow had managed to get a bunch of women's lingerie mixed in with my clothes in my luggage without me noticing. My wife unpacked for me when I got home.

Tommy was also the best man at my second marriage. After that ten-day disaster I fired him permanently from the job.

The two bull riders were quiet on the ride in from the airport to the rodeo arena. In the darkened Cadillac limousine the only sign of life was the glow of Tommy Steiner's cigar. We were in Jackson, Mississippi, and Steiner was putting on the rodeo for the twelfth straight year. He had just been to the airport to pick me up, and as was his habit, he looked around the lobby to see if there were any cowboys who needed a ride into town. He found Bobby Berger and Bryan McDonald, who were both going up on bulls later that night. The bulls, like the rest of the stock at the rodeo, belonged to Tommy Steiner.

Berger, who is a former world champion bull rider, broke the silence. "How's R.L. bucking these days, Tommy?"

Steiner took the cigar out of his mouth. "Pretty good, Bobby. He's had a week's rest."

R.L. is a bull from Matagorda County. Bad to buck and bad to fight, he is one of the best in Steiner's string of bulls, which is saying a great deal, because Steiner has the best string of bulls in the world.

I happen to know this firsthand. I have known Tommy some ten years, but I've known of the Steiners for over twenty-five. I was fifteen when I came out of my first chute on a Steiner bull, at a rodeo in Bay City produced by Tommy's daddy, Buck Steiner. And in all the years I had rodeoed myself, and in all the years I have written about rodeo, I have seen a lot of bucking stock and a lot of rodeo producers. The Steiners are the best.

They got started back in 1941, when Tommy was in the Air Force and doing a little bull riding on the side. Old Buck called him and said he wanted to get into the rodeo-producing business. "Hell, I thought he was crazy," Tommy says. "But then he always had been. Anyway, we decided to give it a shot."

Now Steiner looked back to the rear seat of the limousine where Bryan McDonald sat with his rigging bag between his boots. "What have you drawn, Bryan?"

"Four-forty-four," the cowboy said.

"Good bull," Steiner said, and put his cigar back in his mouth.

He said it the same way a coach might comment on a journeyman halfback who had just barely made the traveling squad. Steiner's attitude toward his bucking stock is much like that of a manager or coach toward his athletes. "Of course they're athletes," he has told me. "They just happen to have four feet and can't argue back. But we feed them like athletes, we rest them like athletes, we condition them like athletes. I like to rest my bulls and horses at least four days between times when they come out of the chute. Some of them as individuals buck better with three days' rest, some do better with five. It depends on the animal." He regards his bulls and bucking horses as his team and the cowboys as the opposition. "Most people who see a rodeo have little idea of what it's all about. It isn't cowboying, it is a basic contest between two athletes, a one-on-one situation with a winner and a loser. My job is to produce rodeo stock that the cowboys can't ride. Theirs is to ride it. Neither one of us ever wins all the way. But if these cowboys got to riding all my stock, it wouldn't be long before I was out of business."

At the arena Steiner went first to the holding pens to check on the stock to be used that night. Steiner, fifty years old, is built in the image of the Western cowboy, with wide shoulders and slim hips. As he walked to the pens he was stopped several times by cowboys who wanted information on the particular head of stock they had drawn for that night. Steiner helped them as best he could. "I tell you, Donny," he said to one cowboy who would be on a saddle bronc that night, "I don't know that much about that horse. We just bought him, and I've only seen him once. I believe he comes out and cuts back to his left about two jumps into the arena."

Steiner's coaching the opponent is something most people don't understand about rodeo. Everyone, from the stock boys to the cowboys to the producer, helps everyone else. A head of bucking stock usually follows a fairly set pattern of moves, so knowing in advance what the animal is likely to do gives a cowboy a decided hedge against getting hurt and also gives him a chance to win some money. A cowboy's worst enemy will tell him the truth about an animal, even if they just had a bloody fistfight the night before in a beer joint.

At the pens Steiner walked up to his chute boss, John Farris, who was leaning against the fence. Farris, a lean, snuff-dipping, stove-up old cowboy, has been with Steiner for twenty years. Together they looked over the six bulls in the pen, all veterans of many rodeos. The bulls stood quietly, their massive heads lowered, chewing their cuds, eyes half-closed. Occasionally one would ripple his skin to disturb a fly, the movement clearly delineating the animal's huge muscles. Over in one corner a brindle bull with a white stripe down the back of his neck stood stolidly, every so often flicking his tail. This was a relaxed, well-traveled bull. He would stand quietly in the chute while a cowboy got down on him, but he exploded with all the pent-up power of 1800 pounds of muscle and gristle when the chute gate opened. This bull was R.L. There was something almost primeval about his enormous head, the curve of his blunt horns, and the way his ears hung down like quart bottles. At the fence, Steiner nodded his head toward the bull.

"Old R.L. looks ready."

"Oh, yeah," Farris said. R.L. had got colicky at the rodeo in

Lake Charles, and there had been some discussion of shipping him back to the Steiner ranch near Austin to recuperate, but he had made a comeback.

"I gave Bobby Berger a ride in from the airport," Steiner said. "He's got R.L. tonight."

Farris smiled thinly. "Then I reckon he's got a night's work planned out."

They were silent for a few minutes more, studying the bulls. Most of the stock had been trucked in four days before from the rodeo in Lake Charles. Even short-haul trucking will draw a head of stock down seventy-five pounds or so to where he needs a few days of good feed and water to regain weight and strength.

The next pen over contained young bulls that Tommy's son, Bobby, had just bought in Florida and Louisiana. They differed from the old bulls who knew the game by being constantly on the prod, always shifting around, fidgeting, hooking a horn at each other, working themselves up to a sweat.

"Look at them," Steiner said disgustedly. "They won't have a thing left tonight. They'll be wore out by show time."

Once the actual performance starts, a rodeo producer has little to do. His work for that rodeo has already been done. He has selected and bought his stock, seen to the care and conditioning of the animals, and worked out, through experience, just what stock will perform best at what rodeo. He has gotten that stock to the right place at the right time with the right accommodations to coax the best performance out of every bull and horse. One of the astounding eccentricities of bucking stock is that they will perform with varying degrees of ability depending upon the town and arena, so the routing of the stock is extremely important for a producer like Steiner, who might have several rodeos going on simultaneously. "There's some ball players hit better in some parks than others, isn't there?" says Steiner. "Why should a bull or a saddle bronc be any different?"

Routing the stock is very important, but it's not the only job. If a rodeo is a big affair, Steiner also has to arrange for and pay the people who draw the crowds—star attractions like Donna Fargo and Loretta Lynn and Michael Landon. Then, of course, he has to oversee his regular crew—the rodeo announcer, the clowns, the timers, the rodeo secretary, and the pickup men, plus the chute boys, feeders, truck drivers, and roustabouts who deliver the stock and get it in shape.

Besides the stock, Steiner and his crew must attend to the noncontestant livestock—horses for the pickup men, horses for the grand entry, and horses for introducing celebrities and other notables. There is also a great deal of paraphernalia to maintain, all the way from portable bucking chutes and pens to tack, feed, hay, and straw. To move everything, Steiner has twenty-eight vehicles, including three huge tractor-trailer rigs for hauling the bucking stock. He doesn't know exactly how much all this costs, but he does know he's got over $1 million in bucking stock alone.

"That's really what you count," he says. "Your permanent— more or less—horses and bulls. Stock you'll be using for eight or nine years. There's a pretty good turnover in dogging steers and roping calves. Obviously, the calves grow up and get too big to rope, and dogging steers smarten up in a hurry. It's not long before they'll start settin' up—stopping just as a cowboy leaves his saddle to dive for the horns. That makes it kind of hard on the cowboy, and we have to get rid of that steer. We buy our rodeo steers down in Mexico. They're called *corrientes*. What you get is a little undersized bull that's run loose on the range. The grazing is so poor that they don't develop big bodies, but they go ahead and put on a nice set of horns. We buy them, bring them back to the States, and castrate them. They make the best dogging steers in the world."

Steiner has, in his active string, about 100 bulls and about 150 head of bucking horses, both saddle broncs and bareback horses. He has about half that many coming up as prospects. These reserve animals are kept on one of his two five-thousand-acre ranches near Austin and Bastrop.

"A rodeo season is a long time," Steiner said, "and your older bucking stock will commence to get tired from all the trailering and moving around. You try to protect them by bringing in your younger prospects and sending some of the old veterans back to the ranch to get a little rest for next year. Besides, you've got to give your younger stock some game time so they can begin to get used to an arena full of people and being bucked out of a chute."

That night Steiner went into the arena, but he just stood around smoking his cigar and watching. John Farris was taking care of getting the bulls to the chute since Steiner's son, Bobby, a former world champion bull rider, had left Jackson to go back to Austin to supervise the testing of some young bulls he'd bought.

Steiner was training Bobby to take over the business, just as Tommy had taken over from Buck, and someone asked Steiner if Bobby was a partner yet. "He *says* he is," Steiner said, talking around his cigar. By that time the bareback riding, calf roping, steer dogging, barrel racing, and other assorted events were all over, and it had finally come time for the bull riding.

We could hear Don Endsley, the announcer, saying, "And now, ladies and gentlemen, we come to what many consider the real part of rodeo, the premier event in the sport. Cowboy bull riding. In this event the cowboy is not required to mark the animal out of the chute. Nor is he required to spur. He must ride the bull for eight seconds and he must not foul him with his free hand. Other than that his only job is to stay aboard."

The mood had changed behind the chutes, as it always did when bull riding was the next event. The cowboys became quiet and the horseplay ceased. Here and there a cowboy was crossing himself or standing alone with his head down and his eyes closed. The bulls came into the chutes with a rumble and a banging. They were huge and immensely strong. John Farris stood at the loading gate, shunting them back and forth so they entered the chutes in the proper order. Against a far wall, Bobby Berger was rosining his bull rope, running it up and down with his gloved hand. As he worked, he glanced over his shoulder to see if R.L. was in a chute yet.

Tommy Steiner came walking by and asked, "How you doing, Bobby?"

"Good," Berger said briefly.

"You ought to win some money on R.L."

"Maybe," Berger answered, still rosining his rope. Berger, thirty-three, has been out on plenty of bulls. He will not say he is afraid of a bull, but he will say that he is concerned about doing his best. "It's a sport," he says. "I'm here to compete."

Bryan McDonald, just down the way, was standing up over Four-forty-four, the bull he had drawn, a boot in the slats of the chute on each side. A friend was gingerly dropping the bull rope around Four-forty-four's huge chest. McDonald looked tense. He kept working his riding glove up tighter on his hand.

Looking at him, Steiner commented, "I don't believe Bryan has got his game face on. He looks to be thinking about something else. Old Four-forty-four may get him."

I thought the same thing. Once a cowboy decides to ride a bull he had better have his mind 100 percent made up that he is going to ride that bull. And Bryan McDonald did not look like he had his mind completely made up. The bull very definitely had his mind made up—he didn't want McDonald on his back.

Down the line, R.L. was crowded into a chute, and Berger climbed up the side and hung his bull rope over the great back, standing astride him as McDonald had done. A helper, using a wire, caught the end of the rope, and passed it up.

Up at Chute No. One, Bryan McDonald dropped down on his bull and asked for the gate. Four-forty-four came out jumping and spinning, not bucking particularly hard, but still making a nice show. McDonald bucked off on the fourth or fifth jump. The bull ran down the arena, looking for the chute gate. McDonald limped over to the fence, disgusted.

Watching, Steiner said, "I told you he didn't have his mind made up. But you watch Berger. He's ready."

At Chute Five Berger was easing himself down on R.L. The bull made no sign other than to shake his head so that strings of saliva went flying. A friend astride the railing behind the chute pulled Berger's rope tight. Before a bull explodes out of the gate, a cowboy must judge the animal's strength and pull his rope correspondingly. If he gets it too tight the bull will snatch the rope right out of his hand.

"A little more," Berger said, watching the rope pull into R.L.'s flesh.

"He's awful strong," the friend said. "Better not take too much."

"A little more," Berger said, frowning, a look that was out of place on his handsome, easygoing face.

Behind Berger, John Farris was rigging the flank rope around the bull's hindquarters. He tied it loosely so that it wouldn't agitate the bull while he was standing in the chute. But it would come tight when the chute gate opened and the bull's muscles expanded. Farris stepped down and tapped the chute with his cattle prod as Berger was working his way down on R.L.

"'Bout ready, Bobby?"

"Yeah," Berger said, his voice getting that slightly breathless quality that comes when the adrenaline starts pumping. He took two wraps of the bull rope around his gloved hand, then used his free hand to pound his fist closed. R.L. still stood calmly, his head swaying from side to side. Berger pulled himself up on his rope, tensed his arm, tensed his face, tensed his body.

"Now direct your attention to Chute Four," Don Endsley began, "where we have a former world champion bull rider who's been to the national finals some seven times. Bobby Berger on—" But he got no further. Berger, tight-mouthed, nodded and said, "Outside." The chute opened, and R.L. exploded.

It was a classic performance by the bull, though his movements weren't as powerful as usual. Standing by the chutes, Steiner said to Farris, "He's still not a hundred percent yet."

Berger was putting on an excellent ride. He'd held his deep seat through R.L.'s first jump, which is the hardest time in a ride. It is usually then that a bull gets a cowboy off balance, and it's next to impossible to regain balance on a good bull. But Berger had survived that, and now he was coordinated with the bull's movements. With his spurs hooked deep under R.L.'s belly, he leaned into the bull's spin as the animal turned back to his left and began to swap ends. The clown was working close to the bull, forcing him to turn back and continue spinning, staying close enough to be there immediately when the cowboy hit the ground. "That's something few people know about," Steiner said later. "How a good clown, by the way he positions himself and the way he works the bull, can get a better performance out of the animal."

Then the buzzer blew and Berger came tumbling off. Instantly, the clown was there, swooping in to take the bull's attention and lead him away from the cowboy and on down the arena. Berger came back to the chutes, coiling his bull rope. Only once did he glance over his shoulder to make sure R.L. wasn't after him.

The judges marked the ride a sixty-nine, good enough for third place in performance money and putting Berger fourth in the overall. A bull ride is scored fifty points on how well the animal bucks and fifty points on how well the cowboy rides. There has never been a one-hundred-point ride because there are no perfect bulls and no perfect cowboys.

Steiner was standing by the chutes as Berger walked by. "Good ride, Bobby," he said.

"Yeah, well," Berger answered, disappointed because he hadn't scored higher. A difference of two points had cost him about $500.

Steiner said to me, "If anybody is going to ride one of my bulls I'd rather it be a good cowboy like Berger." Then he smiled. "Of course, I'd rather didn't any of them sons of bitches ride my bulls."

Next morning we sat in his motel suite drinking coffee. Steiner was working over his stock lists, and his wife, Beverly, was sitting at the other side of the table writing the innumerable checks that go with the rodeo business. Steiner was leaving the next day for Austin, leaving the rodeo in the hands of his son, Bobby, who had just returned from Austin. But before he left he had to decide what stock to send where. He had a rodeo coming up in Montgomery, Alabama, and another in Bay City, Texas. In addition he'd had a call from Mike Cervi, a fellow rodeo producer, who was putting on the big show in Houston.

He told Beverly, "Cervi wants to borrow twenty bulls and twenty-eight bucking horses."

"Have you got them to spare?"

"No, but we'll have to do it. Mike's busted his butt for us enough times."

I asked him what Cervi would pay him for using the bulls, and he said, "Whatever is fair. Last time he used some of my stock there was a check for thirty-six hundred dollars waiting for me in my office when I got back to Austin."

All these contracts for Steiner stock made me wonder about something I'd always just taken for granted. Why do the Steiners, of all the hundreds of rodeo producers in the business, have such consistently outstanding bulls through the years?

"Well," Steiner said, "I don't really know the answer to that myself. We've always been lucky in our selection of untried bulls. And, of course, I've got people around the country who are always on the lookout for bucking stock for me. Scouts, I guess you'd call them. I trust their judgment, and if one calls me and says, 'Tommy, I think I've found you a good prospect,' I'll usually tell him to go ahead and buy the animal. Of course, they don't always work out. But then I think the time they spend on the two ranches helps them. It's rough country, and I think that keeps them in better condition than bulls that are kept in pens or flat pastureland. One of the main things is the way we know each individual bull, know his habits and what will keep him in the right frame of mind so as to give the best performance."

A couple of nights later Steiner was back in his house in Austin. He was sitting in his office taking a call from one of his scouts, a man in Iowa who said he had located three good prospects that looked like they would make good bareback bucking horses.

"What'll we have to give?" Steiner asked, twirling his cigar in his mouth, his feet propped up on his desk. The man thought the horses could be bought for a thousand dollars a head. "Well, go ahead and buy them. Just draft on me and ship 'em to the Bastrop ranch."

He put the phone down and it rang immediately. The call was from a rancher in Louisiana who occasionally sold bulls to Tommy. The man said that he was about to round up his bulls and he wanted to know when Steiner could come down and look them over. "Well, this is a bad time right now," Steiner said. "What do you think you have?"

The rancher said he had six good prospects. "Tell you what," Steiner said, "go ahead and ship what you think is right up here to me at the Austin ranch. We'll give them a little time to get used to the place, then give them a try."

That would be fine, the rancher said, and he told Tommy to pay him whatever he considered the bulls that he wanted to keep were worth.

"Lot of people might think we do business in a kind of loose way, but that's rodeo," Steiner said. "It's probably the only business left where a man will take nothing more than your word on a deal. If you don't keep your word in this business you won't last long."

He went out to the kitchen to get a cup of coffee and stood a moment listening to Farris telling Tommy's lawyer and accountant a story about a speckled Brahman that had gotten loose in downtown Mercedes.

"I remember that," Steiner said, laughing. "We finally hemmed him up in somebody's grocery store. Run all the customers off."

Steiner, like most people in rodeo, thinks that sort of thing is funny. He once turned a bull out in an arena where I was on foot.

I was considerably over the hill to be running from bulls. He had done it, he said, just to see if I could still get to the fence first.

Not too long ago we were in an Austin bar having a few drinks. There were a couple of high rollers sitting just down from us. We were dressed in Levi's and hats and boots, and they asked us if we were cowboys. "No," Steiner said, "we just found the hats."

Well, they commenced putting on the dog a little, and Steiner leaned over to me and said, "I'm going to get these two big shots to buy the drinks." Then he started lamenting to me, in a voice just loud enough for the two dudes to hear, about how we were broke and out of work in a strange town. He let that sink in, then he turned to the two dudes and said he wanted to buy them a drink.

That wouldn't do, of course. They insisted on buying us a drink, which Steiner, after considerable persuasion, allowed them to do. They bought a second and then a third and a fourth round. Steiner thanked them for being kind to two old broken-down cowboys. But outside on the street he said to me, "I'd rather have done that than to have made a deal for a hundred thousand dollars."

Later that evening a call came in from Bay City, from Roger Langford, one of Steiner's stock handlers. Tommy sat down at his desk and lit a fresh cigar while he listened. All around the walls were rodeo memorabilia and plaques, some testifying that a Steiner bull or horse had been voted bronc or bull of the year by the Rodeo Cowboys Association. Last year, of about one hundred bulls voted to the National Finals, thirteen were Steiner's—more than any other stock contractor had on the roster.

The telephone call was about Red Lightning, who had been trucked to Bay City only that morning. A plaque lying on Steiner's desk proclaimed that Red Lightning had been voted the bull of the year for 1978.

On the phone Roger was telling Tommy, "He got a cut above the hoof on his right foot this morning. Don't know how he got it, but he's been bleeding all day and we can't get it stopped. What do you want us to do?" The bull was, after all, worth $10,000.

Steiner, unperturbed, said, "Well, find the best vet in town and do whatever you think is best. Don't get excited. It takes a long time for a bull to bleed to death."

"You can't get excited over every little thing in this business," he told me. "If I got myself in a storm every time something went wrong, I'd wear myself plumb out."

The day before he was to leave for Bay City, Steiner and I went out to his Austin ranch to look over some mares and colts. Driving up to the ranch house, Tommy pointed to the right. "Up there is what we call the sheep camp—big old bunkhouse sort of affair. Any cowboys that come through town can go up there and stay as long as they want to. A bunch of times a year a gang of them will show up to practice on our new bulls. Of course, it gives us a good chance to see how our new stock will do. Most of the cowboys that come are friends of Bobby's and some of them are the best in the world."

When we got to the ranch house, John Farris reported that Roger had called in to say that Red Lightning would be all right. "He said he'd got some old retired vet out of bed at midnight," Farris explained. "He told the old man not to worry about the expense because this was no ordinary bull. Roger said the old man turned around and looked at him like he was crazy and said, 'I ain't doing this for money. I'm doing it for Tommy Steiner.'"

Steiner laughed. "That sounds like Dr. Cornelius. He's a good one. When you taking off for Bay City?"

"Any minute."

"We'll be along in the morning. Bill Ussery says you picked out four of those green bulls to ship to Bay City in the little truck. That ought to help."

Normally Steiner would not go to a small show like Bay City, but he had produced it so long and had so many friends there that he always tried to put in a personal appearance. I went along too, because Bay City also happens to be the first place I ever rodeoed.

"I like Bay City," he said. "It's just a good old-fashioned rodeo. No star, no frills, just rodeo. Only drawback is they've moved into a new arena and it's kind of small. You have to be really careful about where you spot your stock in the chutes."

But at the arena he didn't like what he found. Someone had wet down the dirt in the chutes and it was a foot deep in mud. "Damn," he told Farris, "somebody did a first-class job of making it hard on my stock. If they have to stand around in this they'll be wore out before the gate opens."

Bobby came up to his father that night just before the grand entry, which Tommy always leads. "Stock is kind of drawn down and tired," he said. "We got the bulls and horses in from Houston that we loaned Mike but they've only had two days' rest and Mike bucked some of them out twice down there."

"Yes," Tommy said, "and they're coming into this little arena from a big pasture like the Astrodome. I'll be surprised if any of them buck. How is the stock we shipped in from Jackson?"

"They're a little better off. But we're going to have a big slack."

In each rodeo event, cowboys draw for their times and only ten or twelve compete during public contests. The others, who are called the slack, have their turns after the show.

"How many we got in the bull riding?"

"Thirty-five have entered."

"Huh!" Steiner said, not very humorously. "And we only got thirty bulls. We're going to have some tired stock when the she-bang is over."

In spite of the mud in the chutes and other handicaps, the stock bucked fine. The bareback riding was won on Easy Rider, who did a spectacular job even though he was obviously drawn down from working in Houston and then being trailered for a hundred miles.

"I wish they'd do something about that mud," Steiner told Farris. "See if you can't get some dry dirt in there to help things."

"We done done that, Tommy. But it didn't help none."

Next morning, early, Steiner was awakened by a call from John Farris. "Tommy," Farris said, "I got some bad news. Easy Rider just died."

Steiner swung around and sat on the edge of the bed. "The hell you say! Hell, that horse just won the bareback last night."

"I know it," Farris said. "But he's dead now."

"Well, what the hell did he die of?"

"They're going to do an autopsy, but my guess right now is that he had pneumonia. Probably caught it in Houston."

"I'll be damned. That's five thousand dollars' worth of bucking horse."

"If not more," Farris said.

"Well, I'll be out there in a little while. I'm gonna get a little more sleep."

That afternoon he went out to the trailer that Mildred Farris, John Farris' wife and the rodeo secretary, used for an office, to check what stock would be out that night and who had drawn what. He looked over the list and said, "Huh!" Here's a coincidence. Bobby Berger had R.L. in Jackson and here he's drawn him again. But he won't win no money on that bull this time. Not as tired as that bull is."

Later in the day Bobby told him he had just bought a saddle bronc over the phone for $7200. "Well, I hope he's a good one," was all Steiner said.

"He is," Bobby answered. "And Dad," he added, "I'll bet you right now that out of that bunch of twenty bulls we bought down in Florida, at least four go to the National Finals."

"I'd like that," Steiner said.

But Easy Rider was still on his mind. "You know," he told me, "that was one of the best trades I ever made for a horse. I think I gave nine hundred dollars for that horse and you couldn't have bought him for nine thousand, not as hard as it's getting to find good bucking stock. Used to be we could get some of the best off the Indian reservations up in Iowa and Montana and places like that. But that source has about played out. I tell you, I don't know where all the outlaws have gone to."

That night he said to Bobby Berger, "Say, why don't you quit picking on my little old bull. That bull is tired."

"So am I," Berger said.

Steiner got serious. "He won't be a money bull tonight, Bobby. He's real drawn down. We're bucking most of these bulls out for the second night in a row, and they just haven't got much left."

His analysis was correct. The night before more than half the cowboys had bucked off, but they were now having very little trouble staying on the lethargic stock. Standing in the arena, Steiner fretted about the mud in the chutes. "Look at that," he said. "We're giving them the first jump. Damn stock can barely get out of the chutes in all that mud, much less explode out of there."

Berger's ride on R.L. was anticlimactic. Just looking at the bull, you could see by the way he hung his head that he was tired. When the gate opened, he bucked straight away down the arena, making no attempt to spin. Berger stayed with him, but his score was too low to get him in the money.

Watching, Steiner said, "That's one bull that's going to get a rest."

He and Beverly and I sat late that night in a cafe having steak and eggs. "You know," Steiner said, "this is a very tiring business." He ran a hand over his face. "I should have marked the stock tonight that we'll be shipping out. Some is going back to the ranch, some to Montgomery, and a friend called me night before last and needs some bucking stock for a rodeo he's putting on down in the Valley. I don't know where I'll get it, but I guess I will. Seems like when the season opens there's plenty of time. Then you get two or three rodeos going at the same time and you just run out of everything—hired help, time, stock, everything." He took a drink of coffee and looked across the room. "I wish I'd marked that stock tonight. Now I'll have to get up early and get it done."

Why, I wondered—with all his money, with a couple of ranches worth $15 or $20 million, and a saddle shop he and his daddy own in Austin, and all his range stock—why did he go on doing it? He and Beverly stay on the road for the entire rodeo season, a good ten months of the year. And on top of that they lost almost $85,000 on the stock operation last year. Why, then, should he do it? When I asked him, he looked startled. "Hell, you still hang around rodeo and you don't have to. How come *you* do it?"

I said I didn't know. I said I guessed it was because there was nothing else like rodeo.

He put his cigar back in his mouth and grinned. "Then don't ask me no more stupid questions."

19

Los Pescaderos Puros

I came to write this story at the entreaties of two people I know who wanted, badly, to go fishing with noted Port Aransas, Texas, guide, Smokey Gaines. They knew that I knew Smokey and would be able to arrange it, which, even though I don't much care for fishing, I was happy to do. They were both friends of mine and they are both excellent in their professions. I would trust my life to the skill of Dr. James M. Thompson and I consider Sam Caldwell as fine an artist as I shall ever hope to meet. However, and you will understand it once you read of my experience with the pair, I would sooner go fishing with a twelve-foot white shark as go out on the water again with either of them. In fact, I wouldn't so much as go into a pet store, in the company of either or both, to buy a goldfish.

Sam Caldwell I more or less forgive because he is easily led. But I have plans for Dr. Thompson.

W e went out on the water in the bay just outside of Port Aransas, Texas. We were after the
elusive speckled trout, a breed of fish that is
not only difficult to catch and boat but which
makes excellent eating. In company with
me were the noted fishing guide, Smokey
Gaines, whose boat we were guests on; Sam Caldwell, a water col-
orist from Houston; and a certain Dr. James M. Thompson, a physician from Corpus Christi who had nearly been stuck off the
medical rolls on several occasions for his congenital and unrestric-
tive habit of lying about his fishing prowess.

Actually, I was the mullet on the boat, a mullet being an inexperienced fisherman. That pretty well fit me since the closest
I'd ever come to salt water fishing was getting seasick and managing to lose a rod and reel overboard that was supposed to have cost
some $400. I knew Smokey Gaines was an expert on account of
that is the way he makes his living, but Caldwell and Thompson
both made what I thought were pretty extravagant claims as to
their ability. We went out in a twenty-two-foot open boat called
the *Calliope*. It was powered by a 175-HP engine, would do
twenty-eight knots at full throttle and was, I was told, equipped
with more electronic gear than an F-16. Well, maybe not that
much, but it did have loran, a bottom finder, a fish finder, about
three radios, and an EDT, an emergency distress transmitter
which went off automatically in case you turned over. The last,
since I can't swim, rather disturbed me. Of course we were all
outfitted in the required Coast Guard life vests but I have never
taken much comfort in that sort of gadgetry, having never had the
occasion to try one out.

We met at the dock in Port Aransas, right outside of the Tortuga Flats Restaurant, which was to play a more important role in
that day's fishing than I could have envisioned. It was five-thirty in
the morning. Now I have seen five-thirty in the morning when I
have written all night or been out drinking iced tea with friends
until the early hours, but I can't recall deliberately arising to go out
somewhere at such an hour. At least not since I had been a fighter
pilot in the Air Force. Of course we didn't get up to go fishing.

But there we all were, and the squalls—which I understand is a
term used by seafaring men—started almost immediately. I was

being docile and gentlemanly, but nothing would do except that Caldwell and Thompson had to start smartmouthing about how they were going to show me a thing or two. Naturally that led to me mouthing back a little at them. The upshot was that we decided to form two-man teams and have a ten-dollar bet on who caught the first fish, the biggest fish, and the most poundage of boatable or legal trout. The total of the bet would amount to $30 per man.

Now I had their attention, and Thompson wanted to talk about how we'd choose the teams. His allegiance to his brother in smartmouth had suddenly evaporated. I claimed the right, as the mullet, to the first choice. Thompson denied that right, claiming that I probably knew more about salt water fishing then I was letting on. Caldwell joined him in the argument, as water colorists are wont to do.

So we flipped a coin, a quarter, right there on the dock in the dark. They would later claim that I scooped it up and announced that I had won before they had a chance to see it. Am I responsible for their lack of night vision?

I had played a whole bunch of sandlot football in Texas where you choose up sides, and I'd never seen anybody take the worst player first. Naturally I took Smokey Gaines.

Smokey is a rotund man of some forty years. During the spring and the summer he is a fishing guide. Come fall and winter he is a hunting guide. He seems to have an instinct that none of the rest of us have for where the game is, be it fish or fowl. I guess that's why he gets paid for it. All I know is that he was, in the next hours, to impress me with a degree of expertise that no other sporting professional, be he wearing cleats or not, has matched.

When we got on the boat I drew an imaginary line halfway between the fore and the aft. I told Thompson and Caldwell that they would stay forward of that line, that they would not be allowed to cross it, that I was armed and dangerous. Smokey was standing at the console getting the engine started and watching us cast off. He said, in a sort of amused voice, "You are a bastard, aren't you?"

I said, "I don't care what you call me, just so long as we whip their ass."

He said, "Oh, don't worry about that. They ain't got a chance."

Dr. Smartmouth, forward in the boat, heard the remark. He said, "Hey, we'll be fishing in the same water out of the same boat. I resent that statement."

Smokey said to me, "Don't worry."

I said, "You sure?"

He just said, "Yeah."

But Caldwell was worried about another matter. He said, "Now, wait a minute. We're not allowed aft. But you got the ice chest back there that contains the Snickers bars and the cold drinks. How are we supposed to get at them?"

I said, "Gentlemen, when the sun gets high enough and it gets hot enough the concession stand will open. I am the sole proprietor."

Thompson said, "Oh, yeah?"

I said, "Oh, yeah. At that time cold drinks will be $6 apiece and Snickers bars, of which I know Dr. Thompson is especially fond, will have gone to about $18 apiece. Do I hear any argument?"

There was some garbled talk forward as we headed out, at low speed, into the ship channel that was to take us to Pelican Island. Smokey leaned down in my ear and said, "I hope you're really carrying that pistol because it sounds like mutiny forward to me."

I said, "Not to worry. We're not dealing with serious-minded people here."

The water was blue, the spray across the bow was white, and the people forward had not yet learned that they would soon be turning green with envy. At a grass bed just off Pelican Island Smokey pulled the boat in close to the shore and directed Sam Caldwell to get the anchor over. Then Smokey went forward to the live bait well and took out what he called Molly Perch—small little fish about an inch to an inch and a half long that he bought from the shrimp boats who caught them in their nets and sold them as bait. And, even though I thought he was consorting with the enemy, he showed the motley crew forward the correct way to hook the bait and where to cast. Then he came aft. I was sitting on the fish box, the large chest full of ice where any catch, in case we got lucky, would go. I remember his casting out, distinctly, even though I might have been dozing, and then sticking the rod in my hand and saying, "Now, fish. You understand you got to stay awake to fish?"

Or maybe that was what he said. Hell, I don't know.

Next thing I knew someone was yelling in my ear, saying, "Reel, dammit! Reel!"

Now I know I hadn't been asleep. My attention might have been momentarily diverted but I definitely was not asleep, even though Dr. Thompson and Sam Caldwell were to take a diverse view and make some rather unseemly remarks. But the upshot of the whole episode was that, once I finally started reeling, I brought in a four-and-a-half-pound, twenty-five-inch beauty of a speckled trout. All Thompson and Caldwell could do was cry out in derision, "Luck! Luck! Beginner's luck!"

I had never heard grown men make such poor sports of themselves.

But we fished on. In our end of the boat Smokey and I were doing a very fine trade in three- to three-and-a-half-pound trout. My four-and-a-half-pounder continued, as it would finish, to be the biggest fish of the day. Forward, our companions were strangely not having the same kind of luck even though they were fishing with the same equipment, from the same boat, and in the same water. Dr. Thompson seemed to be specializing in catching "hardheads," a particularly undesirable breed of catfish which Smokey insisted he dehook over the side and fling back as he didn't want to contaminate the boat with such trash. Caldwell, meanwhile, was apparently contenting himself with missing strikes and having crabs take his bait.

I watched Smokey. It was a pleasure to watch the way he fished. He stood in the stern of the boat, slightly hunched over. We were using spinning reels and, with that sort of rig, you turn the reel until the bail is on top and then take the line with your trigger finger so that you can feel the slightest movement on the other end. Speckled trout take the bait very deceptively, moving off slowly with it like a cat burglar making off with your Roby. Smokey had instructed me, as soon as I felt the line move, to count to ten before I set the hook. But, observing him out of the corner of my eye, I could see that he only let the line run for three or four seconds before he popped his rod backwards. I challenged him with this. He said, "Well, I don't have to. The fish know *I'm* not asleep but the word has already spread about *you* down there on the bottom."

Naturally that drew a pretty good laugh from the mutinous crew forward. But they had concerns other than laughing at my expense; namely that they weren't catching any fish. Thompson, after several rejects, had finally boated a keeper trout, but Caldwell was still zero for everything. From my vantage spot on the catch box I could watch him watching Smokey. He was casting close to where Smokey was laying his bait and emulating his every move. If Smokey tightened his line with a few turns of the reel, Sam did the same. If Smokey lifted his rod tip and popped it a few times to give his bait more life, Sam copied him. He did everything Smokey did except, while I was watching, Smokey caught a fish and Sam didn't.

By then Smokey had caught five fish, I had caught two, and the team of Caldwell and Thompson were a bit behind with just the one fish.

It got to be nine o'clock and the sun was good and up. It was August, and we were on the water in an open boat, so naturally it was hot. Pretty soon, despite their sworn inclinations to the contrary, I began doing a pretty brisk business in cold drinks and Snickers bars. We moved often, which was a welcome relief from the sun, having the wind cool us down a little. I was impressed with the way Smokey could read the water. We would be motoring along, the water all looking the same to me, and then he'd suddenly cut the engine and point at a spot and say, "There's fish in there." And there *would* be, though it was generally only he that caught them.

Never once did I see him consult all that expensive electronic gadgetry he had on board. I ventured to inquire why he had it if he wasn't going to use it. He just shrugged and said, "Oh, it impresses the clients. Makes them think they're getting their money's worth." Which I guess was important because Smokey gets $200 for a half day and $50 for each additional person besides the first two. He furnishes all the equipment, lunch, bait, and something you can't buy at Sears and Roebuck, instinct. He says he doesn't know where he got it or how he got it, just that he's always had it. He says, "I just know where the fish live and I know when they want to bite. I just try and accommodate them."

Which I reckon is an ideal situation if you like to catch fish. And apparently there are a goodly number of people out there who do because Smokey stays pretty well booked up most of the fishing season.

He did have one class of equipment that we were using and that was the rigs, the rods and reels. I casually inquired what they cost and Smokey told me just a little over $200 apiece. I said, "Apiece?"

"Apiece."

After that I was a little more careful with my rig, even sometimes being so cautious as to set down my glass of iced tea when the action got a little heavy.

Anyway, Sam kept watching Smokey, trying to imitate his every move. What he couldn't imitate was the stylish way that Smokey could set a hook. Most fishermen, when they feel that telltale tug, jerk the rod tip straight up. Smokey doesn't do this because he says it generally reduces your chances of hooking the fish. Sam was proving him right in this theory. Instead, Smokey, when he sets the hook, makes a sudden sideways whip, tucking his elbows tight into his body and turning his body almost in motion with his arms. I never saw him miss a strike all day.

But it wasn't just the striking motion that Smokey had, it was something else. As I have said, not without a little embarrassment, he was casting my bait for me, an action that invariably caused jeers and catcalls from the motley crew forward. He was also watching my line along with his, so that I never missed a strike and never failed to boat a fish once I had one on the line. How then was he catching twice as many fish as I was?

Smokey couldn't explain it. Neither could I.

One thing he could explain was why he never let me do my own casting. I asked him that very question. He said, as he set the hook for yet another fish, "You remember what I told you these rigs cost?"

"Yes."

"That's the reason."

I shrugged it off, crediting such an attitude to my mistake in jokingly telling Smokey how that $400 rig managed to get away from me on the deep sea fishing trip. I could not believe that the man would expect a simple error to repeat itself.

When eleven o'clock came the sun was picking up ferocity. By now we had caught about twenty-five fish, all but twelve of which we'd released. The keeper score stood nine to three in favor of the good guys. There was no way they were going to reverse the trend even if we were to fish night and day for the next week. We had won the first fish, the poundage, and, short of a miracle, the biggest fish. The motley crew forward was out $30 a man, not counting what they owed the concessionaire for Snickers bars and cold drinks.

So I began dropping subtle hints about my duties as a writer, suggesting that we hasten back to the cool comfort of the Tortuga Flats Restaurant where I could conduct interviews in a more civilized manner and have access to a better grade of iced tea. But even while I was doing this subtle directing, Dr. Thompson, to Smokey's back, was saying, "Oh, no, Captain, I could stay out here all day. I am loving this!" And all the while he was mouthing his deceit he was shaking his head from side to side, violently, and grinning with hypocrisy and smacking his gum, confident that he would get both of his wishes—namely to make me look like a quitter and to get the hell back to dock and into the air conditioning.

He would shortly pay for his duplicity.

We had anchored just off a grassy flat where the water was about four feet deep. But it was a muddy bottom and, after a few casts, Smokey said, "Ain't no fish here. Let's move on."

That's when the good doctor, in an attempt to prove he could do manly things on a boat, hustled over to the anchor chain and began to haul. But the anchor was buried in mud. It had been Smokey's intention to unstick the anchor with the motor before it was hauled in. So there was Dr. Thompson leaning over the right side of the boat, precariously, while Smokey was gunning the engine and swinging the boat to the left. He yelled, "Doc, Doc, let it be! Let it be!"

But it was too late. Gravity took over and, before Dr. Thompson could release the anchor chain, he went overboard headfirst. He came right back up and stood there in waist-deep water, water streaming off him. He tried some inane remark like "It just looked so cool and inviting," but it didn't come off. Smokey and Sam didn't laugh but I made up for the pair of them and, to my credit, I have never mentioned the incident more than three or four hundred times since it happened.

I fear, however, that my attitude toward Dr. Thompson's misfortune may have colored his attitude and caused subsequent events to occur.

We headed in just before noon. Smokey said, "When I set out to give a party a half a day's fishing they are going to get a half a day's fishing." I was wishing he hadn't been so dedicated. I had the ice chest open and had my head halfway in it gasping for air. Thompson would have liked to have done the same but I wasn't about to let him near the back of the boat. I said, "You might trip and fall into the propeller and be chewed to bits."

We finally got into the oasis of Tortuga Flats and got seated. I borrowed a pen from the waitress and wrote out on a paper napkin the sum total of what the losing team lost. Smokey and I had won all three categories so that was $60 right there. Then there was the matter of the concession stand. That added $84, making for a total of $144 from the both of them. They took the account sheet and studied it, nodding and agreeing that it was right in all particulars. Then Thompson suggested that we order lunch, which they would pay for, and then they'd get around to the other bill.

I said, "Now, lunch is not coming off that $144."

"Oh, no, no, no," Thompson said. "We'll pay for that in the spirit of good will."

I should have known something was wrong right then, but I was feeling magnanimous. I was also feeling a little sorry for Sam. Caldwell is a true fisherman. In fact he says he paints to fish and fishes to paint. I guess he says that because he paints a lot of fishing scenes. Of course Thompson is different. He can't fish.

The waitress came and we ordered. About a minute later Thompson suddenly remembered something he'd left in his car. He got up and Sam got up too, volunteering to help. They left. I idly watched them go out the door of the restaurant.

Smokey and I talked. Five minutes passed. Then ten. Thompson and Caldwell did not return. After a little longer the food came. Smokey said, gently, "I guess we might as well eat."

When we were finished Smokey nodded at their plates. He said, "Guess we ought to eat theirs, too."

"Yeah," I said. "You go ahead. I'm not all that hungry." I was getting a kind of hollow feeling inside. I had ridden down with Thompson. Sam had driven straight from Houston. I was afoot.

Smokey said, looking at his watch, "Uh, I've got a redfish charter at two o'clock. It's getting on for that now and I've still got to gas up and get bait. You give any thought to how you're going to get back to town?"

"Cab?"

He shook his head. "Thirty miles. Be pretty expensive."

"Bus?"

"Not that I know of."

About then the waitress came up with the bill and a note. I took both of them. The bill was horrendous, but the note was worse. I had secretly been harboring the hope that it was all just a joke and that the errant pair had been outside having a quiet laugh. But the note said: "Smokey's lunch is paid for. We take the moral position that we do not pay off cheaters nor do we let such ride in our vehicles." It was signed, "Los pescaderos puros." The pure fishermen. They were pure all right, but it wasn't in soul or spirit and it certainly wasn't as fishermen.

I paid the bill, bid Smokey goodbye, and then went next door to a fish-cleaning house where we were having the trout filleted, hoping to salvage what I could from a horrible experience. Naturally the *pescaderos puros* had struck first.

I finally found a high school boy who drove me to Corpus Christi for twenty dollars. When I walked into my house I found Dr. Thompson and his wife and Sam and my wife busily preparing a fish fry with fish they had caught only the slightest percentage of. Dr. Thompson looked around at me as I came into the kitchen and said, without the slightest trace of guilt, "Oh, did you finally decide to come home?"

They had told my wife that I had stayed in the Tortuga Flats Restaurant the whole time, that I had never set foot in the boat, never wet a hook, and certainly never caught a fish. They claimed that I had spent the whole time at the bar drinking iced tea and certain other potables.

What was worse, my wife believed them. She knew I didn't much care for fishing so she said, "If you weren't going to go out on the boat why did you even bother getting up so early and making such a fuss about it?"

She still didn't believe me after I had her call Smokey that night and talk to him. She just said, "Oh, you put him up to that. That's just like you. Besides, Jim is a doctor and doctors don't lie."

Doctors don't lie?

Sure, and Thompson didn't fall overboard either.

Editor's Note: We are in receipt of a letter from one of the gentlemen in question, Dr. James M. Thompson. He writes:

"It is a testament to the virulence of the Fisherman's Virus that noted writer and ex-raconteur Giles Tippette could be infected on his very first fishing trip. The virus affects the parts of the brain dealing with both vision and memory. The distortion caused by the virus explains why Giles could look at the fish he caught and think it was bigger than mine, and why his memory of the events of the trip and who won the bets could be so wrong. The virus also affects the con-science center of the brain —people so afflicted have been known to tell outrageous lies, sometimes without even realizing it.

"On the long trip from Corpus Christi to Port Aransas, Tippette told me repeatedly what a prolific and successful writer he was. Later, I realized that he had been telling the truth and must have been exhausted from overwork, because every time I looked to the rear of the boat he was asleep; just sitting there on the rear cooler (the one with my Snickers and Caldwell's beer in it) dozing in the sun like a lizard on a rock.

"Every now and then when a passing fish would accidently run into his hook and get stuck on it, Tippette's partner, Smokey Gaines, would wake him up and try to coach him into landing the fish. Most of the time Tippette would argue that there was no fish on the line and try to go back to sleep. Only constant prodding and shouting by Smokey could keep Tippette awake long enough to land a couple of sorry specimens of speckled trout. Tippette did, however, set a record for the most crabs caught.

"Tippette showed his lack of sporting instincts by trying to load the bets by taking our guide as his partner. Nevertheless, Caldwell and I emerged victorious. First Fish bet was a tie, Biggest Fish bet was clearly won by Caldwell/Thompson, and Most Fish Caught was won by Tippette/Gaines (mainly because Tippette insisted on counting his crabs as fish, a clear violation of the rules).

"I will save the description of Tippette trying to drive the boat home while simultaneously sticking out his chest and posing for the photographer, and the tales of how Giles got us kicked out of the Tortuga Flats Restaurant, for another time.

Tippette spent so much time bragging in the restaurant after the trip that he missed his ride back to Corpus Christi. It was a long and lonely, but quiet, trip home."

20

"But I Was an Old Five"

I guess, in all men and women, there is the vague wish, every now and then, to have lived in a different era. In a sense I got the chance to do that by reliving the history of the Abernathy brothers that you're about to read. True, I only got to interview one, but, through the depth of his memory and through the experiences they all encountered, I was able to get a long look into a freer time, a more self-reliant time, a time that will never be again, a time not of freeways and concrete and constricting laws and plastics and pastels but a time of freedom of movement and spirit.

Near the end of my research I sat in a little ranch house with Temple Abernathy on his place in central Texas and reminisced about those times. He was aged then, not only by years, but by experience. Yet his mind was still as clear as a bell as he told stories you usually only encounter in history books.

We sat there most of one day, sipping a beer every now and then, while I listened to Temple talk. He was glad to have a listener. He thought what he and his brothers had done had been forgotten.

Not if I have anything to say about it.

The year was 1904, Teddy Roosevelt was President, Archie Hahn was the world's fastest human, Jim Jeffries was the heavyweight champion, the New York Giants under John McGraw had won the National League pennant, and down in the Texas cattle country Jack Abernathy was catching wolves bare-handed.

Which seems a rather interesting occupation and one not to be taken lightly. There had been nothing in Abernathy's background that gave a hint he would become involved in so risky a pastime. At nine, he was a working cowboy and by fifteen he was breaking horses. But for those times and that country this wasn't particularly unusual. The only clue that Abernathy might be subject to aberrant whims came at seventeen when he decided to be a musician.

The question that comes to mind is why he wanted to catch a wolf bare-handed or why *anyone* would want to.

Abernathy caught his first wolf without giving much thought to danger. It was a mistake, done, he said later, in a hasty moment. When he was fifteen he was working as a cowpuncher for an outfit near the Oklahoma border. Working cattle one day, two greyhounds of which he was very fond jumped a wolf. After a chase the wolf turned and bayed. By the time Abernathy rode up, one dog had been disemboweled and the other was being chewed. Abernathy had no gun and, without thinking, jumped from his horse and started for the fight. He was a young man noted for his exceptional quickness and agility, but, even so, a big wolf—and this one weighed about 125 pounds, almost as much as Abernathy—has canines an inch long and jaws that can crush bones. Abernathy later wrote that his only concern was getting the wolf off his dog, and that he expected the beast to run away. Instead, the wolf attacked Abernathy, lunging for his throat. Instinctively he threw up a hand, thrusting it sideways into the wolf's mouth. He then grabbed the wolf with his free arm and threw it on its back, and he discovered that as long as he kept the animal's lower jaw open it could not bite him. They struggled, the animal scratching and clawing. Once, Abernathy lost his hold and had to retake it. The scramble ended in a standoff with Abernathy on top of the wolf, holding onto its jaw for dear life, and the animal sulking beneath him. Abernathy was cut and bleeding when his brother, who had missed him, rode up. Abernathy later told his son that his brother said, "Well, what have you got there,

Jack?" and he said, "I've got something captured I can't get loose
from." His brother wanted to shoot the wolf, but Abernathy decided that since he'd got that far he was going to take the animal
back alive. He made a running hitch with cord around the wolf's
jaws, jerked his hand out, and with a quick pull tied its mouth shut.
Then he slung it over his saddle and took it back to camp.

They say Abernathy caught a few more wolves at this time, but it
was more for the sport of the thing and it wasn't until years later
that he got serious about wolves. Instead, he decided to become a
musician, got married, began selling pianos and raising a family,
including two sons. It's important to take note of these two sons
because they figure in the story later and they were just a bit unusual, too, maybe even more so than their father.

After Abernathy quit being a musician and piano salesman he
returned to cowboying and catching wolves. Only this time he discovered that he had a real knack for wolf catching and he began
doing it full time, selling the animals to zoos, circuses and traveling
shows for $50 each. His fame spread and Teddy Roosevelt heard
about him. Teddy, of course, couldn't let something unusual and
outdoorsy go uninvestigated. A month after he was sworn in for his
second term as President, Roosevelt arrived in Frederick, Oklahoma, to watch Jack Abernathy catch a live wolf. That made everyone nervous, including the governor of Texas, S.W.T. Lanham, who
sent Texas Rangers to provide Roosevelt with added protection.
According to newspaper accounts, Roosevelt was immediately
taken with Jack Abernathy and with Abernathy's famous wolf-
hunting horse, Sam Bass. The President and Abernathy posed for
pictures, the two looking bully and the Secret Service men looking
apprehensive.

The first morning, Roosevelt joined the ten-mile chase over
broken and rocky land. He later wrote: ". . . just as they crossed
the creek the greyhound made a rush, pinned the wolf by the hind
leg and threw it. There was a scuffle, then a yell from the greyhound as the wolf bit it. At the bite the hound let go . . . and at
that moment Abernathy, who had ridden his horse right on them
as they struggled, leaped off and sprang on top of the wolf. He held
the reins of the horse with one hand and thrust the other, with a
rapidity and precision even greater than the rapidity of the wolf's
snap, into the wolf's mouth, jamming his hand down crosswise

between the jaws, seizing the lower jaw and bending it down so the wolf could not bite him . . . with his knees he kept the wolf from using its forepaws to break the hold until it gave up struggling. When he thus leaped on and captured this coyote it was entirely free, the dogs having let go of it; and he was obliged to keep hold of the reins of the horse with one hand. I was not twenty yards distant at the time. . . . It was as remarkable a feat of the kind as I have ever seen."

Of course, they had trouble with Roosevelt because he wanted to catch a wolf, too. The Secret Service finally talked him out of that, and he turned his attention to killing rattlesnakes, one as long as five feet, with his riding quirt. When he couldn't be persuaded to stop, and had, in fact, killed several, Ranger Captain Bill McDonald secretly burned the quirt in the campfire.

Roosevelt wasn't the only one of the party who wanted to try catching wolves. It was reported in the *Daily Oklahoman* that two others attempted it and had their hands badly mangled. When Roosevelt asked Abernathy about his technique, he said, "Well, Mr. President, you must remember that a wolf never misses its aim when it snaps. When I strike at a wolf with my right hand I know it's going into the wolf's mouth."

During his career Abernathy caught about a thousand wolves. He wrote: "Usually I wore a thin glove, the thinner the better. I wore this glove merely to prevent the sharp canine teeth of the wolf from splitting open the skin of my hand. In thrusting my hand into the mouth of a biting wolf, sometimes the sharp teeth would scratch the skin if I didn't have on a thin glove." In a book he wrote called *Catch-'Em-Alive Jack*, Abernathy talked about trying to teach others the process. "Nearly all were able to make the catch so far as letting the wolf have their hand. But when the savage animal would clamp down on the hand, the student would become frightened, fearing the hand would be ruined forever. Instead of holding fast to the lower jaw, the student would quit. Consequently the wolf would then almost ruin the hand."

One of Abernathy's sons, Temple, talks of witnessing such an instance as a small boy: "Dad was trying to teach a Mexican cowhand who was around the camp. The man got the wolf all right, but then he got scared and let go and the wolf bit him viciously. He died a few days later. Loss of blood or some such."

In his book Abernathy claimed that the only time he was badly bitten was when he was catching wolves for a Colonel Cecil A. Lyon near Sherman, Texas. He had caught several wolves successfully, but then he had a few drinks of whiskey and the next wolf bit him. He later said the whiskey had ruined his timing.

Temple says the worst bite his father got was from his very first wolf. "Dad told me he was surprised at how easy he got that wolf down and thought he had a good chance of getting out of a bad spot unharmed. So he went to jerk away, but when he did, the wolf got him by the wrist and bit him pretty bad. Dad pried open his mouth and took his hold again, but the wolf had severed the artery in the wrist, and he was losing blood pretty fast when my uncle rode up. When they got back to camp, that big vessel was sticking out about half an inch and spurting blood. Dad tried to shove it back in under the skin, but it wouldn't go. Finally, he just stretched it and cut it off with some shears they had around the wagon, tied it and stopped the bleeding."

When Roosevelt returned to Washington, he sent for Abernathy and asked him what federal office he would like to hold. Abernathy said he'd like to be the United States marshal for the Oklahoma Territory and Roosevelt appointed him on the spot at a salary of $5,000 a year. Later, the President wrote:

My Dear Marshal:

I guess you had better not catch live wolves as a part of a public exhibition while you are Marshal. If on a private hunt you catch them, that would be all right, but it would look too much as if you were going into show business if you took part in a public celebration.

Give my regards to all your family.

I am sure you are doing well in your position.

This presidential paper has to rank as some sort of first—and last. Surely no head of a government before or since has written to one of his employees telling him to quit catching wolves barehanded.

In 1909 Temple Abernathy was five and his brother Louie was nine. Jack had been out to Santa Fe in the spring of that year, picking up prisoners. On his return he told the boys about the irrigated farmlands in New Mexico and the unbelievable orchards he had seen. Temple says, "Dad got to talking about those fruit trees and it just made my mouth water. He talked about apples as big as grapefruit, and pears and oranges. I loved fruit. We were living in the Oklahoma Territory then and we never saw any fresh fruit. All canned. So the more we talked about it, the more me and Bud, my brother Louie, thought we ought to go out there and see all that and get some of that fruit. Dad had raised us to be independent and resourceful so we broached the subject and he decided it would be all right. We'd been riding horseback most of our lives. When I was eighteen months of age Dad was taking me wolf hunting sitting in front of his saddle. I was now five, but I was an *old* five and Louie was a pretty fair hand at nearly anything he wanted to do. Dad gave Louie his wolf-hunting horse, Sam Bass, and I had a pretty dependable horse named Geronimo that was about half pony. Then Dad gave us a letter saying we weren't runaways and he gave Louie a checkbook so we wouldn't be carrying much cash and we just set out one morning."

For Santa Fe, New Mexico, from Guthrie, Oklahoma—a distance of about eight hundred miles. On horseback. Through rough country that had just barely been cleared of hostile Indians and was still frequented by outlaw bands and was as sparsely settled as any part of the nation.

"We had a side of bacon and some canned stuff and oats for the horses," Temple says. "There weren't any roads. We just rode cross-country, stopping whenever we could with a farm or ranch family. Sometimes we'd get to a little town and stay at the hotel. Lord, that was a pleasure. Don't let anyone tell you a little kid don't like to take a bath. You let him get dirty enough and he'll just think it's pie."

Temple's biggest problem on the trip was mounting his horse. Louie would saddle Geronimo for him, and Temple would pull himself up like a wall climber, starting with the stirrup, then catching the tie-downs that hung off the saddle and finally the saddle horn. In pictures taken at that time Temple looks the size of a bug, sitting on his horse with stubby legs sticking out on each side. "Mostly, I'd find a downed log or a fence or a high porch and get up that way," Temple says. "But that wasn't the worst part. The worst part was getting off. All I could do was catch hold of the saddle horn and swing off and drop. In my high-heeled boots I bet I sprained my ankles half a dozen times."

The brothers got into trouble about halfway to Santa Fe. As they were crossing a stretch of badlands, a black cloud suddenly arose, covering the sky. It began to hail. The boys got off and crouched under their horses' bellies. But the storm worsened and the hail increased in size. Even the unruffleable Sam Bass was becoming hard to hold and Temple's pony was whinnying and jumping. "That hail was about the size of a baseball," Temple says. "A chunk of it hit me on the head and even through my hat liked to knocked me cold. We were right out in the middle of a bald prairie—not a tree, not anything to find shelter under. But over to our right, about half a mile, was a low range of hills and Bud yelled at me he saw something looked like a hole in it."

They tore across the alkali flat and rode straight into a cave in the side of the hill. "It was so black you couldn't see your hand in front of your face," Temple says. "We were pretty beat up and pretty tired and I laid down right there and went to sleep. I don't know what would have happened to us if that cave hadn't been there, because the storm went on for hours."

As they traveled, word began to spread and, often, when they came to a town they found that the news of who they were and what they were doing had preceded them. "As a matter of fact," Temple says, "a lot of women were indignant about anyone letting two small boys cross the country a-horseback. Dad came out there to Santa Fe while we were visiting with the governor, and when he was going back on the train there was a bunch of women wanted to take him off and hang him. Of course Bud and I didn't think anything about it. We didn't know what it was to be scared. Wasn't old enough, I guess."

Except once. "We'd stayed with a ranch family and they showed us the direction to take next morning," Temple says. "The rancher told us if we saw a herd of horses, to give 'em a wide berth. Not to go within half a mile of 'em. What it was was a herd of mares that had been turned out with a big jack to get mules. Now a big jack, especially one with a herd of mares, will kill a horse. Horse hasn't got a chance. Anyway, we topped a little rise and there was the herd. I guess we didn't swing out wide enough because that old jack winded us and here he come. We put the horses in a run, but that jack was gaining. My little pony couldn't keep up and pretty soon the jack was breathing down my neck. I could hear him bawling and hee-hawing right behind me. I looked back and there he was, snapping his jaws. Looked about a foot wide. Bud dropped back and went to quirting my pony and Geronimo put on enough speed so that we got a little lead. Then Bud, who was always a level-headed lad, saw a fence up ahead with a gate. He yelled at me to come on and he put Sam Bass in a high run and got to the fence in time to open the gate for me to sail through and then he slammed it shut right in the face of that jack as he came tearing up. I tell you that scared me. It did."

It took the boys a little more than two months to make the round trip, including a week's stay with the governor of New Mexico. When they returned they discovered they were celebrities. In part, this was because of their famous father, Roosevelt's friend, but what they had done was looked upon as a staggering accomplishment for two children, riding through country that would give grown men pause. But that trip was only a tune-up.

The next year, 1910, Roosevelt, now an ex-President, was returning from a hunting trip in Africa and Jack Abernathy decided to go to New York to welcome him home. During Roosevelt's presidency Abernathy had been summoned to Washington on many occasions. Temple says that when his daddy was there, the President would dismiss his bodyguards, declaring that Jack Abernathy was all the protection he needed.

The boys didn't need any excuse to go to New York. Roosevelt's return was enough. On April 5 they saddled Geronimo and Sam Bass and rode out for New York. Again they took bacon, bread, oats and the checkbook. Along the way Louie cashed many checks for food and lodging, but they were to discover later that a lot of them were never turned in, people preferring to keep them as souvenirs.

Oklahoma had been a state for only three years and much of the eastern part was settled by Indians and inhabited by bandits and people who preferred seclusion. One night, riding late, the boys came on a solitary house on a prairie. Inside were half a dozen rough-looking men wearing guns. "They made us welcome," Temple says, "and took care of our horses and took us in the house. Wasn't any furniture, just an old wood-burning stove. For supper they killed a beef and we had fresh meat. Next day we noticed them following us a few miles back. They stayed with us all that day, never coming any closer than a mile. A long time later, after we got back from New York, there was a letter there for Dad, the marshal. It was from the men, who said that they'd made us welcome and taken care of us and then seen us on through some territory that might have been a little risky. Said if Dad would come out, they'd give him a different kind of welcome. It was a gang Dad had been trying to run down for some time."

Before the boys could get out of Oklahoma, Geronimo began to fail. They had ridden hard one hot day and Geronimo had drunk too much water. The next day he started to founder. They made it in to Hominy, Oklahoma, where one of Jack Abernathy's deputies lived. He took them out to a herd of about forty horses and told Temple to pick one. Temple chose a paint horse that had only been ridden once. The boys stayed there for several days while Louie gentled the horse and then they left. Temple named the paint Wylie Haynes after the deputy. "He was the best horse I ever owned," Temple says. "Never gave me a moment's trouble, and we did get into some tight spots every once in a while."

North of Springfield, Missouri, in the Ozarks, the boys were hit by a spring norther. What began as freezing rain turned into sleet and then into snow. They were miles from anywhere, with a cutting wind blowing. After a time they were forced to dismount and walk to keep from freezing to death. Icicles hung down from the brims of their hats, and the horses' tails and manes were similarly coated. They walked for hours until they came to the town of Union. There was a hotel there, but it was now well into the night and it took a lot of hooting before they could rouse anyone. The clerk, who had gone to bed, couldn't believe that anyone could have survived such a night without shelter.

They crossed Missouri, then Illinois and Indiana and started into Ohio. Once again they were celebrities, with their pictures and write-ups in the papers. Souvenir hunters became a problem, pulling hair from the horses' tails. In Cincinnati, the mayor exclaimed, "Why, they're hardly bigger than seventeen cents!" They got a tour of the zoo that exhibited timber wolves advertised as having been caught by Jack Abernathy, though Temple doubted that. In Dayton they met the governor of Ohio, were given a tour of the Wright airplane factory and met Wilbur.

But once on the trail again the boys were soon in trouble. Outside Wheeling, West Virginia, they came to a creek muddy and swollen by heavy rains. Louie went first on the sturdy Sam Bass to see if he could make it. The old horse carefully picked his way through the current, swimming strongly until he found footing on the other side, whereupon Louie turned him around and reforded the creek. He helped Temple onto Sam Bass, mounted Wylie Haynes himself and they set out. Temple and Sam Bass made the far shore, but Wylie Haynes wasn't strong enough to negotiate the current and was swept downstream. Horse and rider went under, then bobbed up in the swirling current. "Temple yelled at me," Louie says, "'Hang on, Bud!'" Two hundred yards downstream, Wylie Haynes found his footing and was able to scramble ashore. By now the boys were entering well-settled territory with paved roads. They stopped in Washington, D.C. for ten days and were given an official greeting and taken to see President Taft. Louie found him "big and jolly, but he didn't play with us like Teddy did."

They left Washington on June 6 and arrived in Baltimore the same day their father reached New York. Now impatient and tired, they pushed on, making it a one-day ride from Wilmington, Delaware, to Trenton, a distance of seventy-five miles. Their progress through New Jersey was slowed by the large crowds they were attracting, but by the time they reached the New York ferry in Jersey City, their father was there to meet them, along with some dignitaries who had brought collars of roses for the horses. They reached Manhattan at six-thirty that evening, riding their horses through the busy streets. A hundred policemen kept order in the crowds that turned out to welcome them.

The boys were part of the welcoming party that went out to meet Teddy Roosevelt in a cutter as his ship entered the harbor. Then they rode with the Rough Riders in the welcoming parade down Fifth Avenue.

But now it was over—or almost over. Their father asked them how they'd like to drive a car back to Oklahoma. He said that the Brush Motor Car Company would furnish the car and he was willing to let them go, provided they could become good enough drivers. Of course they wanted to try that. The fact that there were very few roads, much less paved ones, was no deterrent. The fact that the automobile was still in its infancy and was a very unreliable mode of transportation, especially on a 2,500-mile trip, was not worth considering. Gasoline stations and garages hardly existed, but no matter. If they could ride a horse cross-country they could drive a car. It was that simple. The Brush, manufactured from 1907 to 1913, was a one-cylinder, ten-horsepower automobile capable of speed up to thirty miles an hour. In the interest of lightness, a great many of its parts, including the axles, were made of wood. Louie and Temple practiced driving up and down Broadway until their father was satisfied they could handle the machine. Sam Bass and Wylie Haynes were shipped home by rail and on July 6 the boys set out.

The boys took a somewhat circuitous route, which ran through Albany, Detroit and Chicago. After leaving that city, they drove over rutted trails but still averaged better than a hundred miles a day. Temple's main complaint about the car was its chain drive: "Nearly all the roads were muddy and that damn chain just slung mud all over us the whole way." Other than that and a goodly number of flats, the boys had a surprisingly easy time on the sixteen-day trip.

Which ought to have wound up their careers as traveling men. No boys of any age could match what they had done, and very few men could claim such experiences. But then the Brush Motor Car Company invited them to New York for an automobile show. At that time there was talk that Roosevelt might become a compromise presidential candidate for the Republican Party. A couple of enterprising promoters from Coney Island named Thompson and Dundee hired the boys to ride an elephant and a donkey from New York to Washington. Louie rode the elephant and Temple the donkey and again they drew huge crowds, but the elephant developed sore feet and the ASPCA made them dismount in Philadelphia.

That definitely should have ended it, except the same promoters were willing to put up a $10,000 prize if the boys could ride horseback from the Atlantic Ocean to the Pacific Ocean in sixty days.

Well, why not? After all, that would only be across the Appalachians, the Rockies, some deserts and whatever smaller mountain ranges there were beyond. Never mind the dearth of roads, of communications, of means of supply. This time they left from Coney Island, first riding belly-deep in the Atlantic surf and then turning and starting west. The indefatigable Sam Bass and Wylie Haynes had been shipped north again and here the boys were, setting out for their longest ride yet.

The rules were simple: get there in sixty days and eat and sleep completely out of doors. No staying in hotels, no having dinner with a ranch family. No support of any kind. Just the boys and their horses and whatever they could carry or buy along the way. Nor were their expenses paid, which is hard to believe today, when a huge caravan of trailers and side men surely would accompany such an expedition and when a man gets paid something close to the national debt for a parachute jump into a canyon. A good crowd was on hand to see them off, but there would be no crowds in the deserts and no newspaper photographers when they were crossing the Rockies. By then Temple was seven and Louie was eleven. The trip would cover 3,619 miles.

They passed through big towns—Albany, Buffalo, Erie, Toledo and Chicago—and received the now-accustomed publicity. In Toledo, Temple remembers, owners of a department store put up a big table in front of their store (so they wouldn't break the rule about eating inside) and laid out a big feed. "Dad used to say we had 'sawmill appetites.' Well, we didn't let him down on that one."

Wylie Haynes, unused to the hard-surfaced Ohio roads, developed sore feet. They changed his shoes and soaked his hooves in neat's-foot oil, taking it slowly. "Each night," Temple says, "Wylie Haynes would just lie down on his side. We'd put feed and water up by his head and next morning he'd be ready to go."

Nothing seemed to bother the indestructible Sam Bass. An iron-gray gelding of sixteen and one-half hands, he had stoically traversed mountains and deserts; the clatter and smell of the automobiles they occasionally met didn't concern him. But he was getting old. He was sixteen and was on his second cross-country trip after a lifetime of hard range work and wolf chasing. "Until he died," Temple says, "the only trouble we ever had with Sam Bass was on that first trip to Santa Fe when he'd want to chase every wolf we saw. He could smell them, you know."

Camping outside of Chicago they ran into a storm and almost froze to death. They had to pack up in the middle of the night and ride through sleet and snow to find shelter. Louie later recalled that it was the coldest he'd ever been. Within a month they would be crossing deserts where the temperature sometimes would reach 120° during the day.

The boys passed through Iowa and Nebraska and then into Wyoming, making good time. Before they had left, their daddy had plotted out checkpoints for them. By the time they quit Nebraska they were running two days ahead. But near Cheyenne, Sam Bass, the old campaigner who ought to have known better, got into a field of new alfalfa and foundered. He died the next day.

Temple says, "We felt pretty bad about that. I guess old Sam was about the best horse there ever was. But we had to keep going. Louie bought another horse, a black, but he wasn't a good traveler. Old Sam and Wylie could go along just like they were in tandem. They had a nice way of going. But this black just couldn't cover any ground."

Crossing the desert flats of Utah, Temple got sick. He loved canned tomatoes and they had bought some at a little store. In the afternoon, with the sun blazing down and the temperature 100°, they had stopped to eat. "I ate that can of tomatoes and I think there must have been something wrong with it." Temple says. "Of course, the tomatoes were hot. Everything was hot, but I remember the can looked kind of swelled out. Right after that I got so sick I thought I was going to die. There wasn't any place to rest. Wasn't even a telegraph pole for shade. Louie got me on my horse and we started riding. I think he got a little scared. Sometime that night we got into a little town that had a store and they put me to bed in a back room. When I woke up they asked what I wanted and I said corn flakes and milk. Right after that I started feeling better. I think it was the milk absorbed the poison. But I was pretty weak for several days after that."

Temple doesn't remember how they navigated. "It wasn't anything exact. We always had a pretty good sense of direction and sometimes we'd find a railroad or a line of telegraph poles that we knew had to be going toward some little town where we could maybe get water and fresh supplies. We only got in a bind once and that was in Nevada. We'd been without water all one day. We weren't worried about ourselves but about the horses. All of a sudden we topped a rise and there was a house. Just a house, nothing else for miles around. It was deserted, but they had a well and it still had water. We were mighty glad to see that place."

But it was all for nothing. Sixty-two days after they'd started they rode their horses into the Pacific at San Francisco. No one was there to meet them except their father and a few of the curious. They were two days late. They got nothing, not even a consolation prize.

And that was the end of their traveling. Or nearly so. A few months later the Indian Motorcycle Company sent a machine to Oklahoma with an offer that they ride it to New York City. Of course, they did. What else could they do? After you've crossed the country by horse and by car and a chance comes along to ride a motorcycle, why, you've got to take it. It was a tandem affair with two seats and two sets of handlebars. Louie drove all the way because the cumbersome cycle was too heavy for Temple to control.

After that, the boys went on the vaudeville circuit for six weeks, finally making some real money. And then it was off to school. "It was pretty hard to take for a while," Temple says, "but we did get used to it."

Jack Abernathy dabbled in motion pictures for a time and later went into the oil business as a wildcatter. He had given up his position of marshal once the careers of his sons showed promise. He died in 1941 at sixty-five in Long Beach, California.

Louie went to law school and ended up an attorney. He is now in a nursing home in Austin, Texas. Temple followed his father into the oil business, working as a lease scout and driller. At seventy-two, he lives quietly in a small town in central Texas. Except maybe it isn't all over for him. He's got some shallow oil wells located and he would like to develop them to get extra money. He wants to buy an airplane and single-hand it across the United States.